Fundamental Studies in Educational Research

# Fundamental Studies in Educational Research

## Edited by
## Paul Vedder

SWETS & ZEITLINGER B.V. AMSTERDAM / LISSE     PUBLISHERS

SWETS & ZEITLINGER INC. ROCKLAND, MA / BERWYN, PA

Institute for Educational
Research in the Netherlands

**SVO**

Sweelinckplein 14
2517 GK The Hague The Netherlands

1965 – 1990   25th anniversary

9 3 1 9 4 6

*Library of Congress Cataloging-in-Publication Data*

(applied for)

*CIP-gegevens Koninklijke Bibliotheek, Den Haag*

Fundamental studies in educational research / ed. by Paul Vedder
Amsterdam [etc]: Swets & Zeitlinger.
Met lit. opg.
ISBN 90-265-1057-8
SISO 450.43 UDC 371.012 NUGI 724
Trefw.: onderwijsresearch : opstellen

Cover design Rob Molthoff
Cover printed in the Netherlands by Casparie IJsselstein
Printed in the Netherlands by Offsetdrukkerij Kanters B.V., Alblasserdam

ISBN 90 265 1057 8
NUGI 724

# Contents

# Introduction:
# Fundamental Studies in
# Educational Research

Paul Vedder *
Institute for Educational Research in the Netherlands
The Hague, The Netherlands

The publication of this book is part of an initiative of the Institute for Educational Research in the Netherlands (SVO) to develop and start up educational research programs that are directed at fundamental issues in education. Eight scholars, internationally respected experts, were invited to present their ideas about the possible contents of fundamental educational research programs. SVO's initiative is an attempt to guarantee room for fundamental studies in the domain of educational research.

Fundamental research derives its value from its eventual contribution to technology development and its intrinsic cultural merit. Regardless of whether or not it will eventually have social or technological consequences, fundamental research constitutes one of the critical innovative forces in a society, and is therefore important. The value of SVO's initiative becomes even clearer when viewed in the light of a recent report from the Organisation for Economic Cooperation and Development (OECD), entitled "Science and Technology Policy Outlook" (OECD, 1988). In this report the OECD expresses its concern about current systems of research and higher education in several OECD countries that have a more practical,

* In editing the contributions I was kindly assisted by Kees Broekhof, who did most of the linguistic editing.

short-term and commercial orientation than they had in the past. The OECD stresses the importance of good education and basic, curiosity-driven research as the essential functions of scientific activity. The OECD countries are warned for jeopardizing these functions.

In this introductory chapter I shall describe SVO's role in educational research in the Netherlands and SVO's particular commitment to fundamental educational research. The ideas about the nature of fundamental research that are expressed in this introductory chapter were also presented to the authors, to guide them in writing their contributions. Of course, each contribution reflects its author's personal ideas about what fundamental research in education is. The result is a rather diverse collection of texts. This diversity is not only the consequence of individual differences, but also of the natural diversity of interpretations of the concept of "fundamental", which is inherently relational and context-dependent. A summary of proposed research problems and some comments on the contributions are presented in the final two sections of this chapter.


### The Institute for Educational Research in The Netherlands

SVO can best be described as a national science council in the field of the educational sciences, which functions at the same time as a research contracting agency. SVO is an independent agency, although it is almost completely financed by the Ministry of Education and Science. SVO's managing board is made up of representatives of the research community and of the main customers (i.e. the three national schools councils and the Minister of Education).

SVO acts as coordinator and project planner, mediating between the demand for research, the research institutations and consumers of research information. Most of the research with which it deals (taking up 80% of the total research budget) is practice or policy oriented. The remaining 20% of the available funds are used in principle for research aimed at the advancement of educational theory, so-called "fundamental" research.

The legislative act by which SVO's functioning is regulated prescribes that SVO shall help in setting up fundamental research and that it shall stimulate the development of scientific knowledge and the development of research instruments. All this, however, is to take place on the condition that SVO shall support research applied for by order of the Ministry of Education or by practitioners in the field of education. The Act does not specify the content or the form of the support SVO has to provide. This circumstance makes room for the development of fundamental research that is planned, realised and evaluated without being directly dependent on the ever-changing wishes for research of educational policy makers and individuals or organisations in the educational field.

## The authors' task

The authors were asked to write about the problems or the type of problems in their subject domain which, in their view, should be subjected to fundamental research. They were asked to focus first of all on the implications of their proposed studies for educational theory. If they wished to do so, they were also free to elaborate on developments in educational technology that might be stimulated by the studies they propose.

In my brief review of the eight contributions I shall address the questions of what types of fundamental research are proposed by the authors and how the authors judge the importance of research directed at the development of technology.

One of the major principles in science is that one looks at the research object from many angles. I have tried to pay tribute to this principle by inviting two authors for most of the topics.

Herbert Walberg (University of Illinois at Chicago) and Douglas Windham (State University of New York at Albany) write about "effective schools", Walberg describes a theory in the domain of effective schools research, while Windham discusses economic aspects of effective schools. Margaret Clifford (University of Iowa) and Franz Weinert (Max Planck Institute, Munich) discuss motivation and learning in school. Clifford addresses problems in diagnosing motivation as a factor influencing learning and learning outcomes; Weinert focuses on theory building. Two authors write about multilingual/multicultural education: Miguel Siguan (University of Barcelona) and Jim Cummins (Ontario Institute for Studies in Education). Siguan gives a description of problems in planning and implementing bilingual multicultural education in Western countries and the Third World and Cummins discusses theoretical notions and their empirical basis. The fourth topic in this volume is from the domain of educational psychology: learner differences in processes of learning. Noel Entwistle (University of Edinburgh) presents research ideas about teacher activities and differentiation strategies in relation to instructional learner differences. Allen Purves (University at Albany), finally, reflects on the importance of international comparative studies as they are set up by the International Association for the Evaluation of Educational Achievement (IEA).

## A summary of proposed research problems

Walberg, the first author in this volume, presents a theory of educational productivity which he justifies by referring to empirical studies and their results and to a special methodology that is used to synthesize research findings. The theory concerns variables that have been found to correlate with academic achievement. Walberg suggests that his theory should be integrated with instructional theories. The problem is clear: How can knowledge of school effectiveness variables be used in attempts to actually improve school effectiveness? A second problem concerns the completeness of a theory of educational productivity: What additional variables should such a theory take into account? Walberg proposes to analyze research on meta-cognitive approaches to reading comprehension. The third problem is more complicated: What are the limits of possibilities to optimize school effectiveness? The optimisation process takes a long time. To be able to measure the growth of effectiveness, evaluators need measures that enable comparisons of effectiveness over time. Such measures do not exist at present. Most curriculum-based tests are content-specific. Only progress within a particular knowledge domain and over a timespan of no more than a few years can be measured. Obviously, new measures need to be developed.

Windham's contribution about the cost of effective schools is in a way futuristic. His research recommendations are prompted by a desire to make changes in the educational practice. It would seem that the educational practice is not yet ready for these changes, however. Windham takes the view that research into the efficiency of education and effective schools research should proceed along the following lines:
1  definition of the desired results of education (target definition);
2  definition and development of indicators and measures for determining the effectiveness with which targets are attained;
3  description of ways in which the set targets might be attained (instructional technology);
4  an analysis of the cost and effort involved in the use of particular instructional technologies.
If these points could be addressed in connection with each other, it should be possible to lay the foundations for a public debate about minimum standards of education. The ultimate goal would be to guarantee that pupils who follow the same type of education will have the same learning experience, aimed at achieving specific common goals. For some groups (ethnic minorities, working class children) and for some regions this will be more difficult to realise than for others. Such differences should be

allowed for in the allocation of funds.

Finally, there are, according to Windham, two associated topics that need to be investigated: the changeability of the educational finance system, and the personal, societal and school characteristics that should be taken into account by a model used for analyzing the effectiveness of education.

Clifford approaches the phenomenon of "motivation" from the viewpoint that it ought to be made an explicit learning topic in school. In her view, research and development work should be aimed both at teachers and at pupils. As regards teachers, their perceptions of how to regulate pupil motivation should be investigated as well as their teaching behavior and the organisational structures they employ in their efforts to regulate pupil motivation. According to Clifford, some of these ideas, behaviors, and forms of instruction are counterproductive. As regards pupils, Clifford argues that a test should be developed to measure pupil motivation in a way similar to that used in measuring achievement. One of the problems which should be clarified by further research is the distinction between achievement and motivation. Clifford proposes to tackle this problem from the angle of attribution theories and ideas about "academic risk-taking", which should be investigated for principles that might be of importance for the motivation of pupils. Moreover, attribution theories should be examined for differences between effort attribution and strategy attribution. As regards risk-taking in learning, Clifford believes that further research should focus on the conditions that encourage or discourage the taking of risks.

Weinert is much less optimistic about the eventual outcomes of risk-taking research. His contribution about motivation is of a more theoretical nature. He stresses the importance of conceptual analyses in the field of research on motivation, which should result in better definitions of a variety of motivational concepts and their interrelations. He further states that theoretical models of learning and motivation should not only explicitly define motivational factors and mechanisms, but should also specify how motivational processes work under classroom conditions. Weinert's contribution addresses many of the current problems and developments in the domain of motivation research. Thus far, studies of the relationship between motivation and learning have focused on single learning episodes and specific achievements on the basis of temporally limited learning activities. Weinert proposes to supplement these studies with studies on the development of motivation over longer time periods. A possible topic, he suggests, might be the role of motivation in the acquisition of expertise. In many studies motivation is measured and analyzed as if it were a strictly personal quality. Most modern motivation theories, however, hold that this is not the case. These theories represent an interactionist view of motivation. In this view, the type of motivation in a learning situation as well as its intensity and the manner in which it manifests itself are seen as depending also on instructional conditions, the value orientation of parents and a variety of other social conditions. Research, according to Weinert, should attempt to contribute to the substantiation of interactionist views of motivation, which might eventually improve possibilities for doing research under real classroom conditions. One of Weinert's main concerns, finally, is the quality of motivation measurement. In his view, improvement of the assessment of various motivational constructs and processes constitutes one of the major challenges for future research.

Siguan, in his contribution about multilingual and multicultural education, starts by pointing to the large body of knowledge that exists about the education and development of pupils from ethnic groups. He states that there is, on the other hand, a lack of knowledge about the economic, political and cultural factors that play a role in the development and acquisition of languages, and that little is known about the relation between language acquisition and cognitive development. He goes on to specify this problematic lack of knowledge in more practical terms: How much attention should be given to children's first language once they have made a start with learning a second language? How do differences and conflicts between the cultures related to different languages affect teaching and learning? What is the influence of different scripts on bilingual education? How can different meanings of reading and writing which are anchored in culture be identified and how and in what degree do these differences affect learning to read or write? Siguan incidentally proposes not to tackle too many problems separately. Research will have to focus on the complex interconnections between economic, political and cultural conditions on the one hand, and on language acquisition and the consequences for cognitive development on the other.

Cummins stresses the importance of theory development in the domain of multilingual and multicultural education. He argues that the impact of research in bilingual education on educational policy has been minimal. Research data and facts from bilingual programs, so he claims, only become interpretable for policy purposes within the context of a coherent theory which allows for the generalisation of research findings across contexts. He presents a theoretical framework and proposes research which is aimed at evaluating and broadening this framework. His ideas are broadly defined, addressing socio-political as well as psycho-educational factors.

He proposes, for instance, to analyze the relation between the power of a cultural ethnic group and the institutional characteristics of schools that are visited by members of this group. He lists four characteristics that should receive special attention:

1 the extent to which minority students' language and culture are incorporated into the school program;
2 the extent to which minority community participation is encouraged as an integral component of children's education;
3 the extent to which the pedagogy promotes intrinsic motivation on the part of students to use language actively in order to generate their own knowledge, and
4 the extent to which professionals involved in assessment support minority students by treating their academic difficulties as a function of interaction within the school context rather than legitimizing the location of the "problem" within the students.

Entwistle stresses the importance of research on the influence of learning contexts on learning. To him, a central research question is: How do students use factual knowledge to develop idiosyncratic forms of representation and personal understanding? He points to the need to investigate the influence of different learning styles on the relationship between, on the one hand, teacher instructions and learning materials and, on the other hand, the development of pupils' understanding of learning content. Other questions concern self-awareness in learning, which is important for the impact of learning and for the students' motivation. Entwistle proposes to investigate the complex relationships between students' age, motivation, mastery of skills, control of meta-cognitive strategies and learning outcomes for a variety of subject areas. Entwistle also goes into the topic of "school climate": How do students experience their school education, for instance with regard to teacher instructions or testing practices, and how does this affect their learning styles?
He argues that the choice of topics for fundamental studies in educational research should not be restricted to theoretically defined problems. The ecological validity and the practical relevance of fundamental studies to policy makers should not be ignored. Therefore, "real" problems that are experienced by teachers and students should also be considered.

Purves' contribution, entitled "The world as an educational laboratory", emphasizes the possibilities and the advantages of international comparative research. Some of the research problems he brings forward have also been discussed by others. To extend the explanatory value of research studies, Purves believes it is necessary to operationalise the concept of "opportunity to learn" with greater precision. Although instruction time and content coverage play a role in this context, these are not the only important aspects. It might be useful to analyze the appreciation of a subject area by a particular cultural community (cf. Siguan). Purves points out two practical problems that should be addressed by future research. First, he argues that greater efforts should be made to develop and evaluate educational programs for the "semi-literate underclass". He points out that many such programs are not offered in ordinary education, but in the army, in factories or in welfare institutions, since the people concerned have left formal education. The second problem concerns the scarcity of resources for education in developing countries. What should be given priority on a budget: school buildings, instructional materials, teacher training, or other types of educational provision?

### Conceptions of fundamental research; some preliminary comments

In the research context, "fundamental" is an adjective that expresses how some research projects are related to others. This relationship can be described in various terms.

Recently two of SVO's consultants concluded, after analyzing research proposals in the field of adult education, that particular projects on reading had better not be executed until other (i.e. fundamental) research in reading comprehension would give a better perspective on the value of the proposed projects (see Houtkoop & Van der Kamp, 1987). Such analyses make clear what kind of research can justly be labelled "fundamental". This kind of relationship may be called conditional. It concerns studies which are fundamental with regard to research that will be carried out at a later point in time. The point of reference lies in the future. The majority of proposals that are put forward in this volume fall within this category.

The second kind of relationship links up with the idea of the growth of scientific knowledge. In this context fundamental studies are studies that add to or further specify knowledge which was obtained in earlier studies. The point of reference lies in the past. This type of relationship implies that scientists should have an idea of a growth dimension along which the progress of knowledge can be measured (see Wohlwill, 1973; Bearison, 1983). Fundamental research of this kind is proposed by Weinert and in a sense also by Siguan.

The third type of relationship is best described in terms of abstractness and generality. Studies of this kind deal with general problems such as the gap between schooling and labour, the discrepancy between home language and instructional language etc. These studies are set up in such a manner that the results are not time-bound or specific of one educational system. A particular instance of this type of fundamental research are studies concerned with the international comparability of research and research findings. Although it is possible to define individual projects in terms of growth of knowledge, it is often better to define growth of knowledge in the widest possible context, i.e. in terms of a review of as many research projects as possible, including projects from abroad. The combination and analysis of data from different time periods and different nations or cultural backgrounds is a check on the value of otherwise single, fragmented pieces of research. Through combined research efforts, investigators may protect themselves against conclusions that may actually be unjustifiable generalisations of historical or local particularities (cf. Boshier & Collins, 1983). This type of fundamental research is proposed by Walberg.

As stated earlier, the authors were asked to focus primarily on the implications of their proposed studies for educational theory. However, most contributions also address technology development or are explicitly inspired by consumer interests. I would like to go into this in some detail here, in the light of what was said about the endangered position of fundamental research in the first section of this chapter.

Fundamental research and technology oriented or policy oriented research are compatible types of research. Moreover, fundamental research is always more or less technology or policy oriented. This is most clearly exemplified in Cummins' contribution, especially where he addresses the relationships between research, theory and policy. He stresses that the sociological context, which he describes in terms of power relations between dominant and subordinate groups in society, plays a major role in determining the choice of issues to investigate, the conduct of the research, the interpretation of the findings, and their relevance for policy.

What principally distinguishes these types of research is their relationship with the scientific world (the forum of scientists) and their relationship with the consumer world, which is often a commercial market. Figure 1 depicts a model of the relationships that characterize the two types of research.

For sake of clarity, I distinguish here only two types of relationships: (1) knowledge gains for the scientific world or the consumer world, and (2) the influence of the scientific world or the consumer market on the contents and structure of research projects. In the case of fundamental research the intended and the realised knowledge gains are substantial for the scientific world, whereas for the consumer market they are, as a rule, limited. In the case of technology and policy oriented research the intend-

Figure 1.    A model characterizing fundamental and
             technology / policy oriented research

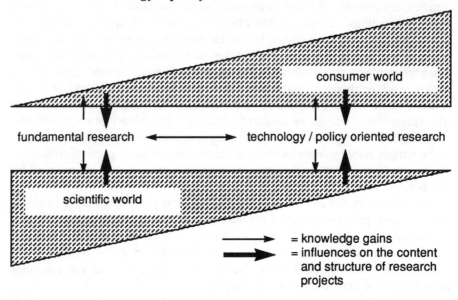

ed knowledge gains for the consumer world are large, but they are small
for the scientific world. Furthermore, as is shown in the model, the consumer world has a relatively strong influence on technology and policy
oriented research, whereas its influence on fundamental research is relatively weak, though certainly not absent. Conversely, scientists have a
strong influence on the form and content of fundamental research, while
their influence on the other types of research, at least where the content is
concerned, is limited.

In a sense the model underscores what was stated earlier about the
OECD's concern about the fact that the position of fundamental research is
jeopardized in some countries by systems of research and higher education that are highly practical, short-term and commercial in their orientation.

The question here is whether the authors' preoccupation with technology
development and policy or consumer interests has perhaps interfered with
their concern with the importance of the fundamental nature of the
research they discuss. In fact, only Weinert and Windham explicitly
emphasize the importance of fundamental conceptual analyses. Nearly all
authors, however, stress the importance of instrument development with
the aim of exploring and assessing various constructs and processes that
are deemed relevant in educational research. Such developments, of
course, implicitly call for conceptual, theoretical analyses. Walberg, Cum-

mins, Clifford, Entwistle and Purves are particularly concerned with measures for the improvement of school practice. It is difficult to tell whether this concern perhaps distracts their attention from fundamental research issues.

Be that as it may, there can be no doubt that emphasizing the importance of improving school practice is not out of place when addressing fundamental issues in educational research. The eventual improvement of school practice is after all an important motive for fundamental research.

## References

Bearison, D.J. (1983) Who killed the epistemic subject? In: W.F. Overton (ed.) *The relationship between social and cognitive development*. Hillsdale, N.J.: L.E.A.

Boshier, R.W. & J.B. Collins (1983) Education participations scale factor structure and socio-demographic correlates for 12,000 learners. *International Journal of Lifelong Education, Vol. 2*, pp. 163-177.

Houtkoop, W. & M. van der Kamp (1987) *Probleemverkenning volwasseneneducatie*. The Hague: SVO.

O.E.C.D. (1988) *Science and technology policy outlook*. Paris: OECD.

Wohlwill, J.F. (1973) *The study of behavioral development*. New York: Academic Press.

# A Theory of Educational Productivity: Fundamental Substance and Method

Herbert J. Walberg
Univerity of Illinois at Chicago
USA

Considerable research shows that education in general and teaching in particular can be made more productive, although substantial increases in efficiency may require new arrangements and incentives. Prior psychological theory suggests that academic learning is a function of five proximal factors - student age, ability, and motivation, and the amount and quality of instruction - and four supportive or substitutive factors - the environments of the classroom, home, peer-group outside the school, and mass media, particularly television, to which students are exposed. More than 100 syntheses of some 8,000 studies of these factors show their consistent association with learning outcomes.

The theory of educational productivity may be considered "fundamental" with respect to the editor's definition of the term. The studies on which it is founded have been conducted largely independent of the immediate demands of policy makers and practitioners. Indeed, we have made special efforts to compile and analyze studies and data from multiple time periods and nations rather than what seems currently fashionable. The theory is not only independent in this sense but also critical of prevailing policy and practices in showing that far better results can be achieved.
The theory of educational productivity might be considered fundamental

in another sense: it is directed to the fundamental purpose of education - learning - as well as specifying its generally well-established influences. It is, however, simple and reductionistic in focussing on the proximal or direct influences in the immediate learning setting rather than more remote organizational and political factors that obviously affect the nine productivity factors.

The theory, moreover, is primarily psychological since it draws on psychologically-oriented experiments in educational settings. It also, however, draws on sociological methodology, specifically, secondary multivariate analysis of national and international surveys, to establish the generalizability of the apparent influences of the nine factors across time and place.

The productivity theory is inspired by economic production functions that call for a full specification of factors that efficiently "produce" desired outcomes. Since we have been preoccupied with causality and generality, however, my colleagues and I have yet to estimate values of outcomes and the costs of the factors. Oddly few estimates of the value and the costs of various educational technologies seem to be available for affluent countries. Much of the best estimation work is by Windham and others in newly industrializing countries (see subsequent chapter).

## Definitions and Fundamental Questions

A few working definitions may be useful at the outset. For the purpose of this chapter, effectiveness may be defined as the attainment of educational goals, mainly the psychological maximization of learning. Learning is viewed in a broad sense, which includes cognitive, affective, and behavioral components; immediate and long-term dimensions; and academic, "life-relevant", and other aspects. Effectiveness, of course, varies by degrees; and the degrees may be measured by the amounts learned. Efficiency or productivity may be thought of as a ratio of the amount learned (or its value) to the resources consumed (or their costs). Resources include not only financial expenditures on buildings, equipment, and staff salaries, but also valuable human time and effort, including that of teachers, parents, and students.

Learning is a psychological process that can be measured and optimized. But it is also useful to ask the essential question of economics: How can competing goals be attained with scarce resources? Educators are unused to thinking economically about values and costs; but such thinking raises policy and practical questions about educational fundamentals that affect national welfare and students' prospects for adult life: What learning is of most worth? What is the relative value of general and special learning?

What instructional methods yield the highest ratios of added learning value to total costs including capital expenditures, operating budgets, institutional changes, and human time? What new incentives and organizations in the educational enterprise would best foster productivity growth?

Thinking about such questions incurs psychological costs of time and effort. Even if education is a vast industry, it cannot be assumed that educators have such incentives and resources to make it as productive as it can be. It may be easier and rationally self-interested to plead for increased public subsidies, the wisdom of tradition, and protection against competition. Classic observations of bureaucracies, especially those unsubjected to marketplace competition, suggest that their means become more important than ends and that incrusted tradition and custom block innovation (Weber, 1905). Bureaucratic functionaries, moreover, may consider their own interests since altruism is hardly infinite.

## New Demands for Productivity

The time seems ripe to ask skeptical questions about the prevalent technology of classroom instruction, which, with its characteristic reliance on recitation and seatwork, has remained essentially the same since the turn of the century in the U.S. (Hoetker & Ahlbrand, 1969). Poor test scores and high costs have elevated the productivity problem to intense national concern in the U.S.; but it is also of high interest in the Netherlands and other countries as shown by intensified interest in national achievement testing and international comparisons.

Estimating educational effectiveness and efficiency may be difficult because educators disagree on the nature, measurement, and value of the content to be learned. Different examinations, moreover, contain various emphases that may not reflect what has been taught; even nationally-standardized mathematics tests used in elementary and secondary schools lack content comparability. In addition, even if learning were well measured, aligned, and calibrated, educators have neither agreed nor estimated values and costs. In order to make more rational and informed decisions on what and how to teach, they would need to know the dollar or time-equivalent value of each item, topic, attitude, or skill to be learned and the full costs of imparting it including the student's foregone opportunities for leisure or learning something else.

These problems of values and research, however, are hardly insuperable; and citizens and politicians throughout the world are obliging educators to do better and avoid unnecessarily increasing costs. In the public sector, where costs are often paid by third-party taxpayers rather than disciplined by consumer choice, the costs advocated may have had few bounds.

Today, however, it is increasingly recognized that efficiency in the public sector is in the national if not the professional interest. Japan and Western Europe are taking the leadership in efficiency efforts including privatization, deregulation, and increased consumer choice in many economic spheres. It appears that large improvements in educational productivity are also possible. Education, for example, is one of the largest service industries in the U.S.; and its rising costs in the past few decades have been associated with declining numbers of students served and, according to the National Commission on Excellence in Education (1983), poor achievement test scores by international standards. Although efficiency may have declined in education, the potential benefits of productivity growth are vast.

The wealth of nations depends on the abilities of people as much as it did two centuries ago when Adam Smith argued that education should be considered a useful investment rather than mere consumption. Moreover, increased international economic competition, as well as the continuing rise in "knowledge industries", means that a variety of abilities will be in greater demand (Walberg, 1983).

Recent studies provide a grim picture of U.S. achievement even in the elementary grades. In mathematics, for example, Stevenson (1983) found that students in the U.S. fall further behind Japanese and Taiwanese at each grade level; and, by fifth grade, the worst Asian classes in his large sample exceeded the best American class. Our research and observations in elementary science classes in Japan corroborates his findings. Recent international comparisons in mathematics and science also showed poor American performance. Even though Americans may be most concerned about these dismal results, policy makers in other countries are also interested in increasing educational productivity in their own national interest. With free trade and communication, countries that increase their human capital will generally benefit not only their own citizens but those in other countries as well.

## Productivity Theory

In recent years, my colleagues and I analyzed large-scale U.S. and international educational surveys and compiled syntheses of thousands of educational research studies (see Walberg, 1984, 1986, and 1988, for details). These surveys and syntheses show that nine factors appear to increase learning. Potent, consistent, and widely generalizable, these nine factors fall into the three groups shown in Table 1. Many aspects of these factors, especially the amount and quality of instruction, can be altered by educators; and these deserve our attention especially in improving educational opportunities for at risk youth.

Each of the first five factors - ability or prior achievement, development, motivation, and the quantity and quality of instruction - seems necessary for learning in school; without at least a small amount of each, the student can learn little. Large amounts of instruction and high degrees of ability, for example, may count for little if students are unmotivated or instruction is unsuitable.

Table 1: Nine Educational Productivity Factors

Student Aptitude
1) Ability or preferably prior achievement as measured by the usual learning tests
2) Development as indexed by chronological age or stage of maturation
3) Motivation or self concept as indicated by personality tests or the student's willingness to persevere intensively on learning tasks

Instruction
4) the amount of time students engage in learning
5) the quality of the instructional experience including method (psychological) and curricular (content) aspects

Psychological Environments
6) the "curriculum of the home"
7) the morale or climate of the classroom social group
8) the peer group outside school
9) minimum leisure-time television viewing

Time or quantity of instruction and study, along with the other factors, should be viewed as a scarce ingredient in learning. Quality of instruction, for example, can be understood as providing optimal cues, correctives, and reinforcement insure the fruitfulness of engaged time. Diagnosis and tutoring can help insure that instruction is suitable to the individual student. Inspired teaching can enhance motivation to keep students persevering. Quality of instruction, then, may be considered as efficient enhancement of allocated or engaged learning time.

Similarly, the four psychological environments can enlarge and enhance learning time. Good classroom morale may reflect match of the lesson to student aptitude, the socially- stimulating properties of the academic group, or, in general, the degree to which students are concentrating on learning rather than diverting their energies, because of unconstructive social climates. Peer groups outside school and stimulating home environments can help by enlarging learning time and enhancing its efficiency; students can both learn in these environments as well as become more able to learn in formal schooling. Finally, television can displace homework, leisure reading, and other stimulating activities; and it may dull the student's keenness for academic work. For instance, some of the average of 28 hours a week spent viewing television by U.S. secondary school students might usefully be added to the mere four or five weekly hours of homework they report.

### Evolution of Theory and Research

Unlike other national studies of education that have relied on hearings and testimony, our investigations of educational productivity followed applied research in the natural sciences in several respects (Walberg, 1983). Since its inception, the theory of educational productivity guided the inquiry. The theory is sufficiently explicit to test; and, using large bodies of national and international data, a wide variety of empirical studies of it were conducted. We published about two dozen of these empirical studies in research journals of the American Educational Research Association and the American Psychological Association that require review by referees as in other scientific disciplines. Only after extensive observation and some modifications of the theory (notably the addition of television and peer group to the list of major factors) were the implications drawn in professional and policy journals such as Daedalus, Educational Leadership, and Phi Delta Kappan. We later worked with several organizations that wanted to bring the findings before their member practitioners; these included the American Federation of Teachers, the National Association of Secondary School Principals, the Council of Chief State School Officers, the U.S. Navy and the U.S. Department of Education (in the "What Works" series), and ministries of education and other agencies in Asia and Europe. Like other theories, however, the theory of educational productivity should be considered open to disproof in part or whole by empirical contradiction.

In our investigations, we tried to follow three scientific canons - parsimony, replication, and generalizability. In this context, parsimony means that the theory converges on the least number of factors that powerfully and consistently predict or explain cognitive, affective, and behavioral learning.

As pointed out above, the theory is reductionistic and psychological: It fundamentally assumes that academic learning is an individual affective, behavioral, and cognitive activity that mainly takes place in the social context of the classroom group as well as in the home and peer group. This is not to deny the influence of Washington, the statehouse, the community, superintendent, and principal but to encourage examination of their effects on the nine factors directly impinging on individual students. Thus, from our view, school and district economic, political, and sociological characteristics and conditions are less relevant to learning because their influences are less alterable, direct, and observable. They are not substitutes for the nine factors, but more distant forces that can support or interfere with them.

More and less productive classes, moreover, may be expected in the same school; and it is somewhat misleading to characterize a whole school or district as effective - just as it is less accurate to characterize an optimal condition of plant growth as the average annual rate of rainfall in a state or farm than the amount of rain and irrigation that reaches the roots of a single plant in a given time period.

The educational productivity theory itself is admittedly over-simplified because learning is clearly affected by school and district characteristics as well as many economic, sociological and political forces at the school, community, state, and national levels. Yet these characteristics and forces - such as the sex, ethnicity, and socioeconomic status of the student, the size and expenditure levels of schools and districts, and their political and sociological organization - are less alterable in democratic pluralistic societies; are less consistently and powerfully linked to learning; and appear to operate mainly through the nine factors in the determination of achievement. Thus, we offer our theory not as a threat to those who see the efficacy of other factors but as a collegial invitation to demonstrate their effects on the nine factors or directly on the outcomes of schooling.

The canon of replication, in my view, means that the findings in similarly designed studies should reproduce one another fairly closely. For example, reinforcement or reward of learning has been implemented in various forms such as candy, tokens, symbols, and social recognition; it can be and indeed is usually operationally defined in detail in various studies. The question is whether these forms are the same or different in their effects. To answer this question, the various implementations or strategies grouped under the same category may be more finely categorized and empirically compared in their effects on learning to see if their magnitudes are the same or different. Usually, simple rather than complicated, detailed classifications serve to summarize the findings; and these relatively simple findings suggest educational implications that are convenient and practical to implement.

Generalizability means that studies should yield similar results in national and international samples of students of different characteristics such as sex and age, in different subjects such as civics and science, and using different research methods such as surveys, case studies, and experiments (Walberg, 1986). For example, the effects of mastery learning on different students and in different school subjects and grade levels may be estimated to determine the extent of their generality. What has been empirically found in hundreds of studies is that generally the results are surprisingly robust. Echoing the folk adage, what's good for the goose is good for the gander. The more powerful factors appear to benefit all students in all conditions; but some students appear to benefit somewhat more than others under some conditions. In addition, some studies report larger effects than the average; others, of course, report smaller effects. The cited research should be consulted for details.

## Methods of Research

Since our concern was productivity, we hoped that our own research would efficiently capitalize on previous inquiry; and, under the support of the National Institute of Education and the National Science Foundation, our team of investigators started by compiling reviews of the 1970s on the productive factors in learning. Next, quantitative syntheses of all available studies of productive factors were conducted; syntheses of several thousand investigations were compiled. Case studies of Japanese and American classes were carried out to compare educational productivity in the two countries. The productive factors were further probed for their significance in promoting learning in three large sets of statistical data on elementary and secondary school students - the National Assessment of Educational Progress, High School and Beyond, and the first mathematics survey of the International Association for the Evaluation of Educational Achievement.

## Secondary Analysis

Re-analysis or "secondary analysis" of previously collected and analyzed data is an important part of productivity research and is becoming prevalent in educational research for several reasons: It is more widely recognized today that political, substantive and methodological assumptions heavily influence the apparent results of quantitative (and qualitative) studies. The term "independent variable," for example, makes a substantive claim of causality that may be difficult to prove or disconfirm in experimental or correlational research, especially that from a single local sample at a single point in time.

Yet educational relevance rests on causality to a large extent because educators seek efficient means that cause desirable ends; and most decisions by policy makers and practitioners are guided only by partial knowledge of conditions and causes. To determine policy and practice, it is often worthwhile subjecting data, especially state, national and international data that have potential for generalizability, to multiple analyses, possibly by several independent teams of investigators, to test the robustness and generalizability of findings rather than taking for granted the assumptions of the first or a single analysis. In addition, some sets of data gathered at great cost and difficulty may be capable of shedding light on more questions than those they were originally collected to answer. Secondary analysis may be fit into a framework or typology of various forms of educational research (Walberg 1986). The definitions below show how secondary analysis and, another new and related form, research synthesis, compare to and contrast with traditional primary research and narrative reviews:

*Primary research*, for the purpose of this chapter, reports an original analysis of raw qualitative or quantitative data. It may include a literature review, theoretical framework, and explicit hypotheses. As mentioned above, secondary analysis is the re-analysis of data by the original or, more often, other investigators for the same purpose for which they were collected or a different purpose.

*Reviews* are narrative commentaries about primary and secondary research. They usually summarize and evaluate studies one by one, but rarely statistically analyze their results. Reviews often contain theoretical insights and practical recommendations, but rarely assess rival theories by their parsimonious accounting of empirical regularities.

*Research synthesis* explicitly applies scientific techniques and standards to the evaluation and summary of research; it not only quantitatively summarizes effects across studies but also provides detailed descriptions of replicable searches of literature, selection of studies, metrics of study effects, statistical procedures, and both overall and exceptional results with respect to experimental conditions, context, or subjects. Qualitative insights may be usefully combined with quantitative synthesis; and results from multiple reviews and syntheses of the same or different topics may be compiled and compared to estimate their relative magnitudes and consistencies. It is also possible to carry out secondary analyses of the data from a research synthesis. Since the data gathered from original reports may be used to calculate "effect sizes," "vote counts," or other indexes of study findings, these data may be obtained to calculate such indexes by alternative procedures.

## Experiments and Surveys

Few intensive experiments (with random assignment to treatment and control conditions) or quasi-experiments are national in scope; and most analyze only one or two factors and sample limited populations within a school or community. They are often strong on observational technique, treatment verification, and measurement of outcomes - in short, internal validity, but they are often weak in generalizability or external validity since they do not rigorously sample from large, well-defined populations. People, moreover, may behave differently in experiments than they do in ordinary circumstances.

Survey research has complementary strengths and weaknesses: it often draws large, stratified, random samples of national populations and measures more factors but sacrifices internal validity since the factors are usually measured cross-sectionally and perhaps superficially with only a few items. Survey research, however, can statistically control to some extent for multiple causes and can be more causally convincing than quasi-experiments controlled only for one or two covariates.

The complementarity of intensive and extensive studies, however, is important. In principle, consistent, powerful effects should consistently emerge from either form of research as well as from case studies. Robust findings give a more solid basis for educational policy and practice. In fact, approximately 70 syntheses of several thousand intensive studies support the consistently positive effects or correlations of the nine productivity factors or their more specific aspects (Walberg, 1986; the expected negative association of achievement with extramural television hours beyond ten per week is the exception). In addition, a syntheses of nine regression studies of extensive survey data on 15,802 13- and 17-year-old students tested in mathematics, science, social studies, and reading by the National Assessment of Educational Progress supports the sign of these findings (Walberg, 1986). The correlations of the factors with achievement and subject-matter interest as learning outcomes varied from -0.45 to +0.68; and 83 (or 91 percent) of the 91 correlations were in the expected direction. Although the magnitudes of the correlations depend slightly on the type of learning outcome (achievement or attitude), subject matter, and productivity factor, they average +0.19, and most range between +0.05 and +0.40. When the factors were controlled for one another in multiple regressions, 58 (or 91 percent) of the 64 coefficients were in the expected direction. The regression weights, moreover, were non-significantly different across age, subject matter, type of outcome, subject matter, and productivity factor. The results, however, reveal colinearity among the factors: students advantaged on one also tend to be advantaged on the others.

The results suggest further that no single factor is dominant in determining learning outcomes (although ability or prior achievement might have been if socioeconomic status had not been used as a cross-sectional proxy for this factor). The prior syntheses of intensive and extensive studies thus suggest that no single factor can serve as a panacea. Improving all the factors using scarce resources of human time and effort as efficiently as possible would seem a more advisable policy than improving only one, which may lead to diminishing returns. Most of the evidence, however, is assembled from U.S. studies from the past decade, and it would be useful to test the generality of the results across countries and historical periods. Our group, therefore, has begun secondary analyses of data archived by the International Association for the Evaluation of Educational Achievement.

## Research Synthesis

Ten years ago, our group wrote an article called "The Quiet Revolution in Educational Research", which provided estimates of the consistency of effects of educational interventions in the review literature of the 1970s. Five years later, the results of nearly 3,000 studies could be analyzed and reported. Last year, an Australian-U.S. team assessed 134 reviews of 7,827 field studies and several large-scale U.S. and international surveys of learning. For instructional design factors, I recently summarized this work under the 15 rubrics shown in Table 2 (Walberg, 1988).

Table 2: Recently synthesized sets of educational methods and conditions

Psychological Elements of Teaching
Methods of Teaching
Patterns of Teaching
Promotion of Learner Autonomy
Open Education
Instructional Systems
Computer-Assisted Instruction
Student Grouping
Social Environment
Reading Methods
Writing Methods
Science Methods
Mathematics Methods
Techniques for Special Populations
Teacher Training Methods

The detailed compilation of effects in the original article allows us to compare the average effects of educational means with one another - including some efficacious ones that are no longer popular. Researchers and policy makers can see that some techniques have enormous effects, while others confer only trivial advantages or even harm learning. To plan and evaluate programs, policy makers can examine the findings in the light of their own experience and circumstances. In practice, however, they might attain results half or twice as good as the average estimates reported: Success may depend not only on their care in implementation but also on their purposes; the best saw swung as a hammer may do little good.

This psychological research provides first-order estimates of the effects of instructional means on educational ends under various conditions. But some practices may be costly - not in dollars but in new or complicated arrangements that may be difficult for some teachers and educational authorities to begin and continue. Thus, the estimates of effects are only one basis for decision making; and we need to consider productivity or values of effects in relation to total costs including the time and energies of educators and students.

Psychology alone cannot suffice to prescribe practices, since different means bring about different ends. Educators must chose among student-, teacher-, and curriculum-direction of effort; facts and concepts; breadth and depth; short- and long-term ends; academic knowledge and real-world application; equal opportunity and equal results; and Plato's triumvirate of thinking, feeling, and acting. Once these choices are made, the estimates of effects can provide one of the bases for choosing the most productive practices.

## Fundamental Research Prospectus

Several fundamental questions remain; much research remains to be conducted. First, the nine constructs have been cross-classified against several instructional theories including those of Bennett, Bloom, Bruner, Carroll, Cooley, Gagné, Glaser, Harnischfeger, and Wiley (Walberg, 1986). This work, however, was carried out more than five years ago; and surveys and experimental results have accumulated. The theoretical formulation of educational performance models of the past two decades since the seminal works of Bruner and Carroll has rapidly advanced. The models are explicit enough to be further integrated theoretically and further tested in ordinary classroom settings by experimental methods and production functions. Future empirical research and syntheses that are more comprehensive and better connected operationally to these theoretical formulations should help reach a greater degree of theoretical and empirical consensus as well as more effective educational practice.

Our group, because of language and time limitations, has thusfar only partly covered research in the U.S. and neglected that in other countries in which English is the primary language. Obviously it would be useful to synthesize research in other Western countries, and indeed, from throughout the world to test the generality of the results. Under the sponsorship of the Ministry of Education, research workers in Sweden are beginning to synthesize European findings.

Another area is disciplinary extension: Cognitive oriented research promises much for improving education, and the rapidly growing area deserves to be synthesized and related to the nine factors. We have begun by synthesizing research on "meta-cognitive" approaches to reading comprehension.

## Mathematical and Conceptual Formulation

The mathematical formulation of the model requires additional theoretical, empirical and measurement development: For example, multiplicative rather than additive economic theories of production dominate economics. The routinely assumed Cobb-Douglas theory assumes that output is a multiplicative, diminishing-returns function of labor and capital. In contrast to the usual linear regressions such multiplicative functions explain why adding more of an input eventually results in diminishing returns. Analogous models of health behavior hold that constructive action is a multiplicative function of perceived threats of disease and of efficacy of action, and the inverse of perceived total monetary and psychic costs.

I originally formulated the productivity theory such that academic learning is a Cobb-Douglas-like (multiplicative, diminishing-returns) function of student ability, motivation, and the amount and quality of instruction. In this mathematical sense, the theory explains why much behavior that is possible for humans to learn cannot in fact be performed by most since ability, motivation, or exposure is lacking and any number multiplied by a zero factor results in zero output. Although extensive evidence from nine regression studies of 15,802 13- and 17-year-old students tested in the National Assessment of Educational Progress as well as quantitative syntheses of hundreds of studies of these factors (Walberg, 1986) show their robust association with cognitive and affective outcomes of learning, little evidence for multiplicativity and diminishing returns can be cited.

The consistent exception, however, is learning returns to time that do reveal diminishing effects with increasing time inthe regressions and syntheses; and time is the only factor measured on a ratio scale (with a zero point and equal intervals). For this reason, the educational theory cannot yet be disconfirmed. The factors are hardly measured over several magnitudes in the way that physical inputs, dollars, and time are measured from zero to more that thousands of equal units in agricultural, biological, economic, and industrial research.

It appears that the theory is undesirably static and should be modified to take account of older theories and recent evidence that future and current values of environmental and individual variables may be dynamic functions of past values. Considerable evidence in communication, developmental and cognitive psychology, and education, shows that early advantages confer future advantages. Students who are behind at the beginning of schooling or slow to start often learn at a slower rate; those that start ahead gain at a faster rate, which results in what has been called "Matthew effects" of the academically rich getting richer, originally noted in *The Bible* (Matthew, XXV, 29: "For unto every one that hath shall be given, and he shall have abundance; but from him that hath not shall be taken away even that which he hath", Walberg and Tsai, 1983).

Such evidence corroborates prior dynamic theories of human behavior and learning. Merton (1968), for example, quoted the Gospel of Matthew in the Bible on the rich-get-richer phenomenon and argued that such Matthew effects operate in scientific productivity: Initial advantages of university study, work with eminent scientists, early publication, job placement, and citation and other recognition combine multiplicatively over time to confer tastes, skills, habits, rewards, and further opportunities that cumulate to produce highly skewed productivity of scientific work. Similarly, it can be hypothesized that outstanding science departments attract distinguished or potentially distinguished faculty staff and students, grants, facilities, intellectual contacts, and other factors over time that lead to probable continuing distinction.

Simon (1954), moreover, postulated a dynamic "Berlitz model" of learning a second language that is testable and may be generalizable. He assumes that the individual can choose the amount of practice, that practice makes the language activity easier, that ease increases pleasantness of the activity, and that pleasantness increases practice. Along with several other interesting assumptions, differential calculus, that has so richly benefitted physics and engineering, enabled him to derive a number of untested but plausible principles. For example, the amount of practice will decrease in proportion to the amount that the rate of practice exceeds the satiation level. Another example of Simon's derivations is that excessive difficulty slows practice because it is unpleasant, but if practice persists through temporary difficulty, practice will become pleasant and persist through mastery.

It can be imagined that relatively early competitive attainments may promote further practice, attract the attention of outstanding teachers and coaches, and lead to the usual positive-skew distribution in competitive sports and other endeavors where absolute measures are available.

## Research and Practice

It will be difficult to confirm or refute convincingly such plausible and potentially highly useful theories unless better measures of educational factors and results can be developed. The eminent psychometrist John B. Carroll (1982) finds little fundamental progress in mental measurement since Thurstone in 1925. Even the recent single- and multiple-parameter item models seem to him rather minor elaborations of earlier insights or mathematically-tractable models of measures wrongly collected or construed (pp. 67, 77). As Carroll ironically notes, computer-assisted "tailored-testing" in which tests are flexible adapted to students over great ranges of ability (rather than the reverse) is a reversion to Binet's turn-of-the-century precedent of suiting items to ability.

It might be further argued that had psychometrists continued Thurstone's efforts to calibrate mental abilities and tasks to the ratio variable chronological age and learning time, educational productivity might be much better understood and optimized today, a half century later. Before research on educational productivity can establish the magnitude and form of the dependence of academic learning on its causal factors rather than simply the sign of de dependence, it may be necessary to develop adaptive, cardinal measures of learning and its factors over many magnitudes. Such a development, following productivity research in agriculture, health, and industry, might lead to similarly great strides in enlarging human achievement and accomplishments.

## References

Carroll, J.B. (1982)  The measurement of intelligence. In: R.J. Sternberg (ed.) *Handbook of human intelligence.* New York: Cambridge University Press.

Hoetker, J. & W. P. Ahlbrand (1969)  The persistence of the recitation. *American Educational Research Journal,* Vol. 6, pp. 145-167.

Merton, R.K. (1968)  The Matthew effect in science. *Science,* Vol. 159, pp. 56-63.

Schiller, D. P. & H.J. Walberg (1982)  Japan: The learning society. *Educational Leadership,* Vol. 39, pp. 411-413.

Simon, H.A. (1954) Some strategic considerations in the construction of social science models. In: P. Lazarsfeld (ed.) *Mathematical thinking in the social sciences*. Glencoe: Free Press.

Stevenson, H. (1983) *Comparisons of Japanese, Taiwanese, and merican mathematics achievement*. Stanford, CA: Center for Advanced Study in the Behavioral Sciences.

U.S. Commission on Excellence in Education (1983) *A nation at risk*. Washington: U.S. Department of Education.

Walberg, H.J. (1981) A psychological theory of educational productivity. In: F.H. Farley & N. Gordon (eds.) *Psychology and education*. Berkeley: McCutchan, (first presented at the 1976 annual meeting of the American Educational Research Association).

Walberg, H.J. (1989) Productive teaching and instruction: An inventory of the knowledge base. *Phi Delta Kappan*, in press.

Walberg, H.J. (1983) Scientific literacy and economic productivity in international perspective. *Daedalus*, Vol. 112, pp. 1-28.

Walberg, H.J., D.P. Schiller & G.D. Haertel (1979) The quiet revolution in educational research. *Phi Delta Kappan*, Vol. 61, nr. 3, pp. 179-182.

Walberg, H.J. & T. Shanahan (1983) High school effects on individual students. *Educational Researcher*, Vol. 12, nr. 7, pp. 4-9.

Walberg, H.J. & S.L. Tsai (1983) Matthew effects in education. *American Educational Research Journal*, Vol. 20, pp. 359-373.

Weber, M. (1902, 1930) *The Protestant ethic and the spirit of capitalism*. London: MacMillan.

# The Cost of Effective Schools

Douglas M. Windham
State University of New York at Albany
USA

It must be recognized at the outset that the issues concerning school costs (and the related issues in regard to school financing) inherently are residual to concerns with the goals of schooling, the effectiveness with which we achieve these goals, and the efficiency with which we mobilize human and material resources within the classroom, individual school, and school system settings. As the title of this paper suggests, our interest here is in determining the cost of providing effective schooling. Thus, there will not be an extensive discussion of such technical cost measurement issues as the valuation of teacher time, facilities provision, or variable-life materials. Other sources (Coombs & Hallak, 1987; Levin, 1983; Tsang, 1988) exist for these purposes. Rather, the focus in this paper will be upon defining the nature of the cost problem within the simultaneous constraints of effective goal attainment and efficient resource utilization. As a result, we will be describing the forms of research and analysis necessary to determine the most efficient, i.e., cost-effective, means of providing a specified form and amount of schooling that is deemed to be effective.

Efficiency in schooling often is confused with the two related concepts of school quality and school effectiveness (Windham, 1988). School quality is one of the most diffuse and confusing terms introduced into educational policy discussions in the last twenty-five years. Depending on the writer, school quality can refer to input measures (aggregate expenditure, per student expenditure, teacher qualifications, availability of facilities, equipment, and materials), process measures (teacher student interaction, student time-on-task, peer effects, use of facilities, equipment, or materials), or output measures (test scores, promotion/graduation rates, later social or economic success). School effectiveness measures, in contrast, normally are restricted to output indicators only.

It is possible to have school quality and school effectiveness without having efficient operation of the school. The efficiency analysis asks the question of whether increased school outputs could be achieved given the available inputs or, alternatively, whether fewer inputs could be used in providing the same level and mix of outputs. Thus, the efficiency concept provides a more inclusive analytical framework than that provided by cost, quality, or effectiveness measures alone. Also it places a stronger emphasis on the scarcity of resources and their appropriate utilization in schooling. It is valuable to note that the efficiency concept can be broadened to include distributional equity and access considerations in process and output measures. The equity and access concerns (for example, participation and attainment by gender, size of place, region, or ethnic/racial group) can be included as output measures along with the more common achievement and attainment standards in defining the nature of an "effective school".

Economic efficiency is related but not identical to the more commonly understood concept of technical efficiency (as used in the study of physics or mechanics). Both efficiency concepts involve a relationship between an output or outputs and a set of inputs. In the case of technical efficiency the relationship consists of a ratio stated purely in terms of physical quantities. Technical efficiency is optimized when one achieves the greatest possible ratio of outputs per unit of inputs. The procedure for dealing with multiple outputs and multiple inputs remains conceptually the same even though the mathematics of the solution is a bit more complicated.

Economic efficiency includes all of the issues related to technical efficiency and adds consideration of the value of the inputs and outputs. This addition of values is required for decision making in that the same physical quantities of different inputs may have dramatically different costs and the same physical quantities of outputs may be valued in terms of benefits quite differently among those who receive the outputs. If the technical relationships among inputs and outputs are known, the calculation of the most economically efficient combination of inputs can be derived if one knows the appropriate costs and benefit values to attach to the inputs and outputs.

The major problems faced in applying the economic efficiency concept in practice are: (1) lack of explicit values (or disagreement over values) for inputs or outputs and (2) the failure to consider alternative technological approaches. The first problem includes the issues related to the propriety of using market prices for valuation, the difficulty of combining individual values into a group valuation or preference, and the inability to deal with purely subjective (psychic) benefits and costs. The second problem is one that, unlike the first, has not received a great deal of consideration by non-economists.

In theory, the process for determining economic efficiency involves three sets of decisions: the desired mix of outputs, the most effective mix of inputs, and the technology to be used in transforming inputs into outputs (Bridge, Judd, & Moock, 1979; Hanushek, 1986). In a case where there is a single output and a given technology, the process of specifying the most economically efficient mix of inputs is quite easy (if input values are given). However, unlike the manufacturing or private service sector, the social service sector (including activities such as schooling) rarely involves choices where outputs are singular or where the appropriate technology is obvious. This is a critical point: the complexity in the economic analysis of effective schooling results not because economic analysis is inherently complex but because the schooling processes - and especially collective social judgments about the effectiveness of schooling processes - are inherently complex.

To summarize: the analysis of the cost of effective schools is congruent with the study of schooling efficiency and must include the following four steps: (1) identification of desired school outputs and outcomes (goals); (2) establishment of indicators and standards for the measurement of effectiveness in achieving the desired goals. (3) identification of the alternative means (technologies) by which the goals may be obtained; (4) analysis of the quantities and costs of the inputs used in each of the alternative technologies.

This research agenda should be understood as inclusive of the productivity topics discussed in the preceding article by Herbert Walberg; thus, the productivity aspects will not be stressed extensively here. Instead, the discussion will concentrate on definition of an effective school, the delineation of resource requirements under varying technologies, and the costing of inputs.

## Definition of an effectiveness standard

The concept of an effectiveness standard is a difficult one to apply in analysis, not because of a difficulty in identifying a definition of effectiveness, but precisely because so many potential definitions exist. When a single term can mean so many things, it ultimately means nothing. A basic requirement for informed debate is a consensus on the meaning of an "effective" school and the adequate financing thereof. If consensus is not attainable, one needs at least a clear understanding of the different definitions being used by various parties to the debate so that real, rather than only apparent (and primarily semantic), disagreements may be highlighted.

The purpose of this presentation is to provide substance to a methodological and policy debate where heretofore there has been little. In doing so certain hazards must be recognized. The more carefully defined and delimited the nature of the effectiveness standard, the greater the danger of losing the political support that has been or may be engendered by the very vagueness of the original definitions of the concept. Many people who may support effective schooling in an abstract way may not be comfortable with a specific definition which has clear implications for treatment of children in schools, higher costs, or for altered fiscal responsibilities for parents, taxpayers, and the various levels of governmental authority.

Still, no progress toward a realization of an effectiveness standard of funding can take place without the consideration of specifics. The first step is to study the alternative definitions of effectiveness and the various formulations for implementing them as a standard for educational costing and finance. A purpose of this paper is to apply certain perspectives of economic analysis to the school effectiveness concept. While social, cultural, political, pedagogical, and methodological perspectives will encroach upon this analysis, the emphasis here will always be on concepts and tools provided by economic science.

Any final formulation of the cost of school effectiveness model undoubtedly will be based upon a more multi-disciplinary perspective than is presented here. This paper is an attempt to emphasize how selected economic perspectives should contribute to that ultimate multi-disciplinary synthesis. Any other approach would fail to exploit the comparative advantage of this writer and of the authors of the companion papers within this volume.

Economists, in their professional as opposed to political roles, normally are not required to engage in the exercise of goal definition. In theory, economic goals are derived from individual preferences, a social welfare function, or a process of political choice. The social welfare function represents the theoretical summation of a group's members' individual preferences across all alternative uses of available resources. Political choice processes represent all decision-rule activities within the range from full-participatory democracy to simple dictatorship. One of the main values of the social welfare function concept is to contrast the goals that would exist if one actually could summarize the individual preferences of the members of a political unit with the goals that result from the existing political decision making structure.

Beginning in the contemporary era of economic thought with the work of Little in the 1950s, continuing through the work of Buchanan and Tullock in the 1960s and culminating in the recent expansion of work in social choice theory (Bowman, 1978, 1982), economists have concentrated increasingly upon the issue of how goals are formed - not what they should be. The purpose of this paper requires a different approach, however. Ultimately, a criterion for effectiveness in school outcomes and finance will be posited; prior to that it is useful to review how most economists would approach the concept of effectiveness.

Economists use the production function as a means of establishing the maximum effects one can achieve from a given set of inputs or the minimum inputs necessary to achieve a given output. The latter concept is most relevant to the understanding of the common view of schooling efficiency. What resources (inputs) are minimally required in order to attain a level of educational outcome(s) that is definable as "appropriate" by some established standard? Once one identifies the necessary resources (teacher, classroom technology, facilities, equipment, etc.) these can be costed and summed to establish the level of funding necessary for "appropriate and effective schooling". The actual process (discussed in more detail below) is complex and not without methodological as well as political problems. But an effectiveness standard can be created and from it can be derived a standard for adequate financing - the cost of an effective school.

The greatest weakness in the economic analysis of educational production relationships has been the excessive reliance upon macro-educational data (national, regional or school district) to examine processes which take place almost exclusively at the micro-educational level (the school, classroom, or individual student). Because both government regulations and school funding often originate at the macro-educational levels (and because data are more readily available for these levels), researchers have been misled into manipulation of numbers that are little more than aggregate artifices for the underlying phenomena they are supposed to represent (Windham, 1980). From such methodological errors were generated the early anti-intuitive findings of Coleman (1966) and of Jencks (1972) on the impotence of schooling generally and the specific assertions about the irrelevance of teachers. To have found any significant positive contribution for schooling variables at these excessive levels of aggregation within largely misspecified equations or equation systems would have been surprising indeed (and subject to just as much skepticism as are the negative findings).

If educational effectiveness of the type discussed here is to have policy relevance it must be based upon an expanded system of micro-educational research. There is a need to merge the structure of the economic model of resource utilization with the educational psychologists' and classroom ecologists' skills of measurement (e.g., see Thomas & Kemmerer, 1983). Only in this way will the production relationships for primary and secondary schooling be established to a degree of methodological confidence necessary for reasoned public policy concerning effective schools.

The problem of determining the cost of an effective education is complicated by the existence of other purposes for primary and secondary education than those that readily may be embodied in the effectiveness standard. If the standard is expanded to include day-care, health, nutrition, safety, and other schooling services in addition to the cognitive, attitudinal, and behavioral aspects, the effectiveness standard becomes both more conceptually complex and increasingly difficult to operationalize and measure. Even if the definition of effectiveness is restricted for the sake of analytical convenience to a few major outputs stated in a specific and measurable way, there is still the problem of optimizing the input mix given the constraints posed by the resources allocated for the goals not included in the formal effectiveness measure.

Thus, a production model standard of schooling effectiveness requires a specific and, where possible, stable definition of outputs, an improved understanding of the relationship between school resources and educational outputs, and a means of optimizing the resource mix within the constraints of availability, costs, and the alternative demands for the resources. In the following section, I will attempt to move from the abstract conceptual emphasis of the present discussion to the more pragmatic issues of generation and use of an effectiveness standard for schooling.

## Toward a schooling effectiveness standard

If there is to be a publicly guaranteed standard of educational effectiveness, the standard must be defined in terms of inputs, processes, or outputs of the schooling system. Over the last twenty years, especially in the United States but to a significant extent elsewhere as well, the increasing trend has been for legislatures, government agencies, and even courts to attempt regulation of education through the specification of outputs. Schools and schooling are acknowledged by most citizens to be among the most powerful vehicles available to promote social change. What is note-worthy is the probability that schools were generally perceived as more powerful agents of change in society (and in the lives of individual children) before they became the recipients of greater and more varied formal social change responsibilities. It is a common bureaucratic phenomenon that any individual or agency that is unduly encumbered with a widening range of responsibilities may end up doing few, if any, of them well. To many educators, parents, and taxpayers this appears to be what is happening with public primary and secondary education systems in the majority of both developing and developed societies.

This analysis may be faulted for ignoring the concomitant change which has occurred in the complexity of society itself in recent decades. In fact, the increased complexity of schools primarily may be only a mirror of the increasingly complex societies in which they operate. The issue now is how schools can retain (or recapture) their traditional cognitive, attitudinal, and behavioral purposes without sacrificing the legitimate gains made in such areas as increased access for minority and disadvantaged populations and adaptation to the special learning needs of individual students.

Schooling effectiveness research can help to do this. There must be explicit consideration of the tradeoffs between and among the traditional peda-gogical goals and the contemporary social goals for primary and secondary education. Where social goals are of such major importance that their pursuit justifies sacrifice of some part of the traditional school goals of cognitive, attitudinal, and behavioral development, that fact should be recognized and clearly stated. To hold schools, and particularly teachers, solely culpable for current failures to achieve desired levels of mathematical (or reading or writing) skills is certainly inappropriate: the school increasingly is a production process from which additional outcomes have been demanded without an adequate compensating change in either the amount of resources or the technology of instruction.

To return specifically to the concept of an effectiveness standard for the evaluation of schools and their requisite costs, such a standard must involve a recognition of the mutual exclusivity of educational goals at the margin when available resources are fixed and resource utilization already is optimized given the inherent constraints. While output standards of schooling adequacy are the most appropriate, the required understanding of the schooling process simply does not exist to allow for use of output measures in isolation. Even if stated quantitatively (in terms of test measures or the like), effectiveness goals are of no use unless schools know how to maximize them given the available resources and technologies. Similarly, the problem with standardizing inputs among schools is that it assumes certain productivity relationships that have not been shown to exist. Thus, equal costs for schooling rarely generate equally effective schools.

Much of the school finance research of the last three decades concentrated upon proving that provision of equal financial resources is not an acceptable proxy for equal educational opportunity. There are three primary reasons why this is so. First, because of a "convergence of disadvantage" in terms of home background, earlier schooling, or physical or mental abilities, some students naturally will require more resources than do other students in order to achieve the same level of learning. Second, situational cost differentials (e.g., variations in land costs, wages, taxes, utility costs, etc.) cause the same level of funding to purchase less schooling resources in some locations (especially in rural areas or large urban centers) than in others. Third, all schools do not operate with the same production technology nor do they attempt to produce the same mix of outcomes (Chapman & Windham, 1986).

In terms of this last issue, there is a need for school research to recognize that the demand for resources (and thus for the financing of school costs) is derived from the form of classroom technology applied (Cummings, 1986). In a single teacher, class-lecture technology, the resource demand may be almost exclusively for teacher time. In a programmed learning format there will be a relatively higher demand for learning materials. Some classroom technologies allow for teacher specialization on pedagogical problems, with a teacher aide assisting in management and discipline. The point is that even within highly regulated public education systems there remains a wide divergence in classroom technology from school to school, subject field to subject field, grade level to grade level, and even from classroom to classroom (Monk, 1984; Thomas & Kemmerer, 1983).

Another problem with standardized resource provision exists when schools have separate production technologies; for example, there is great difficulty in the comparison of schools that produce different combinations of outputs. A vocational technical school may be expected to use a quite different mix of physical and human resources than would an academic preparatory program. Similarly, a quite different mix of resources would be needed for a school with serious student discipline problems than would be required in one without such difficulty. The first school must provide additional physical safeguards for students, teachers, administrators, and property, and this requires use of resources that otherwise could have served pedagogical purposes or alternative social outcomes.

There is a middle ground between the imprecision of output measures and the inappropriateness of input standardization: it is the option of emphasizing the instructional process as a means for determining the effectiveness standard. An "acceptable" instructional process that produces the desired outputs would be defined and then financed. An equivalent instructional process, in terms of outputs, would have to be assured for a school regardless of its location, nature, or special problems. Adding a process emphasis in educational provision can lead to quite large differences in the cost of schooling. To provide the same learning experience for a child in an ethnically mixed, low family income, urban school as for one in a relatively homogeneous and affluent suburban school may require that the pedagogical resources be supplied in addition to the resources necessary to support discipline, compensate for locational cost differentials, etc. Thus, a standardized measure of school effectiveness may require a different process/input mix and thus, a varied incidence of costs and of public expenditure.

Can such a process-oriented system of school effectiveness be designed and implemented and how should it relate to the input and output measures of effectiveness discussed earlier? The best philosophical basis for such a system exists in the Rawlsian model of a "social minimum" (Rawls, 1971). Adapted within a neo liberal framework, this model would imply an obligation on the part of government to supply those resources necessary to assure access to a minimum standard of educational process for all children. Such a system sets aside the debate over whether every inequality is, in fact, an inequity. It also ignores demands by such authors as Williamm Rohwer (1972) that the public school teach only what most adults are capable of mastering. Different social minima could be established at the national, regional, and local levels. There need be no maximums and no requirements for absolute equality.

The primary danger in such a system exists in establishment of the minima at an excessively low level. However, the social minima approach has the dual advantage of making any remaining inequality explicit at the margin (and thus more subject to political demands for justification) and of increasing the potential political attractiveness of educational funding because of its direct link to the learning process. A cynic might well question the last assertion: teacher groups, social elites, and political interest groups may all find the newly "effective" educational system less attractive to support without the present emphasis on the various collectively "ineffective" activities that rebound to their individual or group benefit.

However, an important aspect of a social minima system is that once the social minima are guaranteed (but only then), the regional and local authorities may add on whatever educational "luxuries" they like. This facet of the program gives rise to the central political and economic issue in the social minima debate: is the goal of increasing educational achievement for society's disadvantaged promoted best by a standard of educational provision that has equality of process as its prime criterion? The danger is that the political debate will contrast unfavorably the probable achievements of the social minima provision standards of effectiveness with the idealized but improbable achievements of current equality standards.

The record of the last two decades of court and legislatively mandated educational equality reform in the United States indicates that equality remains as vague and uncertain a standard as ever. Even with a mixture of output measures and input standards of equality, schools and school systems remain vastly unequal without significant gains in the provision of basic or minimally acceptable educational experiences for the disadvantaged. Where equality has made gains, it often has been through a leveling downward that is both a cause and a result of the exodus of many economically advantaged families from the public systems of education.

One simple fact should be faced: the public primary and secondary school system is not an obviously appropriate or effective system for redistributing income or wealth in our societies. The excesses of inequality in income and wealth should be controlled through the laws governing receipt and taxation of income. To those who doubt that such legislation can be achieved, the appropriate reply is to question why they feel society will allow a redistribution of social or economic status through the public schooling function (even if such were achievable) that it fails to support through the tax system.

The public primary and secondary education system is, however, an appropriate institution for establishing improvements in the life chances of a society's disadvantaged members. Such improvements in school effectiveness are more likely to lead to an eventual reduction in social inequality than is any forced equalization of school resources. But is the proposal of social minima in resource provision (based on process needs) any more realistic or politically acceptable than the input or output equality proposals of the last three decades? Probably not. Both courts and political structures would require a period of time to adapt to a new standard for educational provision. Still, the effectiveness minima should be presented, debated, and refined, because there seems little doubt that equalization models will continue to run up against the freedom of parental choice standard and the inherent limits on converting equal inputs into equal results (Behrman, Pollak & Taubman, 1982; Birdsall & Cochrane, 1982).

I stated earlier that a social minima approach to educational effectiveness requires the definition of an achievement standard, the identification of production linkages (instructional technologies), and the supply of financing adequate to obtain the optimum mix of resources. Each of these represent discrete political, as well as analytical, steps that must be taken.

Definition of an achievement goal is an inherently arbitrary activity.

Assume, for example, that the present mean level of national achievement in reading and mathematics for each grade level is accepted as the definition of minimum effectiveness. There is no obvious logic in the choice of such a standard; one could as easily choose the third or ninth decile. Politically, the choice creates a set of very important implications for students, the educational system, and the various levels of government.

Ceteris paribus, the higher the initial definition of minimum effectiveness, the larger the number of students whose education must be improved, the greater the demands on the educational system, and the greater is the potential fiscal impact of the program. The ability and willingness of taxpayers to support the effectiveness standard will determine the ultimate impact. Schooling effectiveness may be viewed as either a collective consumption good or an investment activity; in either case, one can be sure that the taxpayers' support for it will be inversely related to its cost. The higher the initial standard, the harder it will be to generate the political support to obtain the necessary financing to implement and maintain the effectiveness standard.

Even given this political bias toward moderation of goals, a meaningful effectiveness standard for achievement still can be generated. It must be a criterion-referenced standard, of course, to avoid the danger of success through low expectations and poor peer performance. The social minima approach also allows one means of avoiding the problem of dealing with multiple outputs within the educational production function. Minimal standards of effectiveness would be defined separately for each area of achievement. Thus, once the mathematics effectiveness level is achieved, one can behave as if the marginal rate of substitution (the tradeoff of achievement of one goal for achievement of another) of this goal for other goals has been reduced to zero. Additional gains in mathematics would be treated as having no explicit policy relevance in terms of the provision of effective schooling.

With a set of effectiveness minima in place, the next policy issue is clarification of the input requirements for achievement of effectiveness. At present this information does not exist, and traditional production function research offers little likelihood that it will be generated. With ethnographic methods used in a production function context at the classroom and school level, there is no certainty - but some reason for optimism - about what research findings might be obtained. Researchers would have to create a "needs" model that would take student characteristics as given. These would be calculated in terms of both measurable aptitudes and attitudes. The model would then allow one to derive the minimal resources required (based upon the existing state of knowledge of the production relationships) to provide an educational experience that would allow the student to attain the achievement standard.

It takes little sophistication to recognize the implementation problems such an approach implies. Among the obvious are:

1 design of acceptable aptitude, attitude, and achievement tests;
2 avoidance of "moral hazard" issues in that poor performance on the above implies greater resource availability for the school;
3 the implausibility of an effectiveness standard based upon past performance;
4 the existence of fixed resources in the school and classroom;
5 the restrictions on targeting of funds to the needy child;
6 the adjustment of the system to earlier shortfalls.

Each of these issues represents a potential research agenda. The first two issues are subject to treatment in a fairly straightforward technical manner, but the latter four will require significant research and policy adjustments. To implement the effectiveness standard will require the generation of aggregate measures of student characteristics certainly to the school level and probably to the district or regional level. Given the earlier criticism of the aggregate artifices that afflict the present production analysis of schools, these new measures should be designed to elicit the most relevant indicators of student characteristics. Mean measures should be abandoned in favor of percentages of a cohort's population that would have certain characteristics of need as measured by the test instruments. A mean score of 80 per cent on a test imparts less relevant information (for administrative or policy deliberations) than does the knowledge that 22 per cent of the students fell below a score of 60.

The set of necessary resources (costs) for effective schools would have to be adjusted to take into account the existence of fixed resources within a school system. For example, if available teacher quality or physical resources are less than the effectiveness standard anticipates, compensatory increases in other resources must be allowed. One of the major limitations to all attempts to restructure educational production is the extraordinarily small percentage of variable resources within many school budgets. With given physical facilities and long term teacher contracts or obligations because of tenure or union agreements, the primary, if not only, means for altering educational inputs is through increased allocation rather than through reallocation. The implication is that the effectiveness standard will involve a much larger increase in cost than would be the case if all resource inputs to schools were variable in the short run.

An additional problem in implementing the social minima effectiveness formula will be the difficulty of targeting funds to the neediest students. If funds are given to the district or school on the basis of the need for additional resources for presently disadvantaged students, what assurance is there that the funds will be used for those students? Even if the effectiveness funds were treated as a special form of categorical aid - as would be most appropriate - monitoring resource use (or the acceptance of possible misuse) would represent an additional implementation cost.

Finally, in the real world of schools, one would face the problem of the system having to adjust to earlier failures and inadequacies. Some children will still evidence a tendency to fall further and further behind the longer they are in school. In such cases, where compensatory resources have been provided consistently but to little effect, a policy decision must be made as to the extent of societal responsibility under the effectiveness formula. If an eleventh-grade student is still reading at the traditional fourth-grade level, the amount of compensatory educational resources required may prove to be extensive. Resource availability probably will not be adequate to meet this need. In such extreme cases the system must either accept the existence of some rate of residual schooling ineffectiveness and/or create special programs to deal with such students (including consideration of expanded and/or improved out-of-school programs).

Alternative formulations of an effectiveness standard of the social minima type exist, of course (e.g., Carnoy, 1983). One could define adequacy of achievement in terms of a certain percentage of a student group who must achieve the effectiveness goal. Or one could concentrate funds - again within a categorical approach - on the lowest 10 or 20 per cent of a group. The first alternative poses the danger of the least advantaged group of students receiving less attention as more resources are concentrated upon the students closest to the margin of effectiveness. The second alternative would create an extremely sharp division in terms of eligibility for special aid, whereas the need for such aid would be represented by a more continuous function.

Any program to promote effective schooling must take into account the need for compensatory preschool experiences. The earlier that intervention occurs the less will be the future demand for resources to provide compensatory education. It is not sufficient by itself to bring children to the first grade with possession of a preschool level of educational effectiveness, but it is probably the most important single step in the provision of effective schooling for all students and especially for the disadvantaged. If the social minima form of schooling effectiveness were to be implemented, it could be done on a year-by-year basis. Beginning with a given preschool cohort, the effectiveness program could be implemented one school year at a time. Because of the greater diversity in the upper secondary school programs, there might be a decision not to use the effectiveness formula for resource requirements after grade eight or nine.

In the succeeding section, I address several of the central cost issues of policy and practice in regard to the effectiveness standard. My primary purpose is to examine the possibility of transferring the standard described above from the theoretically possible to the politically practical.

## Cost issues in the provision of effective schools

It should be obvious from the above discussion that adequacy of financing can be determined only subsequent to a definition of the costs of the effective schooling process, which itself assumes a prior definition of output standards of effectiveness and sufficient information on the schooling production function. All of this is required before the proper or appropriate schooling arrangements may be defined. Any discussion of school costs without these prior steps is fruitless; to repeat once again: school cost and financing issues inherently are residual issues to those of goals and process.

Just as the polemic critiques of the financial inequity among schools failed to generate acceptable standards for reform, so too might debates on financial adequacy for school effectiveness. A schooling effectiveness research agenda first must be implemented to inform policy in two primary ways. First, it should convince politicians and administrators of the impossibility of a purely objective standard of effectiveness. Second, it should generalize an understanding within the school research community that public policy analysis in this area must be directional and long term.

The limited degree of flexibility within the present school finance systems is such that not all of the goals of effectiveness are readily obtainable. Public policy researchers should try to push the analysis of educational systems in the direction of selected effectiveness goals, but also should act in the knowledge that certain of these goals are distant, arbitrary, vague, and subject to change. The school effectiveness standards, if introduced, should initiate evolution, not revolution, in school cost and finance. The issue of financial adequacy, as a derived product of this cost analysis process, must also be dealt with in a conditional context and within an extended time frame.

Obviously, the issue of equity (whose solution requires a value judgment) must be separated from the issue of equality (involving a measurement problem) in resource availability. The advantage of the effectiveness standard that is discussed here is that equity in terms of the availability of resources (cost and financing) is given a definition in terms of the instructional technology used and the resources available for an acceptable level of output. This standard is no less arbitrary than any other but has the advantage of adjustment to changes in political and social judgments of what the output standard should be, increases in knowledge concerning the nature of the production process in schooling, and changes in the society's wealth and thereby in the available resource base.

This effectiveness standard is not in the tradition of those models wherein equity and efficiency in education are set in contradiction to one another. Rather, efficiency is defined in terms of the equitable provision of the resources required for students to obtain a specified level of educational outcome. There would be (and should be) debates on the outcome standard and on monitoring of resource provision, but this form of effectiveness standard structures the debate in such a way that arbitrariness, where it exists, is made much more explicit. To separate the positivist issues in school policy (what can be done) from the normative (what should be done) would greatly facilitate the resolution of many of the political and administrative problems that exist currently. Certainly, current school finance legislation in most countries could have benefitted in the past from a clearer perception of the distinctiveness of these two issues.

The greatest single barrier to implementation of any schooling effectiveness standard is the insufficiency of our learning theories, of our specification of the school production function and its components, and of our level of methodological sophistication in terms of goal definition. Output measurement is the area where the most work has been done. Two major research activities remain that are prerequisites for effectiveness analysis. First, the definition and measurement of non cognitive goals of schooling require more attention than they have received (especially from economists). Second, the difficulty of dealing with the issue of varying marginal rates of substitution among multiple outputs must be resolved.

The measurement and costing of inputs remains crude. At high levels of aggregation the statistical artifices commonly employed tend solely to reflect resource availability rather than use and often misspecify the nature of the resource itself (e.g., teacher qualifications as a measure of teacher quality). At classroom levels of analysis other methodological and research issues arise. How does one value the flow of teacher resources to students in different instructional settings (lecture, small group, individual discussion)? How does one deal with the issue of the tradeoff between greater methodological precision at the micro-educational level versus the increased data costs and reduced generalizability?

A final measurement issue in an effectiveness system of school finance will be that of evaluation standards. The allocation of funds to schools or school systems on the basis of an effectiveness standard should presuppose the existence of some system of assuring that the resources are used for those students - and in the manner - the effectiveness funding formula emphasizes. For example, if government allocations are distributed to schools on the assumption that economically disadvantaged students require greater resources to attain the effectiveness output standard, then there should be a way of ensuring that the resources are not reallocated away from such students at the school or classroom level. Similarly, the effectiveness standard may provide resources on the basis that disadvantaged learners are operating within an aptitudinally integrated classroom environment. If the classrooms are "tracked" according to aptitude, the resources will not have the assumed impact.

An effectiveness standard requires an understanding by all involved parties of the basic assumptions of the model and it requires monitoring of implementation. Without proper evaluation standards, it is impossible to envision how one could justify the costs of establishing an effectiveness standard for school finance.

The effectiveness standard suggested here inherently and explicitly deals with the issue of variable pupil characteristics. The school cost allocation formula would be designed to provide compensatory resources necessary to bring students with disadvantageous learning characteristics up to the minimal acceptable standard of output performance. The basic standard should not be expected to deal with the extreme disadvantages for which categorical aid programs (for physically and mentally handicapped children, for example) are more suitably designed. The formula could deal with the definition of school funding for the vast majority of students, however.

A crucial research issue is to define what relevant personal, community, and school characteristics should be included in the effectiveness formula. Crude proxies such as race or ethnicity should be avoided in favor of the more specific measures of economic or cultural deprivation. Information costs will continue to restrict the generation of data on the complex and subtle factors of home and school environments. However, greater precision can be promoted if the data used are those closest to our present understanding of learning determinacy. It is not being a member of a social or ethnic minority that restricts learning, but there may be a correlation in certain societies between being a member of such a minority and growing up in an educationally deprived environment. Measures of that environment, approximated in the minimally aggregated way, should be used in determining the requirement for school resources to provide an effective learning environment.

Can our societies afford effective schools for more students? This question is of less relevance than whether legislative bodies will adopt an output-based standard for effective schooling and require administrative adaptation to the process-based input requirements of such a standard. It is doubtful if either type of change will occur fully in the next ten years. However, the problem is more one of political and bureaucratic conservatism than of fiscal capacity or even of research competence to produce the needed information.

The current issues dominating the debate on public schooling in many countries are school discipline, teacher unionism, tax inequities, equalization of resources, and subsidization of private schools. While each of these issues could be dealt with more adeptly under an effectiveness system, there is no sign that the issue of school effectiveness itself has enough immediate political currency, and certainly not enough acceptance under a given definition, for adequate political action to be forthcoming. Effectiveness, like equality, is a political issue whose resolution could threaten the advantages of those individuals and groups whose economic and political power is greatest. If resources for education were more readily available, an effectiveness program that involved a "leveling-up" process might be designed so as to be politically acceptable to a wide audience. The current international environment, however, is one of fiscal constraint (Windham & Wang, 1986). Most parties to educational reform are likely to view the process, quite correctly, as a zero-sum game. Since the politically advantaged have the most to lose, there is little reason for optimism concerning a change that appears as "revolutionary" as does the imposition of a schooling effectiveness standard.

In addition, primary and secondary schooling are entering a period in many nations when an increasing proportion of citizens will be non-users of the system in any direct manner. Especially in developed nations, the increasing relative as well as absolute numbers of elderly voters and younger adult but childless voters make the prospects for any future reform of policy less likely unless it can be achieved at great savings through enhanced efficiency. While effectiveness-based school systems might provide great efficiencies in the long run, the transition cost for a high fixed-cost, low-flexibility system such as public education in the United States or most of Europe is likely to be too high for general public support.

### Summary and conclusion

In what manner can studies of the cost of effective schools, structured on the model I have advocated here of developing social minima based on the linkage of school outputs to process and of process to requisite inputs, be considered as fundamental research? First, the studies suggested here focus directly on the development of new knowledge in each of four areas:

1  the determination of the mix of school outputs deemed to be effective (a
   political choice/social choice research agenda);
2  the analysis of how school inputs combine with school process to produce alternative mixes of school outputs (an educational technologies
   research agenda);
3  the determination of cost levels required for the achievement of the
   school effectiveness standard within different contexts of external environment, resource use, and student characteristics (a cost analysis/edu-
   cation production function research agenda);
4  the analysis of school financing based upon who pays for schooling
   costs and in what amounts and forms (an incentive/fiscal capacity
   research agenda).

These various agenda will call into question a wide range of contemporary
research from the fields of psychology, political science, economics, sociology, management science, and pedagogy. The school effectiveness model
is a framework within which the existing and emerging data bases from
the various disciplines can be integrated, one hopes with a synergistic
effect.
Consideration of the school effectiveness standard for cost provision will
create a demand for new forms of instrumentation and measurement, only
some of which can be anticipated now. But the work on the cost of effective schools can be truly foundational in that from it will flow not just a set
of new research and instrumentation needs, but a justification for the
activities to meet these needs and a structure for their use once the
research and the instrumentation are realized.
But what of the legitimate consideration of whether a program of social
minima cost standards for school effectiveness is "politically realistic"?
First, a foundational study does not require immediate political determination of the study or support for it. However, one must be able to indicate eventual political relevance for the outcomes of the study and that is
what I have attempted to do in this paper. Second, new knowledge and
instrumentation can have the effect of changing dramatically that which is
considered politically realistic. The goal of the researcher must be to help
determine future political realities, not simply to adapt to the current definition of such realities.
Finally, the "cost of effective school" meta research agenda is one that can
promote a greater comparability of national and international school data
to the extent that greater standardization of output measures are achieved
on an intra rather than inter-national basis but, in concert with multi
national assessment of the type promoted by UNESCO and the International Evaluation Association (IEA), even the latter form of comparability

is a realizable expectation (see the discussion in Postlethwaite, 1987, and Purves, 1987. See also Purves, this volume).

To summarize, the concept of an effective school suffers from a plethora of definitions. Within the philosophical construct of social minima, I have developed in this paper a concept of effectiveness linked to the economic model of the education production function. For any given output or set of outputs desired from the schools, an acceptable minimal level of achievement will be defined. Then, for varying qualities of initial student achievement and aptitude, the effectiveness model would define the most efficient instructional process and input mix that would allow attainment of the output achievement level. This required input mix then would have to be costed to determine the financial requirements for the school system and these requirements would then be compared with fiscal capacity and tax payer willingness to finance the new forms of schooling.

Present research and understanding of the determinants of school production initially would constrain specification of an effectiveness standard in any but the crudest manner. Even so, the rationality of the new effectiveness cost standard would be no less than that which exists for the present systems of financing primary and secondary schooling. However, the long-term benefits from an effectiveness standard would be substantially greater - especially for the culturally and economically disadvantaged school populations. Also, resource provision based upon an effectiveness standard makes more explicit the societal obligations to school learners and would provide a more objective standard for administrative accountability to taxpayers than now exists.

Philosophically, there are a multitude of effectiveness options. In this paper I have attempted to clarify the advantages of the social minima approach. Technically, there are serious methodological limitations to refinement of the effectiveness production function approach. A substantial research investment would be required prior to full implementation if this standard is to be used properly. However, the greatest barriers to acceptance of the schoo leffectiveness approach are political.

Political (and bureaucratic) conservatism in regard to education would limit any reform of the present systems and would be especially hostile to an approach that would change the basic assumptions and responsibilities of the systems. Such conservatism is very understandable. Education is one of the most central and participatory social institutions. It affects, directly or indirectly, the lives of all citizens. Within education, students, parents, teachers, administrators, and taxpayers each represent significant constituencies that must be satisfied.

No single politician or political group is perceived as responsible for the

present educational system. Anyone advocating a new system of schooling, however, would be held accountable for its failures. The politician(s)
would have to share the credit for success with each of the constituencies
mentioned above, but would be "free" to take full responsibility for the
failures. Under such a political cost/benefit calculus it is not surprising
that dramatic educational reform has little political support except in crisis
periods.

The research and policy issues to be resolved, e.g. definition of outputs,
costing of inputs, specification of the production function model, definition of intergovernmental responsibilities, modification of constitutional
education guarantees, etc., are all so subjective in nature and controversial
in content that it is impossible to imagine any substantial political support
for an educational effectiveness standard in the near future. Research on
the cost of school effectiveness however, still can produce some significant
benefits. The importance of the debate over effectiveness lies in the clarification of research and policy issues. If nothing else results, more people
should come to the understanding that the present educational system is
not the only alternative that exists, that it is just as subjective and dependent upon capricious specification as the weakest effectiveness standard
would be, and that the impacts of the present systems upon the disadvantaged are the result of implicit choices made by societies and do not reflect
inevitable circumstances.

The issue in the schooling effectiveness debate is similar to the effectiveness standard itself in one way: an expectation that one will fail to achieve
all that is possible should not deter efforts to move to an improved position. Continued research and discussion of the cost of school effectiveness
will clarify many of the contemporary questions of schooling, even if it
does not provide the solution to all of them.

## References

Arlin, M. (1984) Time, equity, and mastery learning. *Review of Educational Research*, Vol. 54, pp. 65-86.

Bas, D. (1987) *A cost-effectiveness of training in the developing countries.* Geneva: ILO Discussion Paper No. 19 (December).

Behrman, J.R., R. Pollak & P. Taubman (1982) Parental preferences and provisions for progeny. *Journal of Political Economy*, Vol. 90, pp. 52-73.

Birdsall, N. & S.H. Cochrane (1982) Education and parental decision-mak-
ing: A two-generation approach. In: L. Anderson & D.M. Windham (eds.) *Education and Development.* Lexington: Lexington Books.

Bowman, M.J. (1978) Choices by and for people. In: *Learning and earning:*

*three essays in the economics of education.* Stockholm: National Board of Universities and Colleges, pp. 9-52.

Bowman, M.J. (1982) (ed.) *Collective choice in education.* Amsterdam: Kluwer-Nijhoff Publishing.

Bloom, B.S. (1976) *Human characteristics and school learning.* New York: McGraw Hill Book Company.

Bridge, R., C. Judd & P. Moock (1979) *The determinants of educational outcomes: The impacts of families, peers, teachers and schools.* Cambridge: Ballinger Publishing Company.

Buchanan, J.M. & G. Tullock (1962) *The calculus of consent.* Ann Arbor: University of Michigan Press.

Carnoy, M. (1983) Educational adequacy: Alternative perspectives and their implications for educational finance. *Journal of Education Finance,* Vol. 8, pp. 286-299.

Chapman, D.W. & D.M. Windham (1986) *The evaluation of efficiency in educational development activities.* Tallahassee, Florida: Learning Systems Institute, Florida State University.

Cohen, D.K. (1987) Educational technology, policy, and practice. *Educational evaluation and policy analysis,* Vol. 9, pp. 153-170.

Cohn, E. & R.A. Rossmiller (1987) *Research on effective schools: Implications for less-developed countries.* Washington, D.C.: World Bank Discussion Paper, Education and Training Series.

Coleman, J.S., et al. (1966) *Equality of educational opportunity.* Washington, D.C.: U.S. Government Printing Office.

Coombs, P.H. & J. Hallak (1987) *Cost analysis in education.* Baltimore, Maryland: Johns Hopkins University Press for the World Bank.

Cummings, W.K. (1986) *Low-cost primary education: Implementing an innovation in six countries.* Ottawa, Canada: International Development Research Centre.

Eicher, J.C. (1984) *Educational costing and financing in developing countries.* Washington, D.C.: World Bank Staff Working Papers, No. 655.

Hanushek, E. (1986) The Economics of schooling: Production and efficiency in public schools. *Journal of Economic Literature,* Vol. 24, pp. 1141-1177.

Jamison, D., S.J. Klees, & S. Wells (1978) *The cost of educational media.* Beverly Hills: Sage Publications.

Jencks, C. (1972) *Inequality: A reassessment of the effect of family and schooling in America.* New York: Basic Books.

Klees, S.J. (1986) Planning and policy analysis in education: What can economics tell us? *Comparative Educational Review,* Vol. 30, pp. 574-607.

Klees, S.J. & S. Wells (1978). *Cost analysis for educational decision making.* Palo Alto: EDUTEL Communications and Development.

Lankford, R.H. (1985) Efficiency and equity in the provision of public education. *Review of Economics and Statistics*, Vol. 67, pp. 70-80.

Lau, L.J. (1979) Education production functions. In: D.M. Windham (ed.) *Economic dimensions of education*. Washington, D.C.: National Academy of Education.

Levin, H.M. (1983) *Cost-effectiveness: A primer*. Beverly Hills: Sage Publications.

Little, I.M.D. (1950) *A critique of welfare economics*. London: Oxford University Press.

Mingat, A. & J.P. Tan (1986) Who profits from the public funding of schooling? *Comparative Education Review*, Vol. 30, pp. 260-270.

Monk, D.H. (1984) Interdependencies among educational inputs and resource allocation in classrooms. *Economics of Education Review*, Vol. 3, pp. 65-73.

Postlethwaite, T.N. (1987) Comparative educational achievement research: can it be improved? *Comparative Education Review*, Vol. 31, pp. 150-158.

Purves, A.C. (1987) *Student performance as an educational indicator*. Paper prepared for the OECD conference on educational indicators, Washington, D.C., November 3-6.

Rawls, J. (1971) *A theory of justice*. Cambridge : Belknap Press.

Rohwer, W.D. (1972) Decisive research: A means for answering fundamental questions about instruction. *Educational Researcher*, Vol. 1, pp. 5-12.

Rosenholtz, S.J. (1985) effective schools: Interpreting the evidence. *American Journal of Education*, Vol. 93, pp. 352-388.

Theisen, G.L., P.P.W. Achola & F.M. Boakari (1983) The underachievement of cross - national studies of achievement. *Comparative Educational Review*, Vol 27, pp. 46-68.

Thomas, J.A. & F. Kemmerer (1983) *Money, time, and learning*. Washington, D.C.: Report prepared for the National Institute of Education.

Tsang, M. C. (1988) *Cost analysis for educational policy making: A review of cost studies in education in developing nations*. Cambridge: Harvard Institute for International Development.

Walberg, H.J. (1984) Improving the productivity of american's schools. *Educational Leadership*, Vol. 41, pp. 19-30.

Windham, D.M. (1980) Micro-educational decisions as a basis for macro-educational planning. In: H.N. Weiler (ed.) *Educational planning and social change*. Paris: International Institute for Educational Planning.

Windham, D.M. (1988) *Indicators of educational effectiveness and efficiency*. Tallahassee: Learning Systems Institute, Florida State University.

Windham, D.M. & J.-L. Wang (1986) *Fiscal capacity constraints and quality/quantity trade-offs in educational development*. Paper prepared for the conference on economics of education, Dijon, France, June.

Ysander, B.C. (1987) Public policy evaluation in Sweden. In: *The Economics of Institutions and Markets*. Stockholm: The Industrial Institute for Economic and Social Research.

Windham, D.M. (1988) *Indicators of educational effectiveness and efficiency*. Tallahassee: Learning Systems Institute, Florida State University.

Windham, D.M. & J.-L. Wang (1986) *Fiscal capacity constraints and quality/quantity trade-offs in educational development*. Paper prepared for the conference on economics of education, Dijon, France, June.

Ysander, B.C. (1987) Public policy evaluation in Sweden. In: *The Economics of Institutions and Markets*. Stockholm: The Industrial Institute for Economic and Social Research.

# Student Motivation and Academic Achievement

Margaret M. Clifford
University of Iowa
USA

Psychologists view motivation as a force that accounts for the initiation and persistence of behavior. Educators view it as a problem that accounts for teacher burn-out and student drop-out. Student motivation consistently ranks among the top two problems plaguing schools (Brown & Payne, 1988; Gallup & Elam, 1988; Kloska & Ramasut, 1985). While psychologists are developing and refining theories of motivation at an encouraging pace, student motivation is becoming increasingly problematic.

To address this concern, we must first examine current school motivation practices and their limitations. There is reason to believe that motivational strategies currently used in schools are, in fact, a major cause of the problems they are intended to resolve. Next, we must select from current research, motivational findings that are relevant to the improvement of student motivation. We must identify and exemplify the relevance of these findings and suggest educational implications. Finally, we must continue to evaluate and refine theory, while we simultaneously field-test principles derived from theory-oriented research. Upon successful completion of field-tests, the development and dissemination of programs, practices and materials can be undertaken.

Thus, the purpose of this chapter is threefold: (a) to assess and evaluate prevailing views and practices related to student motivation, (b) to examine selected motivation processes and their implications for improved student motivation, and (c) to identify practical and theoretical issues relevant to student motivation that are in need of further study, in the field as well as the laboratory.

## Characteristics of school motivation

### *A Narrow and confused focus*

A literature search on motivation as it relates to schoolpractices and classroom activities reveals that student motivation continues to be predominantly associated with classroom management and/or discipline (e.g., Aho, 1978; Ayllon, Garber & Pisor, 1975; Burns, 1977; Woodward, Allendick & Butcher, 1981). It is discussed more frequently in the context of controlling and directing social behaviors rather than cognitive behaviors. Discussions of student motivation that do involve academic achievement, tend to focus more on performance (demonstration of previously learned material) than on learning (use of skills to acquire new information and skills). Furthermore, I have observed that performance, learning and motivation are often assumed to have near-perfect correlations. This assumption is reflected in comments such as, "I can tell from your performance that you are not trying," or "If you just keep trying, I know you will succeed," - comments often used to motivate students.

Discussions on topics such as self-regulation of behavior, attribution, perceived competence, achievement expectations, self-efficacy, and metacognitions - elements currently thought to be at the heart of student motivation - are found primarily in psychological journals and publications designed for researchers (e.g. Ames & Ames, 1984, 1985), as opposed to periodicals or self-help books likely to be read by educators.

Educators must gain an improved understanding of motivational processes and be encouraged to discriminate between motivation for learning and motivation for performance (Brophy, 1987; Dweck, 1985). Improving educators' conceptual framework of student motivation is a prerequisite for resolving problems in student motivation.

### *Behavioristic Orientation*

For several decades now, behavioristic techniques and programs have been prominent in schools. Contracting, token economies, and other behavior modification programs, consistent with Skinnerian principles (Skinner, 1971) have been used to achieve such target behaviors as improved time-on-task, assignment completion, school attendance, rule compliance, and high performance. While operant techniques account for many success stories in education (e.g. Alschuler, 1968; Cohen, 1973), their limitations are well documented. The permanency of conditioned behaviors is often short-lived and the generalizability of the behaviors is limited (Kazdin & Bootzin, 1972; O'Leary & Drabman, 1971).

While Skinner (1984) continues to suggest ways to maximize the benefits of operant techniques (e.g. clarification of goals, improved sequencing of material, individualized pacing), he persists in viewing the teacher as a behavioral engineer and the student as a robot in need of more sophisticated mechanical engineering. He stands by the assertion, "A person does not act upon the world, the world acts upon him," (Skinner, 1971, p. 211). However, there is an abundance of evidence indicating that operant techniques - as typically used in schools - will not resolve student motivation problems, and they might even accentuate these problems.

The obstacles traditionally associated with the use of operant techniques (e.g. haphazard distribution of reinforcers, ambiguous links established between reinforcers and target behaviors) are not the primary source of trouble. Rather, disregard for cognitions and cognitive processes, proliferation of unnecessary reinforcement programs, use of task-irrelevant reinforcers, and the salience and instrumentality of the teacher as a behavioral engineer are among the major obstacles that limit the effectiveness of many reinforcement techniques.

Reward-induced behavior programs have been shown to have "hidden costs" (Lepper & Greene, 1978). Fortunately, research is making these hidden costs transparent; many of them can now be reliably predicted. For example, it is well documented that rewards for initially-liked tasks reduce intrinsic motivation (Lepper & Greene 1975; Ryan, Connell, & Deci, 1985); that extrinsic incentives impair learning (McGraw, 1978) and prompt students to select easy tasks (Harter, 1982; Pittman, Emergy & Boggiano, 1982; Shapira, 1976); and that strong extrinsic regulation is associated with low mastery-orientation (Dweck, 1985).

It is not operant techniques, as such, that are the culprits. It is the excessive, exclusive, and inappropriate use of these techniques that best accounts for many of the motivation problems characterizing our schools. Operant conditioning programs currently used in schools must be modified and supplemented to accommodate research findings that expose their limitations and that document the motivational power of cognitions.

### Faulty assumptions

The assumptions underlying school motivation practices may be a greater source of trouble than over-dependency on operant techniques. My observations suggest there are at least four faulty assumptions that underlie and undermine student motivation efforts. The first assumption is that, with regard to learning, students are passive and must be given detailed directives if learning is to occur. Evidence of the passivity assumption can be found in the decision-making processes that occur in schools. Assignments, learning activities, strategies, criteria, task-difficulty, and performance evaluation are usually determined by teachers, with little if any student input.

A second assumption is that learning is aversive and engaged in only when mandated by external forces. Evidence of this assumption is found in the practice of designating recess, early dismissal, and exemption from class and assignments as reinforcers and incentives for satisfactory academic performance.

The maxim, "Nothing succeeds like success", and publications such as, Schools Without Failure (Glasser, 1969) are indicative of a third misleading assumption: that student success, operationally defined as high performance, is the best of all motivation potions! The premium typically placed on error-free performance and "perfect papers", coupled with the proliferation of easy tasks and reinforcement programs to accentuate success, is consistent with the success-motivation assumption. Evidence also indicates that distorted feedback, signaling relatively positive outcomes for a failed task, is likely to be given especially to individuals judged to have limited ability (Ilgen & Knowlton, 1980). There is reason to speculate that success has become an end in itself, has been given priority over learning, and may actually be a deterrent to learning.

A related assumption contributing to the school motivation problem is that error-making and failure are necessarily detrimental and reduce self-esteem, motivation, and learning. However, within the context of many motivation theories, error-making and failure serve a multitude of positive functions (Clifford, 1979, 1984). Within the context of reactance theory (Brehm, 1966, 1972), such outcomes threaten freedom and stimulate renewed determination and increased effort. Within the framework of learned helplessness (Abramson, Seligman, & Teasedale, 1978), modest doses of error-making and failure "inoculate" the individual against personal helplessness. Within the framework of self-efficacy theory (Bandura, 1977a, 1986), these outcomes strengthen coping skills: a determinant and product of strong self-efficacy.

It is essential to recognize that these faulty assumptions are not inherent to, or necessary by-products of operant techniques. They are, however, consistent with ineffective operant conditioning programs found in our schools. And it is unlikely that effective program changes will occur unless such assumptions are exposed, challenged, and replaced with more valid ones.

## Limited instrumentation

While there are a variety of school indices - such as rank in class, grade-point average, aptitude scores, and standardized achievement scores -
with which to describe, compare, and predict student learning, there are no comparable statistics for assessing and describing student motivation. Most motivation instruments designed to assess self-concept, locus of control, self-efficacy, attributions, achievement motivation, intrinsic motivation, failure tolerance, school liking, and so forth, have been developed for and limited to research activities. Fifty-some years after standardized achievement tests were introduced, we find ourselves without any comparable instruments with which to assess school motivation, a major determinant of academic achievement. Psychologists have recognized the need for such instrument development for some time (Scarr, 1982), yet little progress has been made toward the standardized measurement of student motivation.

Theorists may argue that it is dangerous to develop standardized instruments aimed at measuring motivational constructs still in need of refinement. But, I contend it is unreasonable and perhaps more dangerous to have educators operate in the absence of motivation measures. Is it not highly probable that school-wide use of motivation instruments might accelerate theory development while simultaneously increasing teacher awareness of motivational factors? Standardized assessment of school motivation is long overdue, and although it is not without risk, the potential benefits outweigh the potential liabilities.

## Resistant attitudes

Changes in school motivation practices will not be easily accomplished. The hidden-costs-of-reward findings will not be readily or automatically accepted by educators. A series of studies showed that even in the face of conflicting evidence, adults believe that interest in school can be best achieved with the use of tangible rewards for successful task performance (Boggiano, Barrett, Weiher, McClelland & Lusk, 1987). Another recent study showed that kindergarten, elementary school and high school teachers indicated that verbal reprimands are commonly used to correct deviant behavior, and 75% of these teachers believed corporal punishment should also be used (Brown & Payne, 1988). In short, the task of persuading educators to adopt more effective motivation practices will require more than scientific evidence. My inservice work with teachers suggests that this persuasion task can only be achieved by offering practical, concrete alternatives for student motivation, alternatives that exemplify the scientific evidence we discuss.

In summary, improved student motivation must begin with an evaluation of current school motivation practices including:

A improved distinctions between learning, performance, and motivation;

B recognition of the hidden costs of rewards and limitations of operant techniques;

C exposure and correction of faulty assumptions;

D development of standardized motivation instruments and measurement programs;

E inservice programs that contain not only evidence and reasons for adopting alternative motivation strategies, but also examples of such strategies.

## Clues for student motivation alternatives

### Themes from current motivation research

There is no shortage of motivation theories and research applicable to student motivation. Several books synthesizing these works attest to that (e.g., Ames & Ames, 1984, 1985, 1989; Ball, S., 1977; Paris, Olson & Stevenson, 1983; Stipek, 1988). Among the common messages contained in such texts are:

A the need to recognize the function of cognitive processes, emotions, and self-regulatory processes;

B the need to explicate the nature, determinants, and effects of intrinsic motivation;

C the need to anticipate and provide for individual and developmental differences;

D the need to acknowledge that effective student motivation will require complex, interactive models.

Evidence demonstrating the explanatory power of cognitive, emotional, and self-regulatory factors is impressive. For example, it has been shown that beliefs about reinforcement schedules explain behavior better than reinforcement itself (Baron, Kaufman & Stauber, 1969; Kaufman, Baron & Kopp, 1966). Expressions of anger and pity on the part of a teacher lead students to conclude whether their failure is being blamed on lack of effort or on lack of ability (Graham, 1984). Providing students with opportunities to make choices has been found to increase intrinsic motivation as well as learning (Perlmutter & Monty, 1977).

However, does current motivation research provide a basis from which to derive improved classroom practices? If so, what changes can be inferred from this work? What implications does motivation research have for curriculum development, learning activities, testing, the nature and use of rewards, and so forth?

It has been argued that, "we must remain hesitant in suggesting practical recipes for enhancing student motivation" (Ball, 1984). It has also been argued that educational research cannot have direct and immediate application to practice; it cannot prescribe policy or practice (Shavelson, 1988). I concur that neither recipes nor prescriptions can be directly derived from motivation theories, or from any other theories. However, there is enough data to warrant the identification of new and emerging principles of student motivation. The sharing of principles is a professional obligation. Such principles can serve as alternatives to operant conditioning principles. They can be used as guidelines to improve and/or replace reinforcement programs.

Educators should be given the opportunity and encouragement to field-test emerging principles. By sharing and encouraging cautious, informed use of these principles, and by suggesting examples of effective implementation, researchers are likely to achieve three objectives: (1) narrow the gap between theory and practice, (2) accelerate the refinement of theory and practice, and (3) enhance the receptivity of educators to psychological findings.

It is not the purpose of this chapter to identify an exhaustive list of emerging motivation principles to be field-tested, but only to exemplify, with the discussion of two topics, the type of emerging principles that I believe are ready for field-testing. The research topics I have chosen are attributions and risk taking.

### Outcome Attributions

More than thirty years ago, Heider (1958) convincingly argued that attributions (i.e. causal explanations) for success and failure have a major impact on our behavior. He identified the four most prominent attributions or explanations as ability, effort, task difficulty, and luck. He classified the first two as internal and the latter two as external, establishing locus of control as an important attributional dimension. Weiner (1979, 1980a) suggested an alternative classification for Heider's four attributions which led to the identification of the dimension of stability (the ease with which the explanatory factor could be changed). Globality (the extent to which the explanation was applicable to a single or several situations) (Abramson, Seligman & Teasdale, 1978), control (the extent to which the explanatory factor could be modified) (Rosenbaum, 1972; Weiner, 1979) and intentionality (the extent to which the attribution implies deliberate, preplanned behavior) (Weiner, 1979) were also identified as attributional dimensions useful in predicting behavior following success and failure events.

## The Role of Attribution Dimensions

That behavior is a function of the attributional dimensions has been well-documented. Pride for success and shame for failure is experienced when internal attributions are made, and gratitude is experienced when positive outcomes are explained by the contributions of others (Weiner, Russell & Lerman, 1978; 1979). Future expectations are high when success is attributed to stable factors and failure is attributed to unstable factors, and expectations are low when success is attributed to unstable factors and failure is attributed to stable factors (Fontaine, 1974; Kovenklioglu & Greenhaus, 1978; McMahan, 1973). Hopelessness, resignation, and depression tend to accompany stable attributions for failure (Weiner et al., 1978; 1979). Guilt feelings are the product of attributing negative outcomes to personally controllable factors (Weiner, Graham & Chandler, 1982) and pity results when misfortunes are attributed to uncontrollable factors (Weiner, 1980b, 1980c; Weiner, et al., 1982).

In short, emotions, expectations, and affect are influenced and can be reliably predicted on the basis of the attribution dimensions. And while Weiner (1979, 1985, 1986) contends that dimensions predict behavior and emotions better than do individual attributions, there is enough uncertainty about the number and nature of relevant dimensions and attributions (Clifford, 1986a, 1986b; Weiner, 1984, 1986) that the continued study of both is warranted.

## Strategy: The Neglected Attribution

Strategy has never emerged as a major explanation for failure in studies designed to identify attributions (Bar-Tal & Darom, 1979; Cooper & Burger, 1980; Frieze, 1976; Weiner, et al., 1971). It is also worth noting that most subjects participating in attribution-identification studies are college students or teachers, and most failure situations described as a means of eliciting attributions are educational in nature and setting. Effort and ability are the most frequent explanations given for academic outcomes (Arkin & Maruyama, 1979; Bailey, Helm & Gladstone, 1975; Frieze, 1976; Simon & Feather, 1973).

As has been emphasized previously (Clifford, 1986a), the absence of strategy attributions in the educational world is probably no accident. Few teachers or students are knowledgeable about learning, memory, reading, study, or motivation strategies. But this may only demonstrate a point made earlier: Well-developed psychological principles fail to make their way to the classroom in a timely fashion.

Despite its infrequent use, strategy may be the most promising attribution for enhancing student achievement. Diener and Dweck (1978) found that children who attributed failure to lack of effort (i.e. "mastery-oriented" children) tended to change and improve their problem-solving strategies more than children who attributed failure to ability (i.e. "helpless children"). They concluded, "Helpless children ruminate about the cause of their failure and, given their attributions to uncontrollable factors, spend little time searching for ways to overcome failure. Mastery-oriented children, on the other hand, seem to be directed towards the attainment of a solution. They are less concerned with explaining past errors and more concerned with producing future success" (p. 460).

The work of Diener and Dweck implies that strategy and effort are strongly correlated. Consistent with this view, Anderson and Jennings (1980) compared strategy with ability attributions, and Anderson (1983) examined a combined effort-strategy attribution in contrast to an ability attribution. In both instances, strategy was found to produce more favorable behavior following failure than did ability.

### The Strategy Attribution Advantage

In a series of studies (Clifford, 1986a, 1986b; Clifford, Kim & McDonald, 1988) designed to examine the separate effects of effort and strategy attributions, the superiority of strategy was repeatedly evidenced. These studies generally supported the prediction that academic failure attributed to poor strategy, leads to more favorable evaluations and expectations for future performance than failure attributed to lack of effort. Several possible explanations for this effect were offered:

"...first, strategy attributions might allow one to reduce or escape the guilt associated with not trying or attending. Second, they may enable one to escape the embarrassment and public shame associated with being stupid. Third, and perhaps most importantly, strategy attributions might turn failure outcomes into problem-solving situations in which the search for a more effective strategy becomes the major focus of attention. This search and exploration for improved strategy can be expected to elicit increased effort without the fear that subsequent failure will automatically and immediately imply low ability" (Clifford, 1986a, p. 76).

But an even stronger case can be made for the merits of strategy attributions: First, they guard against dysfunctional expressions of egotism (Frankel & Snyder, 1978; Snyder, Stephan & Rosenfield, 1976) and the self-worth motive (Beery, 1975; Covington, 1984; Covington & Beery, 1976), which, in the face of failure, often prompt the individual to reduce effort as a means of avoiding low-ability judgments. While lack of effort provides protection against such judgments, it also retards learning; it is, therefore, an expensive ego defense relative to strategy attribution.

Second, strategy attributions elicit increased effort. Attributing failure to strategy encourages the search, discovery, creation, testing, comparing,

and modifying of alternative strategies. Such activities require attentive-
ness, concentration, and commitment expressions of effort.

Third, strategy attributions are likely to yield a repertoire of problem-solving strategies. A search for strategies for various problems in various subject areas, should yield an ever-increasing repertoire of strategies. This
repertoire, coupled with increased awareness and monitoring of strategies,
may be the most beneficial effect strategy attributions produce - an effect
much less likely to result from effort, task-difficulty, or ability attributions.

Fourth, strategy attributions should increase one's willingness to perform
challenging academic tasks. It is reasonable to postulate that the tendency
to seek challenging tasks is more strongly correlated with the use of strategy attributions than the use of effort attributions. Armed with an explanation for failure that protects self-worth while simultaneously encouraging
effort expenditure, an individual is likely to find challenging tasks not
only less threatening, but also more satisfying. This prediction is highly
consistent with self-efficacy theory (Bandura, 1977a, 1986; Schunk, 1984)
as well as theories of intrinsic motivation (Csikszentmihalyi, 1975;
Kruglanski, 1975, 1978).

*Behavior attributions*

Heider's (1958) theory was originally developed to clarify the nature of
explanations given to success and failure outcomes. The majority of attribution research continues to examine the nature of such causal explanations, their antecedents, and their consequences. However, in addition to
explaining success and failure outcome, people also attempt to explain
their behavior. Bem's (1967, 1972) self-perception theory, Lepper's (Lepper
& Greene, 1976; Lepper, Greene, & Nisbett, 1973; Lepper, Sagotsky &
Greene, 1977) overjustification hypothesis, and Kruglanski's (1975) endogenous attribution theory address this phenomenon.

I suggest that behavior attribution is at least as relevant to student motivation as is outcome attribution. But, space does not permit me to offer more
than a few comments on behavior attributions and their implications for
education.

Kruglanski (1975) contends that the major determinant of intrinsic motivation is the degree to which an action is endogenously attributed (i.e.
judged to be an end in itself) in contrast to exogenously attributed (i.e.
judged to be a means to an end). The more salient and numerous external
forces appear to be, the more easily and readily we attribute our behavior
to them, and judge our behavior to be a means (e.g. a way to avoid punishment, obtain reward, passify authority) in contrast to an end in itself.
Exogenously attributed behavior is associated with feelings of compul-
sion, lack of freedom, and negative affect. Such behavior tends to be gov-

erned by the minimax strategy: exert the minimum effort and level of performance needed to obtain the maximum desired outcomes. Evidence of
this phenomenon is well documented (e.g. Kruglanski, Stein & Riter,
1977). Finally, endogenously attributed behavior is associated with feelings of freedom and positive affect, and it is assumed to reflect the actor's
personal intentions or goals, since it is not viewed as forced or mandated.
With regard to student motivation, endogenous attribution theory presents the challenge of identifying ways of minimizing exogenous attributions and maximizing endogenous attributions for learning activities.
What type of materials, and classroom procedures are likely to evoke
endogenous attributions?
Suggestions consistent with existing research include the following:

1 Maximize the use of self-selected and optional learning activities.
2 Do not equate learning activities with evaluation activities (e.g. tasks
   used to determine report cards, grade promotion).
3 Avoid teacher mandates, threats, and bribes.
4 Provide for self-scoring and self-evaluation, especially on practice exercises and formative evaluation activities.
5 Avoid the use of extraneous rewards.

Behavior attributions are expected to have a more direct and powerful
impact on behavior; whereas, outcome attributions are expected to have
the greater effect on affect and emotion (e.g. liking for school, fear of failure). The value of attribution theories for student motivation will not be
fully realized until both outcome and behavior attribution research are
integrated, and thoroughly evaluated in the context of school tasks and
settings. Attribution research has suggested a whole new approach to student motivation. Practitioners must be invited and enticed to explore these
newly discovered and highly promising cognitive processes.

### Risk-taking

Risk-taking has been examined more in the context of lotteries, chance
events, and games than in the context of learning. Although it has become
a central part of nearly every current theory of motivation, research on
risk-taking is limited in scope and value. Lopes (1983) suggests that goals
and aspirations have not played a prominent enough role in psychological
research on risk taking. I would add that risk taking has not played a
prominent enough role in research on learning.

### Theoretical Function of Moderate Risk

Theories that attempt to explain achievement behavior, imply or expressly
state that moderately difficult tasks (i.e. probability of success = .50) char-

acterizes the intrinsically motivated and achievement-oriented individual. Such theories emphasize that success at moderately difficult tasks provide maximum satisfaction (Atkinson, 1964; Atkinson & Birch, 1978), enhances self-efficacy (Bandura, 1982; 1986), elicits constructive attributions (Meyer, Folkes, & Weiner, 1960; Weiner, 1980a), provides valued information about competence (Schneider, 1973; Weiner, Frieze Kukla, Reed, Rest, & Rosenbaum, 1971), elicits constructive responses to error-making and failure (Clifford, 1984; Kim & Clifford, 1988), and is associated with optimum concentration, task commitment, and process-orientation (Csikszentmihalyi, 1975, 1978; Kruglanski, 1975, 1978). Engaging in achievement activities representing more than moderate challenge or risk is predicted to result in anxiety; whereas, engaging in activities representing less than moderate risk or challenge will likely produce boredom, (Csikszentmihalyi, 1975).

The functions of moderate risk-taking (i.e. free selection of moderately challenging tasks) as proposed in theories of motivation must be evaluated in terms of classroom instruction and student learning. Csikszentmihalyi's emergent motivation theory (1975; 1978) offers several clues regarding the functions of risk-taking and its potential for enhancing school learning and performance. Csikszentmihalyi contends that moderate risk is not only essential for intrinsic motivation, but can also be used to arouse and increase intrinsic motivation, even for relatively aversive tasks.

Risk is postulated to increase attention, concentration, and process-orientation, while decreasing self-consciousness and concern for reward or recognition. He postulates that moderate risk helps ensure a "flow state" - a state in which behavior flows relatively independent of external props, contingencies, or controls, and the individual is consumed with the task process. Goals, feedback, and rewards continually emerge from action and guide behavior. Each act is undertaken in light of a goal, expectation, and criteria. The consequences of an act are immediately self-evaluated against the criteria, giving rise to a new goal, expectation, and criteria for a subsequent act. Positive evaluation of an act serves as a reward that fuels the flow. Negative evaluation prompts a change in goal, expectation, criteria, and strategy; it redirects and reignites the flow process. Thus, motivation - the direction, amplitude, and duration of behavior - emerges from the task, provided a moderate level of risk or challenge is maintained. The minimizing of external constraints (e.g.bribes, rewards, threats) helps ensure the flow experience rather than an externally driven behavior and a concentration on powerful others.

### Risk-Taking Evidence
Many of the determinants and consequences of risk-taking have been doc-

umented. The risky-shift phenomenon (i.e. increased risk-taking following group discussion) has been repeatedly demonstrated (e.g. Knowles, 1976; Wallach, Kogan & Bem, 1962). Three explanations and supporting evidence have been offered: The value hypothesis states that discussion increases risk-taking because we value risk taking and desire to perceive ourselves at least as daring as the next individual (Brown, 1965; Teger & Pruitt, 1967; Wallach & Wing, 1968). The information hypothesis states that it is the increased information obtained through discussion that prompts an increase in risk-taking (Knowles, 1976). The diffusion of responsibility hypothesis states that discussion provides a sense of shared responsibility for possible failure, which in turn encourages increased risk-taking (Bem, Wallach, & Kogan, 1965; Kogan & Wallach, 1967; Wallach & Kogan, 1965). Thus, risky-shift research indicates that risk-taking is valued, and that a clarification of the nature of risk, as well as reduced responsibility for failure, increases risk-taking.

Other factors found to influence risk-taking are certainty of risk-probability, modeling, rewards, evaluation, and self-regulation: People tend to prefer explicit, well-defined risks to those that are ambiguous (Ellsberg, 1961). They take higher risks after viewing a high risk-taking model (Montgomery & Landers, 1974), and set higher standards after observing a model self-rewarded for high standards (Bandura & Kupers, 1964). Subjects take lower risks when performance is rewarded than when it is not rewarded (Condry & Chambers, 1978; Pearlman, 1984; Pittman, Emery & Boggiano, 1982; Shapira, 1976). When performance is to be evaluated, subjects select easy tasks (Harter, 1978; Maehr & Stallings, 1972); under nonevaluative conditions they choose relatively moderate risks (Buckert, Meyer & Schmalt, 1979; Raynor & Smith, 1966; Trope, 1979). They choose easier tasks when performance is teacher-evaluated in contrast to self-evaluated (Hughes, Sullivan, & Mosley, 1985; Salili, Maehr, Sorensen & Fyans, 1976). Self-regulation in the form of option has been found to increase the selection of moderate risks (Danner & Lonky, 1981), persistence at challenging tasks (Zuckerman, Porac, Lathin, Smith, & Deci, 1978), and learning (Perlmutter & Monty, 1977).

Subjects choose less challenging tasks when instructed to demonstrate learning or ability than when they are instructed to choose whatever level they most enjoy (Maehr & Stallings, 1972). Furthermore, subjects avoid moderate challenge more when asked to demonstrate ability than when they are simply encouraged to learn (Elliott & Dweck, 1981). Dweck (1985) discusses this latter distinction in terms of performance-goals (ability oriented) and learning-goals (skill-development oriented). Nicholls (1984) uses the distinction, ego-involvement (attention focused on self-portrayal) and task-involvement (attention focused on task-mastery). With learning-goals, subjects generally begin with low-to-moderate risk and gradually increase risk, as if to test their limits or secure maximum positive information about ability (Schneider & Posse, 1982).

Among the most powerful factors affecting risk-taking is payoff. Ettenson & Coughlin (1982) demonstrated the payoff effect with a simulated money-decision task. Subjects were given the option of avoiding risk and receiving low payoff, or choosing risks of various levels, each with a possibility of increased payoffs. Subjects took higher risks when payoffs increased systematically with levels of risk, than when payoffs remained fixed regardless of risk level. In other words, variable payoffs (i.e., payoff increases with level of risk) lead to greater risk-taking than fixed payoffs (i.e., payoff remains constant regardless of risk-level).

In summary, moderate risk-taking is facilitated by deemphasizing reward, minimizing external evaluation, providing variable payoffs, allowing for self-regulation, option, and self-evaluation, and focusing on learning rather than on the demonstration of ability.

### Current Observations of Academic Risk-Taking

Most teachers probably attempt to match task-difficulty with student ability. But, even when that objective is fully achieved, moderate academic risk-taking cannot be assumed. Moderate task-difficulty must not be confused with moderate risk-taking. The latter implies choice or option (presumably associated with some degree of personal commitment) in addition to a challenge or moderate (i.e. 50%) probability of failure. Furthermore, to ensure moderate risk-taking, there must be accurate self-knowledge, tolerance for error-making and failure, and constructive responses to failure - rare commodities in most classroom settings. The degree to which students can independently and validly assess their skill (provide self-feedback) is also questionable.

Rewards for high success, the assignment of easy tasks that ensure success, ambiguous feedback for low performance, lack of option in assignments and procedures, and lack of opportunity for self-evaluation are classroom characteristics guaranteed to discourage academic risk-taking. To whatever extent these characteristics are manifested in schools, there is a motivation dilemma: Moderate risk-taking, which predicts highly positive outcomes in achievement situations, is all but prohibited in a setting exclusively designed to promote cognitive achievement.

To examine this dilemma more thoroughly, a series of studies was conducted; studies involving teacher-administration of typical school-related instruments presented as risk-taking activities to intact classes. Data were collected in realistic settings under realistic conditions.

In the first of these studies (Clifford, 1988), fourth-, fifth-, and sixth-graders from two midwestern states were instructed to select six of 35 to 40 multiple-choice items for each of three content areas: mathematics, spelling and vocabulary. Each set of items was arranged on a single page in order of increasing difficulty. To signal item-difficulty, each item was identified as being typical of problems worked at a given grade level (second through eighth). All items were selected from retired forms of a standardized test; thus, the designation of item-difficulty was considered valid. (See Clifford, 1988 for a full description of the instrument.) Subjects were instructed to choose the six items on each page they would "most enjoy working". Risk-taking was defined in several ways. One operational definition was the average item-difficulty (i.e. the average grade-level assigned to the chosen items). A second definition was response accuracy defined as percentage of correct responses. Results showed that students chose items as much as one and a half-years below their achievement levels as measured by standardized achievement tests. The mean absolute success level for various grades and content areas ranged from 77% to 92% - levels far in excess of that associated with optimum challenge (i.e. 50%). Furthermore, academic risk-taking decreased significantly with grade level.

These results confirmed our suspicion that students generally minimize academic risk, value error-free performance over academic challenge, and manifest these tendencies with increasing intensity with increased age. To examine the influence of payoffs on academic risk-taking, a follow-up study using similar-aged subjects from two additional schools was conducted (Clifford, Lan, Chou, & Yang, 1989). Classroom teachers administered the instrument described above with one modification - variable payoffs were provided (i.e. items were assigned point values that corresponded with item-difficulty). Results showed that students selected items more closely approximating their achievement levels.

In a subsequent study (Chou, 1989), fixed and variable payoffs were simultaneously compared with the use of acognitive skill test. Results showed that Taiwanese fourth-graders chose significantly more difficult problems when the value of a correct response varied with item difficulty than when all problems were assigned the same value. This study also confirmed a finding reported by Harter (1978) ten years earlier; namely, that a game context in contrast to an ability or test context increases academic risk-taking.

Harter presented a set of anagrams either as a measure of spelling ability or as a word game. The spelling-ability instructions prompted sixth-graders to select easier problems than did the word game instructions. Furthermore, the anagrams were judged to be significantly easier when presented in the game context. At the conclusion of the experiment, the nature of both conditions was described to subjects who were asked if they would have chosen different problems had they been in the other condition. As expected, subjects indicated they would have chosen more difficult problems in the spelling condition and easier ones in the game condition. Their explanations focused on the anticipation or unanticipation of teacher evaluation and grading. Another independent verification of the game-test finding was reported by Lan (1988).

In addition to payoffs and game context, task-familiarity has been found to influence academic risk-taking. Swineford (1941) reported that male high school students had a 27% higher risk-taking score on unfamiliar test material than on familiar material, and girls had an 18% higher risk-taking score on the less familiar material. Lan (1988) verified this task familiarity finding: Fourth- through sixth-graders were asked to select items either from the mathematics, spelling, and vocabulary tasks described earlier, or from sets of spatial-judgment problems, which represented novel tasks. Students took significantly more difficult items and had higher error rates on the spatial-judgment problems.

In summary, research with elementary school children and conventional school-like tasks, indicates that academic risk-taking is low. This classroom-based research has also demonstrated that academic risk-taking can be increased by game context, novel or unfamiliar tasks, and variable payoffs. Yet despite such interventions, selected problems yield a success level consistently greater than .50.

### Explanations for Academic Risk-Taking

I have already suggested a major explanation for low academic risk-taking, namely, problematic reinforcement practices. However, self-worth theory (Covington, 1984; Covington & Beery, 1976) provides another explanation, especially for low risk-taking on familiar academic tasks or tests. Failure on such activities is more threatening to self-worth than failure on novel, game-like activities. Thus, risk-taking on the former would be expected to be low.

There is also a metacognitive explanation that warrants attention, and it implies that academic risk-taking is even lower than the above reported results indicate. To the extent that students overestimate their ability and/or underestimate item-difficulty, they will choose difficult items, judge them to be easy, and experience high error rates. That is, error-rate may be a function of one's ability to make valid judgments about item difficulty and personal ability. Indirect support for this metacognitive hypothesis is present in a pattern of findings observed in several studies (Clifford, 1988; Clifford, Lan, Chou, & Yang, 1988; Lan, 1988) involving the use of the mathematics, spelling, and vocabulary tasks described above.

Whether students selected items under game or test conditions, with variable or fixed payoffs, they consistently chose items that resulted in fewer errors on mathematics problems than on vocabulary problems, and fewer errors on vocabulary problems than on spelling problems. This pattern has now been observed in five samples, each including two or three grade levels, and drawn from four different states. Self-worth theory or the protection of self-esteem does not adequately explain this content-dependent phenomenon. However, the metacognitive hypothesis might account for this finding.

It can be argued that in answering a multiple-choice mathematics item, students independently calculate a response and match that self-generated response with available options. This provides a fairly high degree of certainty concerning the correctness of the chosen option. If the calculated response is not available as an option, students are likely to recalculate their answer and/or choose to work an easier problem. With a vocabulary item, a student is likely to pronounce the word and perhaps generate a phrase that includes the term and implies the meaning of the most attractive available option. The "usage example" provides less response certainty than does a mathematical calculation, however. Thus, more errors would be expected in vocabulary than in mathematics. Spelling - a relatively rote and low-meaningful type of learning - allows for the least amount of self-generated error-detection. Few test criteria or examples can be generated to facilitate response evaluation; thus, more errors would be expected in spelling than in vocabulary.

This validity-judgment factor might explain high risk-taking associated with novel in contrast to familiar tasks, as well as developmental decline in academic risk-taking. Since one is less able to detect errors and judge ability and item-difficulty on a novel task, one is more likely to choose difficult items and experience high levels of error-making. Similarly, if younger students have less well-developed error-detection and item-judgment skills, they are likely to choose items beyond their ability level and make more errors.

The strongest support for this metacognitive hypothesis was found in Lan's (1988) study. He required subjects to rate the difficulty of each mathematics, vocabulary, and spelling item they chose to work. Mean perceived difficulty ratings across all three tasks ranged from 1.9 to 2.3 on a scale for which values of 1, 2, and 3 represented ratings of, "VERY VERY EASY", "Very Easy", and "easy", respectively. Furthermore, while objective error-rate differed significantly with content, subjective difficulty ratings did not vary, suggesting that subjects thought they had chosen equally difficult items for all three content tasks.

To whatever extent academic risk-taking is a function of underestimating task-difficulty and/or overestimating ability, we have a spuriously high measure of risk-taking. Item-by-item feedback would be predicted to lower risk-taking relative to a no-feedback condition. The effects of game versus test context and variable vs fixed payoffs cannot be easily explained by the metacognitive hypothesis. Nonetheless, these factors might affect the tendency to overestimate ability and/or underestimate item-difficulty. For example, in a variable payoff condition, subjects have an incentive to select the most difficult item they can answer correctly. In any event, caution is warranted in interpreting any measure of risk-taking that is not accompanied by an independent measure of the subjects' intentions.

### A Profile on Academic Risk-Taking

Based upon evidence generated from various theoretical frameworks, we can tentatively conclude the following about academic risk-taking:

1 Students are low risk-takers in academic situations and prefer success over challenge.
2 Both game context and variable payoffs increase academic risk-taking.
3 Task novelty increases academic risk-taking, but perhaps the greatest portion of this effect is explained by underestimation of task-difficulty and overestimation of ability.
4 Academic risk-taking decreases with increased age, but a portion of this effect may be explained by underestimation of task-difficulty and over-estimation of ability.
5 External constraints such as rewards, imposed evaluation, and an emphasis on the demonstration of ability, discourage moderate risk-taking.

Risk-avoidance on academic tasks needs to be further studied. Among the factors that warrant immediate attention are, the extraneous, external reinforcement of success in contrast to learning, and teacher knowledge about risk-taking and the hidden costs of rewards. These factors should be examined with both basic and field studies.

## Fundamental research needs

There are at least two types of fundamental research needed to ensure proper diagnosis of student motivation problems, and development of solutions. Theory must be advanced, and emerging principles must be field-tested and refined. To ignore or unduly favor either of these objectives is almost certain to hinder the goal attainment of both.

My concluding remarks and suggestions will focus on the two topics discussed in this chapter, namely, attributions and risk-taking. However, there are at least another dozen motivation topics worthy of consideration. Each needs to be reviewed with the objective of identifying its emerging principles and specifying the relevance of these principles for student motivation. Thus, my first recommendation is that such an extended review be undertaken.

### Advancement of motivation theories

The advancement of theory is unquestionably a "fundamental" research activity. It ensures improved understanding, prediction, and control of events. When theory refinement is undertaken as a means of solving practical problems (e.g. the improvement of student motivation), the "fundamental" nature of the research is magnified.

### Attribution Research

The abundance of attribution research (See reviews, Harvey & Weary, 1984; Kelley & Michela, 1980) and the integration of attributional concepts with other motivation theories (e.g. Abramson, Seligman & Teasdale, 1978; Kruglanski, 1975; Miller & Norman, 1979; ) are testimony to the functional and practical importance of this concept and related theories.

The integration of attributional and educational processes is attracting increasing attention and eliciting exciting student motivation research (see Ames & Ames, 1984, 1985). Much credit must be given to Weiner who has formulated an attribution theory for education (1979) and identified many of its salient principles (1984). However, the work on linking attribution and education is far from completed. Theorists must continue to refine attribution-education models, examine the relative merits of attributions, determine a parsimonious set of dimensions, and pursue greater theoretical integration. Research on developmental patterns in outcome attributions and behavior attributions (e.g. Nicholls, 1978, 1983, 1984) must be expanded.

The function of strategy and its dimensional nature must be more thoroughly examined. Weiner (1986) suggests that strategy and effort share the characteristics of low stability and controllability, and that they differ primarily on the dimension of intentionality. He contends that while reduced effort is a common device used to protect self-worth, the intentional use of poor strategy is unlikely. Yet, intentional use of strategy, previously found to be ineffective, does occur. Low-ability students sometimes spend an exhorbitant amount of time in non-productive study activities (e.g., recopying notes, copying terms and definitions from books, cramming for exams, rote memorization of facts), knowing that they are unlikely to produce the desired grade effects, but satisfied that these activities will minimize the guilt feelings that might otherwise accompany failure. Faulty strategies provide better insurance against guilt feelings and depreciation of self-worth than does reduction of effort (e.g. reduced studying, inattentiveness, increased absenteeism).

Thus, dimensions other than intentionality are needed to distinguish between effort and strategy attributions. I would suggest, that strategy attributions imply more creative, problem-solving responses than do effort attributions. While effort attributions are likely to evoke "resolution" responses (e.g. I'll do my homework, pay attention, and not skip class), strategy attributions evoke search-and-discovery responses. Both sets of responses imply internality, intentionality, and control. But perhaps it is the nature of control that differs, with effort attributions implying a need for resolute self-control and strategy attributions implying a need for creative, task-oriented control.

Another basic research need is the integration of outcome-attribution theory and behavior-attribution theory. Behavior attributions are expected to have more immediate effects on behavior; whereas, outcome attributions are expected to have more immediate effects on affect and emotion. In addition, the nature of the outcome attribution effects can be expected to differ for endogenously and exogenously attributed actions. For example, failure attributions for a self-selected task are likely to be more constructive than failure attributions for an imposed task (Clifford, 1984). Not only is the nature of outcome attributions expected to vary with the nature of the behavior attribution, but the response to the outcome attribution (e.g. the resulting guilt, pride, dissatisfaction) is likely to differ. Responses for endogenously attributed acts should be more constructive than responses for exogenously attributed acts. The integration of outcome and behavior attribution theories might further validate established attribution principles and facilitate the development of new principles.

An additional research need is the identification of efficient, effective attribution training procedures. While several attribution training studies have been conducted (e.g. Andrews & Debus, 1978; Dweck, 1975), they have primarily identified factors that influence attribution, rather than defined procedures with which to change attributions or ensure the generalizability of changes in attributions.

### Risk-Taking Research

The study of risk-taking as it relates to learning must be more thoroughly and systematically examined. Its antecedents and determinants must be identified, and its effects on learning, memory, transfer, and task-liking assessed. The risk-taking effects of motivation programs that reinforce success and those that reinforce learning should be contrasted and compared.

Procedures for modifying motivation programs that discourage moderate risk-taking need to be identified. Relationships between metacognitive skills, strategy usage, self-regulation, attribution, risk-taking, and school achievement must be studied. A theory of academic risk-taking will undoubtedly be a hybrid of intrinsic motivation theories, self-regulation theories, achievement theories, attribution theories, self-perception theories, and learning theories. The development of such a theory should trigger exciting research and productive controversy, for it will probably oppose many existing motivational practices.

### Field tests for emerging principles

One of the major shortcomings of psychology is the dissemination of its findings and principles. It is ironical that those of us who study human behavior - often with missionary zeal - devote so little effort to promoting the practical value of our discoveries. It is as if we are satisfied to develop theories that serve only the functions of explanation and prediction, with little concern for whether they fulfill the ultimate function of controlling events. In time - often more by accident than design - psychological findings filter into society. But many psychologists are indifferent to this filtering process. They are unconcerned whether it occurs, when it occurs, or how it occurs. I suggest it is both a professional and moral obligation for psychologists to play an assertive role in the translation, dissemination, and implementation of psychological knowledge.

The field-testing of emerging principles is one means of meeting this dissemination-implementation responsibility. We must identify, in a timely fashion, emerging principles. We must work with practioners to field-test these principles. Such field-testing qualifies as fundamental research because; first, it must precede and influence the development of products, programs, and strategies; and second, it is a necessary step in validating and refining theories.

### Attribution Principles

It has been said of attribution theory, "the field is alive with controversy and issues" (Harvey & Weary, 1984, p. 453). Such controversy is often the major focus of attention, but it must not distract us from acknowledging and "marketing" well-established principles. Among the attribution principles that warrant field-testing are the following:

A Ability attributions for failure have undesirable effects on performance, emotions, and self-perception.

B Effort attributions lead to more desirable behaviors and attitudes than ability attributions.

C Strategy attributions lead to more desirable behaviors than effort attributions and evoke less guilt when used to explain failure.

D Outcome attributions primarily influence affect and secondarily influence behavior.

E Endogenous behavior attributions predict positive affect and self-motivated achievement behavior. Exogenous behavior attributions predict negative affect and use of the minimax strategy.

F Endogenous behavior attributions are more probable under conditions providing option and encouraging self-regulation (e.g. self goal-setting, self-evaluation).

These outcome and behavior attribution principles will be of most value when combined with principles derived from theories of social learning, informational processing, self-regulation, learning strategy, and intrinsic motivation theories. For example, in classrooms where learning and study strategies are taught, modeled, and reinforced, and where students are encouraged to select and develop their own strategies, it should be relatively easy to ensure the use of strategy attributions for failure.

In addition to field-testing attribution principles, there is a need to measure student attributions. Only with systematic measurement can we reliably observe the effects of attribution training and modeling. The selection and/or development of instruments and the interpretation of scores should be a cooperative venture between researchers and educators until the standardization of attribution instruments has been realized.

### Risk-Taking Principles

Despite its motly nature, risk-taking research has yielded findings that appear to have immediate relevance for student motivation. Taken as a whole, risk-taking research raises a fascinating question: Can learning in educational settings be presented as a risk-taking activity with the potential of evoking flow state experiences? I am inclined to answer this in the affirmative. However, caution must be used in introducing risk-taking practices in classrooms currently governed by reinforcement programs focused on successful performance (in contrast to learning). Such programs need to be modified so that they are compatible with risk-taking principles. Among the principles ready for field-testing are the following:

1 Learning activities presented within the context of games increase academic risk-taking.

2 The use of extraneous rewards for high levels of performance decreases risk-taking.

3 Variable payoffs for achievement outcomes increases risk-taking.

4 Nonevaluated, learning-oriented activities (e.g. practice exercises and daily assignments) elicit more moderate risk-taking than teacher evalu-

ated, ability-focused activities (e.g. tests, competitive contests, qualifying exams).

5 Risk-taking is greater on newly introduced material (implying the learning phase of instruction) than on familiar material (implying the fine-tuning phase of instruction).

6 The modeling and reinforcement of moderate academic risk-taking will increase risk-taking.

## Summary

Student motivation is a wide-spread concern. Schools have not yet found adequate solutions to motivation problems. But research continues to provide clues regarding the limitations of current practices and potentially-promising alternatives. Principles of motivation are not "sure bets", they are "good bets". In this chapter I have identified several motivation principles that are ready for large-scale field testing. While we continue to develop motivation theories, we must also refine and field-test established principles. Research that contributes to either of these objectives can rightfully be designated as "fundamental studies". Such research will advance theory and practice.

## References

Abramson, L.Y., M.E.P. Seligman & J.D. Teasdale (1978) Learned helplessness in humans: Critique and reformulation. *Journal of Abnormal Psychology*, Vol. 87, pp. 49-74.

Aho, S. (1978) Modification of disruptive behavior: The adaptation of token reinforcement, model learning and role playing methods to overcome disruptions of orderly working conditions at school. *Scandinavian Journal of Education*, Vol. 22, pp. 49-64.

Alschuler, A. (1968) *How to increase motivation through climate and structure* (Working Paper No. 8-313). Cambridge, MA: Achievement Motivation Development Project, Graduate School of Education, Harvard University.

Ames, C. & R. Ames (1989) (eds.) *Research on Motivation in Education*, volume 3. New York: Academic Press.

Ames, C. & R. Ames (1985) (eds.) *Research on Motivation in Education*, volume 2. New York: Academic Press.

Ames, R. & C. Ames (1984) (eds.) *Research on Motivation in Education*, volume 1. New York: Academic Press.

Anderson, C.A. & D.L. Jennings (1980) When experiences of failure promote expectations of success: The impact of attributing failure to ineffective strategies. *Journal of Personality*, Vol. 48, pp. 393-407.

Anderson, C.A. (1983) Motivational and performance deficits in interpersonal settings: the effect of attributional style. *Journal of Personality and Social Psychology*, Vol. 45, pp. 1136-1147.

Andrews, G.R. & R.L. Debus (1978) Persistence and the causal perception of failure: Modifying cognitive attributions. *Journal of Educational Psychology*, Vol. 70, pp. 154-166.

Arkin, R.M. & G.M. Maruyama (1979) Attribution, affect, and college exam performance. *Journal of Educational Psychology*, Vol. 71, pp. 85-93.

Atkinson, J.W. & D. Birch (1978) *The dynamics of action*. New York: Wiley.

Atkinson, J.W. (1964) *An Introduction to Motivation*. Princeton, N.J.: Van Nostrand.

Ayllon, T., S. Garber & K. Pisor (1975) The elimination of discipline problems through a combined school-home motivational system. *Behavior Therapy*, Vol. 6, pp. 616-626.

Bailey, R.C., B. Helm & R. Gladstone (1975) The effects of success and failure in a real-life setting: Performance, attribution, affect, and expectancy. *Journal of Psychology*, Vol. 89, pp. 137-147.

Ball, S. (1977) *Motivation in Education*. New York: Academic Press.

Ball, S. (1984) Student motivation: Some reflections and projections. In: R. Ames & C. Ames (eds.) *Research on Motivation in Education*, volume 1. New York: Academic Press.

Bandura, A. & C.J. Kupers (1964) Transmission of patterns of self-reinforcement through modeling. *Journal of Abnormal and Social Psychology*, Vol. 69, pp. 1-9.

Bandura, A. (1977a) Self-efficacy: Toward a unifying theory of behavioral change. *Psychological Review*, Vol. 84, pp. 191-215.

Bandura, A. (1977b) *Social learning theory*. Englewood Cliffs. N.J.: Prentice-Hall.

Bandura, A. (1982) Self-efficacy mechanism in human agency. *American Psychologist*, Vol. 37, pp. 122-147.

Bandura, A. (1986) *Self-efficacy. Social foundations of thought and action*, Englewood Cliffs, N.J.: Prentice Hall.

Bar-Tal, D. & E. Darom (1979) Pupils attributions for success and failure. *Child Development*, Vol. 50, pp. 264-267.

Baron, A., A. Kaufman & K.A. Stauber (1969) Effects of instructions and reinforcement-feedback on human operant behavior maintained by fixed-interval reinforcement. *Journal of the Experimental Analysis of Behavior*, Vol. 12, pp. 701-712.

Beery, R.G. (1975) Fear of failure in student experience. *Personnel and*

*Guidance Journal,* Vol. 54, pp. 190-203.

Bem, D.J. (1967) Self-perception: An alternative interpretation of cognitive dissonance phenomena. *Psychological Review,* Vol. 74, pp. 183-200.

Bem, D.J. (1977) Self-perception theory. In: L. Berkowitz (ed.) *Advances in experimental social psychology.* volume 6. New York: Academic Press.

Bem, D.J., M.A., Wallach & N. Kogan (1965) Group decision making under risk of aversive consequences. *Journal of Personality and Social Psychology,* Vol. 1, pp. 453-460.

Boggiano, A.K., M. Barrett, A.W. Weiher, G.H. McClelland & C.M. Lusk (1987) Use of the maximal-operant principle to motivate children's intrinsic interest. *Journal of Personality and Social Psychology,* Vol. 53, pp. 866-879.

Brehm, J.W. (ed.) (1966) *A Theory of Psychological Reactance.* New York: Academic Press.

Brehm, J.W. (ed.) (1972) *Responses to loss of freedom: A Theory of Psychological Reactance.* N.J.: General Learning Press

Brophy, J. (1987) Synthesis of research on strategies for motivating students to learn. *Educational Leadership,* October, 40-48.

Brown, R. (1965) *Social Psychology.* New York: Free Press of Glencoe.

Brown, W.E. & Payne T. (1988) Policies/Practices in public school discipline. *Academic Therapy,* Vol. 23, pp. 297-301.

Buckert, U., W.U. Meyer & H.D. Schmalt (1979) Effects of difficulty and diagnosticity on choice among tasks in relation to achievement motivation and perceived ability. *Journal of Personality and Social Psychology,* Vol. 37, pp. 1172-1178.

Burns, R.B. (1977) Teachers' beliefs on the relative effectiveness of reforms for motivating pupils and alleviating behavior problems. *Educational Studies,* Vol. 3, pp. 185-190

Chou, F.C. (1989) *Academic risk-taking as a function of payoff and task context.* Unpublished manuscript, The University of Iowa, Iowa City, Iowa.

Clifford, M.M. (1979) Effects of failure: Alternative explanations and possible implications. *Educational Psychologist,* Vol. 14, pp. 44-52.

Clifford, M.M. (1984) Thoughts on a theory of constructive failure. *Educational Psychologist,* Vol. 19, pp. 108-120.

Clifford, M.M. (1986a) The comparative effects of strategy and effort attributions. *British Journal of Educational Psychology,* Vol. 56, pp. 75-83.

Clifford, M.M. (1986b) The effects of ability, strategy, and effort attributions for educational, business, and athletic failure. *British Journal of Educational Psychology,* Vol. 56, pp. 169-179.

Clifford, M.M. (1988) Failure tolerance and academic risk-taking in ten- to twelve-year-old students. *British Journal of Educational Psychology,* Vol. 58, pp. 15-27.

Clifford, M.M., A. Kim & B.A. McDonald (1988) Responses to failure as influenced by task attribution, outcome attribution, and failure tolerance. *Journal of Experimental Education*, Vol. 57, pp. 19-37.

Clifford, M.M., W. Lan, F. Chou & Q. Yang (1989) *Cross-cultural observations on academic risk-taking with variable payoffs*. Unpublished manuscript, University of Iowa.

Cohen, H. (1973) Behavior modification in socially deviant youth. In: C. Thoresen (ed.) *Behavior modification in education*: Seventy-second yearbook of the National Society for the Study of Education, Part I. Chicago: University of Chicago Press.

Condry, J.D. & J. Chambers (1978) Intrinsic motivation and the process of learning. In: M.R. Lepper & D. Greene (eds.) *The Hidden Costs of Rewards*. N.J.: Lawrence Erlbaum Associates.

Cooper, H.M. & J.M. Burger (1980) How teachers explain students' academic performance: A categorization of free response and academic attributions. *American Educational Research Journal*, Vol. 17, pp. 95-109.

Covington, M.V. & R. Beery (1976) *Self-worth and school learning*. New York: Holt, Rinehart & Winston.

Covington, M.V. (1984) The motive for self-worth. In: R.E. Ames & C. Ames (eds.) *Research on Motivation in Education*, volume 1. New York: Academic Press, Inc.

Csikszentmihalyi, M. (1975) *Beyond Boredom and Anxiety*. San Francisco: Jossey-Bass.

Csikszentmihalyi, M. (1978) Intrinsic rewards and emergent motivation. In: M.R. Lepper & D. Greene (eds.) *The Hidden Costs of Rewards*. N.J.: Lawrence Erlbaum Associates.

Danner, F.W. & D. Lonky (1981) A cognitive-developmental approach to the effects of rewards on intrinsic motivation. *Child Development*, Vol. 52, pp. 1043-1052.

Diener, C.I. & C.S. Dweck (1978) An analysis of learned helplessness: Continuous changes in performance strategy and achievement cognitions following failure. *Journal of Personality and Social Psychology*, Vol. 36, pp. 451-462.

Dweck, C.S. (1975). The role of expectations and attributions in the alleviation of learned helplessness. *Journal of Personality and Social Psychology*, Vol. 31, pp. 674-685.

Dweck, C.S. (1985) Intrinsic motivation, perceived control, and self-evaluation maintenance: An achievement goal analysis. In: C. Ames & R.E. Ames (eds.) *Research on Motivation in Education*, volume 2. New York: Academic Press.

Elliott, E.S. & C.S., Dweck (1981) *Children's achievement goals as determinants of learned helplessness and mastery-oriented achievement patterns: An experimental analysis.* Unpublished manuscript. Harvard University.

Ettenson, R.T. & R.C. Coughlin (1982) Effects of type of payoff and instructions on individual risk-taking behavior. *Psychological Reports*, Vol. 51, pp. 855-860.

Fontaine, G. (1974) Social comparison and some determinants of expected personal control and expected performance in a novel situation. *Journal of Personality and Social Psychology*, Vol. 29, pp. 487-496.

Frankel, A. & M.L. Snyder (1978) Poor performance following unsolvable problems: Learned helplessness or egotism? *Journal of Personality and Social Psychology*, Vol. 36, pp. 1415-1423.

Frieze, I. H. (1976) Causal attributions and information seeking to explain success and failure. *Journal of Research in Personality*, Vol. 10, pp. 293-305.

Gallup, A.M. & S.M. Elam (1988) The 20th annual Gallup poll of the public's attitudes toward the public schools. *Phi Delta Kappan*, Vol. 70, pp. 33-46.

Glasser, W. (1969) *Schools without failure.* New York: Harper & Row.

Graham, S. (1984) Communicated sympathy and anger to black and white children: The cognitive (attributional) consequences of affective cues. *Journal of Personality and Social Psychology*, Vol. 47, pp. 40-54.

Harter, S. (1978) Pleasure derived from cognitive challenge and mastery. *Child Development*, Vol. 45, pp. 661-669.

Harter, S. (1982) The perceived competence scale for children. *Child Development*, Vol. 53, pp. 87-97.

Harvey, J.H. & G. Weary (1984) Current issues in attribution theory and research. *Annual Review of Psychology*, Vol. 35, pp. 427-459.

Heider, F. (1958) *The psychology of interpersonal relations.* New York: Wiley.

Hughes, B.H., H.J. Sullivan & M.L. Mosley (1985) External evaluation, task difficulty, and continuing motivation. *Journal of Educational Research*, Vol. 78, pp. 210-215.

Ilgen, D.R. & W.A. Knowlton, Jr. (1980) Performance attributional effects on feedback from superiors. *Organizational Behavior and Human Performance*, Vol. 25, pp. 441-456.

Kaufman, A., A. Baron & E. Kopp (1966) Some effects of instructions on human operant behavior. *Psychology*, Vol. 81, pp. 243-250.

Kazdin, A. & R. Bootzin (1972) The token economy: An evaluative review. *Journal of Applied Behavior Analysis*, Vol. 5, pp. 343-372.

Kazdin, A. (1975) Recent advances in token economy research. In: M. Hersen, R. Eisler & P. Miller (eds.), *Progress in behavior modification.* New York: Academic Press.

Kelley, H.H. & J.L. Michela (1980) Attribution theory and research. *Annual Review of Psychology*, Vol. 31, pp. 457-501.

Kim, A. & M.M. Clifford (1988) Goal source, goal difficulty, and individual difference variables as predictors of responses to failure. *British Journal of Educational Psychology*, Vol. 58, pp. 28-43.

Kloska & Ramasut (1985) Teacher stress. Special Issue: Disruptive behavior in the comprehensive school. *Maladjustment & Therapeutic Education*, Vol. 3, pp.

Knowles, E.S. (1976). Information weighting familiarization, and the risky shift. *Social Behavior and Personality*, Vol. 4, pp. 113-192.

Kogan, N. & M.A. Wallach (1967) *Risk taking as a function of the situation, the person, and the group.* In: New directions in psychology III. New York: Holt, Rinehart & Winston.

Kovenklioglu, G. & J.H. Greenhaus (1978) Causal attributions, expectations, and task performance. *Journal of Applied Psychology*, Vol. 6, pp. 698-705.

Kruglanski, A.W. (1975) The endogenous-exogenous partition in attribution theory. *Psychological Review*, Vol. 82, pp. 387-406.

Kruglanski, A.W. (1978) Issues in cognitive psychology. In: M.R. Lepper & D. Greene (eds.), *The hidden costs of reward.* Hillsdale, N.J.: Erlbaum.

Kruglanski, A., C. Stein & A. Riter (1977) Contingencies of exogenous reward and task performance: On the "minimax" strategy in instrumental behavior. *Journal of Applied Social Psychology*, Vol. 2, pp. 141-148.

Lan, W. (1988). *Academic Risk-Taking as a Function of Task Content and Task Context.* Unpublished thesis, University of Iowa.

Lepper, M.R. & D. Greene (1975) Turning play into work: Effects of adult surveillance and extrinsic rewards on children's intrinsic motivation. *Journal of Personality and Social Psychology*, Vol. 31, pp. 479-486.

Lepper, M.R. & D. Greene (1976) On understanding overjustification: A reply to Reiss and Sushinsky. *Journal of Personality and Social Psychology*, Vol. 33, pp. 25-35.

Lepper, M.R. & D. Greene (eds.) (1978) *The hidden costs of reward.* Hillsdale, N.J.: Erlbaum.

Lepper, M.R., D. Greene & R.E. Nisbett (1973) Undermining children's intrinsic interest with extrinsic rewards: A test of the "overjustification" hypothesis. *Journal of Personality and Social Psychology*, Vol. 28, pp. 129-173.

Lepper, M.R., G. Sagotsky & D. Greene (1977) *Overjustification effects following multiple-trial reinforcement procedures: Experimental evidence concerning the assessment of intrinsic interest.* Unpublished manuscript, Stanford Univeristy.

Lopes, L.L. (1983). Some thoughts on the psychological concept of risk. *Journal of Experimental Psychology*, Vol. 9, pp. 137-144.

Maehr, M. & W. Stallings (1972) Freedom from external evaluation. *Child Development*, Vol. 43, pp. 177-185.

McGraw, K.O. (1978) The detrimental effects of reward on performance: A literature review and a prediction model. In: M.R. Lepper & D. Greene (eds.) *The hidden costs of reward.* Hillsdale, N.J.: Erlbaum.

McMahan, I.D. (1973) Relationships between causal attributions and expectancy of success. *Journal of Personality and Social Psychology*, Vol. 28, pp. 108-115.

Meyer, W.U., V.S. Folkes & B. Weiner (1960) The perceived informational value and affective consequences of choice behavior and intermediate difficulty task selection. *Journal of Research in Personality*, Vol. 10, pp. 410-423.

Miller, I.W. & W.H. Norman (1979) Learned helplessness in humans: A review and attributional theory model. *Psychological Bulletin*, Vol. 86, pp. 93-118.

Montgomery, G.T. & W.F. Landers (1974) Transmission of risk-taking through modeling at two age levels. *Psychological Report*, Vol. 34, pp. 1187-1196.

Nicholls, J.G. (1978) The development of the concepts of effort and ability, perception of own attainment, and the understanding that difficult tasks require more ability. *Child Development*, Vol. 48, pp. 800-814.

Nicholls, J.G. (1983) Conceptions of ability and achievement motivation: A theory and its implications for education. In: S.G. Paris, G.M. Olson, & H.W. Stevenson (eds.) *Learning and motivation in the classroom.* Hillsdale, N.J.: Erlbaum.

Nicholls, J.G. (1984) Conceptions of ability and achievement motivation. In: R.E. Ames & C. Ames (eds.) *Research on Motivation in Education*, volume 1. New York: Academic Press.

O'Leary, K. & R. Drabman (1971) Token reinforcement programs in the classroom: A review. *Psychological Bulletin*, Vol. 75, pp. 379-398.

Paris, S., G. Olson & H. Stevenson (eds.) (1983) *Learning and motivation in the classroom.* Hillsdale, N.J.: Erlbaum.

Pearlman, C. (1984) The effects of level of effectance motivation, IQ, and a penalty/reward contingency on the choice of problem difficulty. *Child Development*, Vol. 55, pp. 537-542.

Perlmutter, L.C. & R.A. Monty (1977) The importance of perceived control: Fact or fantasy? *American Scientist*, Vol. 65, pp. 759-765.

Pittmann, T.S., J. Emery & A.K. Boggiano (1982) Intrinsic and extrinsic motivational orientations: Reward-induced changes in preference for complexity. *Journal of Personality and Social Psychology*, Vol. 42, pp. 789-797.

Raynor, J.O. & C.P. Smith (1966) Achievement-related motives and risk-taking games of skill and chance. *Journal of Personality*, Vol. 34, pp. 176-198.

Rosenbaum, R.M. (1972) *A dimensional analysis of the perceived causes of success and failure.* Unpublished doctoral dissertation. University of California, Los Angeles.

Ryan, R.M., J.P. Connell & E.L. Deci (1985) A motivational analysis of self-determination and self-regulation in education. In: C. Ames & R.E. Ames (eds.) *Research on Motivation in Education,* volume 2. New York: Academic Press.

Salili, F., M. Maehr, R. Sorensen & L. Fyans (1976) A further consideration of the effects of evaluation on motivation. *American Educational Research Journal,* Vol. 13, pp. 85-102.

Scarr, S. (1982) Testing for children: Assessment and the many determinants of intellectual competence. *Annual Progress in Child Psychiatry & Child Development,* pp. 277-290.

Schneider, K. & N. Posse (1982) Risk taking in achievement- oriented situations: Do people really maximize affect or competence information? *Motivation and Emotion,* Vol. 6, pp. 259-271.

Schneider, K. (1973) *Motivation unter Erfolgsrisiko.* Göttingen: Hogrefe.

Schunk, D.H. (1984) Self-efficacy perspective on achievement behavior. *Educational Psychologist,* Vol. 19, pp. 48-58.

Shapira, Z. (1976) Expectancy determinants of intrinsically motivated behavior. *Journal of Personality and Social Psychology,* Vol. 34, pp. 1235-1244.

Shavelson, R. J. (1988) Contributions of educational research to policy and practice: Constructing, challenging, changing cognition. *Educational Researcher,* Vol. 17, nr 7, pp. 4-11.

Simon, J.G. & N.T. Feather (1973) Causal attributions for success and failure at university examinations. *Journal of Educational Psychology,* Vol. 64, pp. 46-56.

Skinner, B.F. (1971) *Beyond freedom and dignity.* New York: Alfred A. Knopf.

Skinner, B.F. (1984) The shame of American education. *American Psychologist,* Vol. 39, pp. 947-954.

Snyder, M.L., W.G. Stephan & D. Rosenfield (1976) Egotism and attribution. *Journal of Personality and Social Psychology,* Vol. 33, pp. 435-441.

Stipek, D.J. (1988) *Motivation to Learn.* Englewood Cliffs, N.J.: Prentice Hall.

Teger, A.I. & D.G. Pruitt (1967) Components of group risk taking. *Journal of Experimental Social Psychology,* Vol. 3, pp. 189-205.

Trope, Y. (1979) Uncertainty-reducing properties of achievement tasks. *Journal of Personality and Social Psychology,* Vol. 37, pp. 1505-1518.

Wallach, M.A. & N. Logan (1965) The roles of information, discussion, and consensus in group risk taking. *Journal of Experimental Social Psychology,* Vol. 1, pp. 1-19.

Wallach, M.A. & C.W. Wing, Jr. (1968) Is risk a value? *Journal of Personality and Social Psychology*, Vol. 9, pp. 101-106.

Wallach, M.A., N. Kogan & D.J. Bem (1962) Group influence on individual risk taking. *Journal of Abnormal and Social Psychology*, Vol. 65, pp. 75-86.

Weiner, B. (1979) A theory of motivation for some classroom experiences. *Journal of Educational Psychology*, Vol. 71, pp. 3-25.

Weiner, B. (1980a) *Human motivation*. New York: Holt, Reinhart & Winston.

Weiner, B. (1980b) A cognitive (attribution)-emotion-action model of motivated behavior: An analysis of judgments of help-giving. *Journal of Personality and Social Psychology*, Vol. 39, pp. 186-200.

Weiner, B. (1980c) May I borrow your notes? An attributional analysis of judgments of help-giving in an achievement-related context. *Journal of Educational Psychology*, Vol. 72, pp. 676-681.

Weiner, B. (1984) Principles for a theory of student motivation and their application within an attributional framework. In: R.E. Ames & C. Ames (eds.) *Research on Motivation in Education*, volume 1. New York: Academic Press.

Weiner, B. (1985) An attributional theory of achievement motivation and emotion. *Psychological Review*, Vol. 92, pp. 548-573.

Weiner, B. (1986) *An attributional theory of motivation and emotion*. New York: Springer-Verlag.

Weiner, B., I. Frieze, A. Kukla, L. Reed, S. Rest & R.M. Rosenbaum (1971) *Perceiving the causes of success and failure*. New York: General Learning Press.

Weiner, B., S. Graham & C. Chandler (1982) Pity, anger, and guilt: An attributional analysis. *Personality and Social Psychology Bulletin*, Vol. 8, pp. 226-232.

Weiner, B., D. Russell & D. Lerman (1978) Affective consequences of causal ascriptions. In: J.H. Harvey, W.J. Ickes & R.F. Kidd (eds.) *New directions in attribution research*, volume 2. Hillsdale, N.J.: Erlbaum.

Weiner, B., D. Russell & D. Lerman (1979) The cognition- emotion process in achievement-related contexts. *Journal of Personality and Social Psychology*, Vol. 37, pp. 1211-1220.

Woodward, G.L., D.G. Allendic & K.J. Butcher (1981) A rapid, effective technique for controlling disruptive classroom behaviors. *Journal of Educational Research*, Vol. 74, pp. 397-399.

Zuckerman, M., J. Porac, D. Lathin, R. Smith & E.L. Deci (1978) On the importance of self-determination for intrinsically motivated behavior. *Personality and Social Psychology Bulletin*, Vol. 4, pp. 443-466.

# Theory Building in the Domain of Motivation and Learning in School

Franz E. Weinert
Max Planck Institute for Psychological Research
Munich, F.R. Germany

If one were to ask experts in educational psychology for their opinion of the current state of theory and research concerning the influence of motivation on school learning and academic achievement, there would be many different answers. Some experts would highlight the progress in educational research in the areas of achievement motivation, test anxiety, self-concept, and the self-regulation of behavior. Others would stress that theories addressing motivated learning agree with many common sense notions and are therefore highly plausible. Yet others would be dissatisfied with the fact that there are too many competing theories, the validity of which is seldom assessed. Motivation theories provide at best moderate predictive and explanatory power for learning and achievement under classroom conditions. Because of this, theory-based recommendations to practitioners in the field are often too vague, too contradictory, and too abstract to be really useful.

However, despite the fact that the current state of theory construction in the domain of motivation and learning is not ideal, there is a good deal of scientific interest in the area and it is possible to see a number of novel theoretical approaches that offer interesting new perspectives for future research. For example, the emphasis in modern cognitive psychology on the long-term acquisition of knowledge and skills as a necessary condition for expertise has raised new questions concerning the motivation for cumulative learning. Issues that have been dominant to date, such as motivationally based explanation and prediction of single learning episodes, specific achievement, and temporally limited learning activities must be supplemented by analyses of motivation in the acquisition of expertise, a process that develops over many years and that is essential for the mastery of complex tasks in science, arts, technology, economics and sports.

If we do not want to limit the development of comprehensive and substantive theories, it is necessary to provide a broadly defined conceptual framework for studies of motivation and learning in schools. Of course, it is possible to identify some features of school learning that allow a specification of the phenomena to be investigated. For example, a typical feature of school learning is the fact that students' participation in instruction is not voluntary: learning goals, learning conditions, and classroom characteristics are governed more by external factors than by intrinsic factors such as the needs and wishes of the individual learners. In general, school learning may be characterized by the following: There are curriculum-based requirements implying that knowledge and skills be acquired sequentially; learning takes place primarily in groups; a teacher supports and controls the learning process; there are formal rules for assessing achievement, which have a more or less important impact on the learner's further school career and on later professional opportunities and limitations.

What we do not know, however, is what differences there are between learning in the classroom and learning outside it, nor how general or specific the motivational regularities across situations are. Because of this, the school must be seen as a specific case in the more general analysis of the relation between motivation and learning. Whereas learning is largely regarded as limited to the acquisition of knowledge and skills, motivation is understood to involve all the needs, tendencies and goals that initiate, maintain, direct, and modify human activity within the context of cognitive learning. Thus motivation includes such diverse and fuzzy concepts as need for achievement, motivation to learn, anxiety, anger, stress, worry, confidence, doubts, personal perception of control, intrinsic motivation, extrinsic motivation, reward, reinforcement, commitment, expectancies, causal attribution, attitudes toward school, effort expenditures, and so on.

In formal models of school learning, motivational concepts are seldom invoked as separate components for explaining individual achievement differences (Gagné & Dick, 1983; Haertel, Walberg, & Weinstein, 1983). Rather, models tend to favor variables such as learning time, time on task, persistence of learning activities, and so on. It is only in analyses of individual variations in the quantity, intensity and use of learning time that models of school learning look at differences in students' motivation in addition to the preferred cognitive and instructional variables. But the role of motivation in learning theories increases the less learning is regarded as resulting from direct instruction and the more it is regarded as active information processing and a form of self-regulation under changing task demands (Paris & Cross, 1983; Pintrich et al., 1986; Shulman, 1982; Weinert & Helmke,1988). Such changes in theoretical orientations in school learning models are based on recent developments in motivational research.

## The present state of motivational research in the domain of school learning and academic achievement

If one looks at motivational psychology not from the perspective of a motivational psychologist but from the perspective of a scientist who wants to gain a deeper understanding of school learning, one will get both a negative and a positive impression of the present state-of-the-art. On the one hand, several theoretical approaches in motivational research appear to be directly relevant to the psychology of learning and instruction. On the other hand, the empirical results are unsatisfactory because it is not possible to predict, explain and influence differences in students' learning and achievement primarily on the basis of motivation theories. The discrepancy between the internal and external validity of many of the results obtained in motivational research will be briefly outlined in the next sections.

### Important lines of research

There is no unitary theory with a consistent set of core assumptions that explains why and how people seek various goals, activities, and experiences and avoid other goals, activities, and experiences. Rather, there are many theoretical approaches with some similarity to one another, but also with serious differences. Most modern theories of motivation agree on the basic assumption that motivational processes are more strongly influenced by personal perceptions, interpretations and judgments than by objective facts. Where the theories differ is mainly in the information processing mechanisms they postulate to explain this phenomenon.

### Achievement motivation

What determines the large intra- and inter-individual differences in approaching or avoiding achievement-relevant situations? One influential answer to this question was provided by Atkinson's risk-taking model (1957), a model that belongs to the large family of expectancy x value theories (see Heckhausen, 1980). In its simplest form, the model assumes that in any choice situation, an individual will prefer and intensively and persistently work on those tasks that offer the greatest subjective value. The incentive value of these tasks arises from anticipation of self-related emotions aroused by success (pride, satisfaction) or failure (shame, dissatisfaction). In general, success is valued more highly as subjectively perceived task difficulty increases and failure is experienced more negatively as subjective task difficulty decreases. According to this model, tasks of medium difficulty should excite the strongest motivation. However, because individuals develop stable dispositions to give more weight to success or to avoidance of failure, this prediction does not always hold. That is, there is a general approach or avoidance tendency depending on the combination of the strength of the "hope for success" and the "fear of failure" dispositions and the perceived task difficulty.

Clearly this risk-taking model has not only stimulated extensive experimental research but has also been used in motivational analyses of school learning. For the most part, such analyses use dispositional differences in the strength and direction of the achievement motive to predict effort, persistence and success in learning behavior. Occasionally, the entire model has been tested in studies where students were also given the chance to choose tasks varying in difficulty. On the whole the results from all these studies have been disappointing. In short, for many problems, the Atkinson model proved too simple. Correspondingly, practical recommendations derived from the model have also been too simple and vague: "Empirical studies, based on Atkinson's episodic model, make it possible to draw a general educational conclusion. The interaction found between motive constellation and task difficulty supports a concept of education as basically an interaction between personality characteristics of the pupils and characteristics of the educational setting and suggests that teaching ought to be individualized, at least to a certain extent" (Rand, 1987, p.219).

Over the last two decades Atkinson's initial theory of achievement motivation has been elaborated and revised. However, for it to be applied in the field of education, it is necessary to eliminate three restrictions contained in the original model.

First, Atkinson's initial model considers only expectancies and incentives for success and failure for single tasks. Sequences of learning activities and cumulative achievements were first considered in the dynamic action theory (Atkinson & Raynor, 1974). Atkinson himself, for instance, has used the amplified model to explain the phenomena of underachievement and overachievement (Atkinson & Lens, 1980). Students are labelled as under- or overachievers when they obtain higher or lower achievement levels than expected on the basis of aptitude measurements (e.g., IQ). According to Atkinson and Lens, both immediate test performance and cumulative school achievement are influenced by motivation - although in different ways. Whereas motivation strength in a test situation stands in an inverse U-shaped relation to perceived task difficulty, the relation between cumulative learning processes and task-related motivation depends on the number and strength of competing goals. Therefore, it is impossible to predict academic achievement solely on the basis of aptitude tests. For example, an underachiever might be an intelligent and highly (but not too highly!) motivated student who shows low effort and low persistence in school learning due to his engagement in many extracurricular activities. In contrast, an overachiever might be a student who obtains relatively low scores in an intelligence test but who is a persistent and intense learner as a result of individual interests or stimulating instruction. The first student would show lower achievement than predicted on the basis of intelligence test scores, the second higher.

Second, the original Atkinson model only considers one class of expectations, namely the perceived probability of being able to master the particular task presented. In an elaborated cognitive model of motivation Heckhausen (1977) distinguished three types of expectancies, as illustrated in Figure 1.

Figure 1. An extended motivation model of different types of expectancies (from Heckhausen, 1977, p. 287; in a simplified version of Rheinberg, 1988, p. 300).

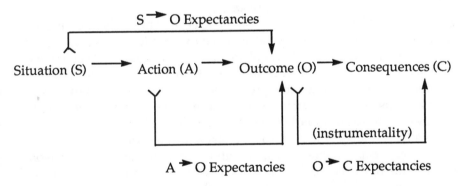

Heckhausen's model assumes that the action tendency is strong (a) when situation-outcome-expectancies (i.e., the perceived probability of an outcome independent of personal action) are low and (b) when both action-outcome-expectancies and outcome-consequence-expectancies are high. Heckhausen and Rheinberg (1980) have provided several practical examples illustrating how the model can be applied to analyses of learning motivation within the school context. The applicability, however, presupposes that a third restriction of the risk-taking model can be overcome.

Third, Atkinson originally considered only the anticipated self-evaluative emotions resulting from success and failure as incentives. In more recent models, outcome-consequence-expectancies are attached to several different classes of values. In addition to emotional self-evaluations, they include social acceptance, personal profit, achievement of superordinate goals, and the experience of a deeper understanding of the subject matter. Of course, students might show considerable individual differences in their preference of different outcome-consequences. However, Helmke (1988a) found that the rank ordering of incentive values was remarkably stable across subjects and time, and for success as well as for failure in a study with fifth and sixth graders. One important result of his study was that "the incentive value...does make a difference in subsequent scholastic achievement. The higher the value-laden consequences of achievement-related outcomes, the higher the level of achievement" (p.14). Superordinate goals and evaluation by parents and teachers appeared to play a greater role as incentives than do anticipated peer- and self-evaluations. Consistent with other recent investigations, Helmke's study suggests that modern conceptualizations of achievement motivation can contribute importantly to our understanding of individual differences in cumulative learning.

### Test anxiety

Atkinson's expectancy x value model of achievement motivation included "fear of failure" as a dispositional variable that, under certain task conditions, would make an individual to perceive avoidance behavior as a "rational response". To measure this trait, both TAT scores and scores on various anxiety questionnaires were used. However, test anxiety has not only been investigated within the context of achievement motivation, but represents a separate, rapidly growing research tradition.

Generally, test anxiety is held to be a stable disposition that leads one to experience achievement-assessment and test situations as a personal threat. This threat is typically reacted to with proprioceptively perceived physiological arousal and tension, a typical anxious feeling state, worry-filled cognitions, with task irrelevant thoughts and avoidance behavior (Helmke, 1983; Sarason, 1980; Sarason & Sarason, 1986). Correlations between trait and state measures of test anxiety and academic achievement scores are consistently negative and range between .00 and -.60. Performance impairments due to test anxiety are particularly high when the actor perceives that the test situation is self-relevant, and when the task to be mastered is difficult and must be performed under speed conditions, so that there are high demands on working memory (Eysenck, 1985).

Certainly, there are substantial individual differences in how students deal with anxiety-inducing situations. These differences in turn depend on the type of task, for example, whether it is possible to do some preparatory work (Krohne, 1978). In view of these findings, it is not surprising that the correlations between test anxiety and academic achievement show substantial differences for different classrooms. Helmke (1988a), for example, found correlation coefficients that ranged from highly negative (r = -.81) to slightly positive (r = .36) for different classrooms. The "achievement-impairing effect of test anxiety ... was found to be particularly high in classrooms characterized by (1) a high intensity of use of time and a low degree of structuring (few previews and reviews) ... and (2) a high incentive of achievement in the classroom,indicating a high salience of success and failure" (p.37). Given that training studies designed to reduce the level of students' test anxiety show on average only weak, inconsistent, and unstable effects, the variables that influence the achievement-impairing effect of test anxiety (e.g., such factors as the social atmosphere, value-orientation, and forms of instruction in the classroom) should play an important role in future research.

### Causal attribution

In expanded cognitive models of achievement motivation, causal attributions for success and failure play an important role in self-evaluation and in task-directed behavior (Heckhausen, 1980). Indeed, the role of causal attributions has in the last few years developed into an independent research area, with special recognition in educational psychology (Weiner, 1984; 1986; Meyer, in press). The basic assumption of attribution theory is that the impact of events, in particular success and failure, on experience and behavior is not a direct one, but rather is mediated by the causal attributions an actor intuitively makes. The attributed causes vary on several dimensions: they may have an internal (abilities, effort) or external (task difficulty, good or bad luck) locus; they may be stable (ability, task difficulty) or variable (effort, chance); they may be global (intelligence, personality) or specific (particular knowledge, temporary motivational state). Different emotional, cognitive, and behavioral effects derive from the particular pattern of causal factors used in attributions for success and failure in any given situation.

However, causal attributions do not vary across situations only on the basis of realistic or even logical judgments, but also on the basis of stable and generalized individual biases in attribution style. These trait-like attributional tendencies can augment or lower self-evaluation, can be functional or dysfunctional, realistic or unrealistic. The syndrome of learned help-lessness for instance has attracted considerable attention in basic and applied research (Abramson, Seligman & Teasdale, 1978). A simplified summary of the model is that individuals who attribute failure to internal, stable, and global causal factors (and who also tend to explain success by external, variable and/or specific factors) suffer from a permanent sense of loss of personal control over their environment. So far little is known about the emergence, development, situational consistency and temporal persistence of generalized negative expectations concerning the effects of one's own actions on outcomes (e.g., learned helplessness versus self-effi-cacy), or on action-outcomes and consequences (hopelessness). However, there is a substantial body of literature concerning the effects of learned helplessness on cognition, emotion, motivation, behavior, and achieve-ment.

J.E. Nicholls (1984) has aptly pointed out that a set of plausible and valid predictions does not constitute a theory. This warning applies in some respects to causal attribution models: this approach requires more sophis-ticated theoretical development, not just refined empirical investigations of the basic processes and functions of causal attribution.

## Goal orientation

Individuals' reactions to success are as similar as their reactions to failure are different. Even when one takes into account dispositional factors such as fear of failure or test anxiety and their associated attributional biases, the variability of behavioral patterns after failure remains high. In a series of studies Dweck (1983, 1986; Dweck & Leggett, 1988; Elliott & Dweck, 1988; Licht & Dweck, 1984) has proposed and tested the hypothesis that the variability in reactions after failure results from the fact that different learners have different goal-orientations. She focussed on two specific goal-orientations: If performance is an actor's central goal, his prime con-cern will be to demonstrate and experience his own abilities. When fail-ures that cannot be overcome by short-term efforts accumulate, this frame of orientation will quickly lead the actor to make an attribution of deficient competence, resulting in the typical reactions of learned helplessness. In contrast, when learning is an actor's central goal, his main concern will not be experience and demonstration of one's own ability, but rather improve-ment in performance and competence. With this orientation, failures are more frequently regarded as opportunities to learn from one's errors, to increase one's effort, to ask for help from others, and to show mastery reac-tions.

The different orientations toward performance or learning goals appear to have a dispositional basis. From Dweck's findings it appears that such goal-orientations may be linked to intuitive theories about intelligence. Those individuals who interpret intelligence as a stable ability which they cannot modify, tend to be oriented more to performance goals, and regard classroom learning as an opportunity to evaluate their own abilities by means of social comparison. When this type of orientation is associated with the subjective perception of high ability, failure leads to a mastery orientation of effective problem solving. In lower ability individuals (or in people who perceive their abilities as low) failure frequently will lead to learning difficulties and to related defensive and depressive reactions. In contrast, those individuals who interpret intelligence as a cumulative, learning-related competence, will tend to adopt learning as a goal-orientation, and difficulties will be experienced as a challenge.

According to Dweck's and her associates' assumptions and findings, goal orientations are determined not only by personal preferences, but are also triggered by environmental cues. For example, if a teacher indicates that her main concern is to assess students' aptitude, ego-related goals (e.g. performance goals) will dominate. Support for this argument comes from empirical findings of typical differences between task-oriented and ego-oriented classrooms, differences which in turn considerably affect the learning behaviors of the students (Nicholls et al., in press).

Generally speaking, students are necessarily concerned with simultaneously attaining two primary goals: Acquiring new and better competences, and maintaining or renewing individual well-being (Boekaerts, 1988a). An important topic for future research is to look in detail at individual and instructional conditions and the effects of different goal-orientations. With such analyses it might be possible to design instructional conditions to promote optimal learning goals.

*Intrinsic motivation*

For several decades, theories of learning motivation have been dominated by the assumptions that needs are satisfied through achievement, social support, rewards, self-evaluation, and so on. Frequently the motivational mechanisms were those underlying expectancy x value models, cost-benefit calculations, or instrumental models. In comparison, intrinsic motives for learning have played a much smaller role in theories of motivation. Intrinsic motivation addresses goals and needs that are satisfied by the process of learning itself and by the possibility of experiencing and enjoying one's own expression of competence and increasing knowledge. In this framework, working and learning are not a means to an end, but are more or less an end in themselves; learning activities and learning goals are not clearly distinguished.

For some time, the questions arising from a consideration of intrinsic motivation have been explored by a relatively separate and small theoretical camp outside the mainstream of motivation research. A number of concepts, such as "effectance motivation", "exploratory drive", "optimal cognitive incongruity", "experience of flow", "self-determination", "personal causation", "interest excitement", and so on, epitomize this work. Underlying these concepts is the assumption that "intrinsic motivation is based in the innate, organismic needs for competence and self-determination. It energizes a high variety of behaviors and psychological processes for which the primary rewards are the experience of effectance and autonomy" (Deci & Ryan, 1985, p.32).

The reason for a careful consideration of intrinsic motivation is that in educational philosophy intrinsic motives are regarded as the most important conditions for, and essential goals of school learning. The worry is that strengthening extrinsic motivation by making external incentives and rewards available is likely to be detrimental to achieving these goals. The reasons underlying such fears come from the results of studies investigating the so-called "overjustification" effect, which show that the use of rewards can undermine intrinsic motivation (for a comprehensive review of these studies see Deci & Ryan, 1985; Heckhausen, 1980). DeCharms (1968) proposed two provocative theses that prompted these studies: (1) intrinsic motivation is weakened if one is rewarded for doing something that one enjoys doing anyway; and (2) intrinsic motivation is strengthened if a reward is withheld for activities performed only to get the reward.

These claims appear to be supported by empirical findings from classroom situations. For example, Harter (1982) reported that an initial curiosity, the spontaneous need to seek new information, and a tendency to master skills independently decrease monotonically with increasing age and time in school. Correspondingly, awareness of external demands and incentives and the internalization of evaluation standards increase with age and time in school. Of course, the actual empirical results are far more complex and contradictory than they seem in such studies. There are many indications that the contrast between intrinsic and extrinsic motivation is neither inherent nor irreconcilable. What is required is research exploring how the two sources of motivation interact, and more complex theoretical models that integrate intrinsic and extrinsic motivational components. Such a line of inquiry is especially urgent, for example, for the systematic investigation of the acquisition of expertise, a process that stretches over many years, and that must incorporate motivational analyses. The significance of motivation in attaining the goal of expertise in sports, in arts or in science is unquestioned. The phrases "Skill and will" or "No pain, no gain" are frequently quoted slogans, expressing a clear appreciation of the importance of motivation for the development of expertise.

## The explanatory and predictive power of motivational variables in school learning: Some disappointing results

The explanatory and predictive power of motivational constructs is the strongest under the following conditions: when the goal is to provide empirical verification for specific hypotheses derived from a specific theory; when the selection and operationalization of independent and dependent variables are based on theoretical assumptions; and when the research design is experimental or quasi-experimental. Models of learning and achievement motivation have proved their worth under these conditions. Unfortunately, however, it has proved consistently difficult to generalize the results from this sort of research to classroom situations.

On the whole, four strategies have been used to apply theoretical models to learning in school:

A  Measurement instruments developed in motivation research are used in studies on the development of school achievement, so that the contribution of motivational variables to overall achievement variance can be estimated.

B  Observed classroom differences are used to test theoretically derived hypotheses concerning the relation between specific teaching conditions and students' motivational reactions and the effects of these reactions on academic achievement.

C  In cooperation with teachers in specially chosen classrooms, an attempt is made to initiate instructional and learning conditions that correspond to a specific theoretical model. The subsequent effect of changes in the classroom situation on students' behavior and performance is then observed.

D  Students with behavioral, learning or achievement problems are observed to determine whether theoretically relevant motivational deficits can be found. If so, training programs are designed to change the relevant factors. The training programs are then evaluated for effectiveness and to establish how improved motivation affects learning and achievement levels.

Each of the four strategies has advantages and disadvantages in terms of testing the theory, of the generalizability of the empirical findings, and the applicability of the results to the reality of the school situation.

### Motivational variables as predictors of academic achievement

Over the last decades many motivation measures have been used as predictors of academic achievement in empirical research in schools. The results have been inconsistent and generally disappointing. In a statistical meta-analysis performed on 40 studies covering the first to the twelfth grade, Uguroglu and Walberg (1979) found that the mean correlation between motivation and achievement was .34. The authors concluded that "motivation measures appear to be associated with less variance in educational achievement on average than are other factors in learning" (p.386). Low correlations were also found in a more recent meta-analysis by Hansford and Hattie (1982) and in a meta-meta-analysis by Fraser et al. (1987). In these reports, the correlation coefficients were positive, as expected, when the strength of achievement motivation, self-concept, and internal locus of control were used as predictors for academic achievement; the correlation coefficients were negative for motivational variables such as test anxiety, learned helplessness and neuroticism.

These weak empirical findings clearly contradict the intuitive judgments of teachers, students, parents, and scientists. If the probable causes for high and low academic achievement are ranked and weighted, a prominent role is consistently ascribed to motivational effects. We may ask then, whether these intuitive judgments are false or whether there is another explanation for empirical results that suggest that "personality variables, including motivation, are not very important in predicting achievement" (Maruyama & Walberg, 1984, p.219).

In the discussions concerning this question, various reasons are provided to explain why the influence of motivation on learning and achievement is possibly underrated. These reasons include methodological weaknesses (e.g., the predominant use of questionnaires to measure motivation; studies limited to dispositional motives without consideration of incentives and other situational factors) and theoretical deficits (e.g., the absence of cognitive moderator variables, failure to use theory-based process measures, disregard of context conditions).

*Testing hypotheses on motivational functioning under real classroom conditions*
As mentioned earlier, one weakness in empirical studies of motivational variables as predictors of academic achievement is that only student characteristics and not instructional characteristics are assessed. This is problematic because no theory would assume that temporary states of affect, motivational processes and motivational effects are not determined by special person-environment interactions. The external validity of motivation models can therefore be evaluated, using classroom differences in relevant patterns of instruction to test the hypothesized dependent motivational effects.

One example of this research strategy is a study by Helmke (1988a), the results of which have already been briefly reported. The study was concerned with the achievement-impairing effect of test anxiety. Three aspects of this study are important for the present discussion: First, the correlations between test anxiety scores and (math) achievement scores were not computed across all classrooms together but separately for each single class. Significant differences between the correlation coefficients for the 39 classrooms show how arbitrary and useless average correlations can be. Second, on the basis of classroom differences in the correlations between motivation and achievement, it was possible to specify several covarying instructional and teacher factors that are consistent with the theory of test anxiety (e.g., the incentive value of success and failure; task orientation of the teacher; use of teaching time; degree of instructional structuring). Third, and most important, it was possible to use these data to test the validity of the interactive model of test anxiety.

Admittedly, this last point is somewhat problematic, because alternative hypotheses cannot be ruled out through control or manipulation of the relevant variables in a correlational study. In principle, however, this research strategy can be improved so that it is a useful way to test theories of learning and achievement motivation.

### Implementation of prescriptive motivational models in classrooms

Comparisons on the basis of existing differences among classrooms are often not sufficient to investigate the basic features of a theoretical model. For example, it is not always possible to identify classrooms with theoretically optimal conditions for successful learning. In such instances it may be advisable to gain the cooperation of teachers to modify the classroom atmosphere and the quality of instruction to provide the optimal conditions in a methodically controlled way.

This strategy was chosen by DeCharms (1976) to test his model of personal causation. The model assumes that "the feeling to be an origin" (and not to feel a "pawn") is the most important motivational condition for successful learning. To experience personal causation, students must have opportunities (a) to set themselves demanding but realistic goals, (b) to recognize their own strengths and weaknesses, (c) to have self-confidence concerning the efficacy of their own actions, (d) to evaluate whether they have reached the goals they have set themselves, and (e) to assume responsibility not only for their own behavior but also, for example, for the behavior of their peers in the classroom.

According to DeCharms' conception, the development of such a motivational pattern depends on the social atmosphere in the classroom. He first tested this hypothesis by using self-designed measurement procedures to assess the "origin" atmosphere in different classrooms. He found that this variable correlated significantly with mean achievement gains in the classrooms. This result was then the basis for a training program designed to modify the "origin conditions" in several classrooms.

First the teachers were given an opportunity to familiarize themselves with the "origin experience". Then, with the help of skilled psychologists, the teachers planned their instruction so that the students would have sufficient opportunities to make decisions independently, to assume responsibility, to set goals for themselves, and so on. This program was carried out in a sample of classrooms over different timespans (from three weeks to two years).

DeCharms' results were impressive: The "origin" atmosphere in the classroom, the reported students' "origin experiences", the choice of realistic aspiration levels, and average academic achievement all improved significantly. However, it is still not clear how widely these findings can be generalized nor whether the experiences reported in this study can be useful in classrooms with worse preconditions. Such problems are, of course, typical for this type of research, and it would be advisable for future research to include generalization studies from the outset.

### Training studies to enhance student motivation

Even though it contradicts cognitive learning theories and most instructional models, many researchers assume that there is a direct relationship between learning motivation, learning behavior and learning achievement. From this perspective, a general research strategy has been to ask whether students who had learning problems also had motivational problems, and whether these motivational problems might be responsible for their learning problems. The answer to this question was generally "yes". Subsequently, a number of training programs in motivation were designed. These were intended to change level of aspiration, perceived locus of control, personal patterns of causal attribution, anxiety in achievement situations, feelings of helplessness, self-concept or self-evaluation strategies. In some programs, learning strategies, mastery reactions to failure and good study habits were included in addition to the motivational variables.

The results from a large number of training studies have been published in the last 25 years (for reviews see Allen, 1980; Heckhausen & Krug, 1982; Krug, 1983; Rand, 1987). Overall, these results are somewhat disappointing. To be sure, the expected changes in motivational level were achieved in many programs. However, as a rule these changes did not have a strong or stable impact on learning behavior or academic achievement. This general result is sometimes interpreted as a failure of the entire training approach. However, this conclusion is too broad and possibly even false. It is more likely that the theoretical assumptions underlying most of the training studies were somewhat naive, because they proceeded from an egocentric standpoint of considering only motivation. However, many educational studies have convincingly demonstrated that learning activities and school achievement are strongly influenced by cognitive factors (prior knowledge,metacognitive competencies, general aptitudes) and by the quality of instruction (Fraser et al., 1987; Weinert & Helmke, 1988).

Even when students' motivation does play an important role in learning, it cannot be expected that increasing motivation will have immediate effects on learning performance, especially when cumulative achievement is the focus. Immediate effects cannot be expected even when, in addition to motivation training, good study habits are included in the training program. Wide-ranging deficits in prior knowledge cannot be compensated in the short term by stronger motivation or by better learning techniques. However, training programs based on more complex models of school learning, including motivational, metacognitive, and domain-specific learning components are not yet available. For this reason, it is not possible to estimate the utility of motivational training programs at this time.

## Deficits of motivational research in an educational framework

Motivation research is currently a very lively area. This extends to the analysis of motivation in the context of school learning. There are various theoretical approaches and empirical paradigms and discussions between the different theoretical camps are by now open-minded. And scientific progress has been made. However, a critical evaluation of this area will reveal several characteristic problems. It is useful to briefly summarize these deficits in order to use this summary to sketch out fruitful areas for future research.

### Conceptual deficits

Two approaches typify motivational research in the context of school learning: In the theoretically oriented approach a researcher examines a motivational model, already substantiated in experimental studies, under classroom conditions. For example, numerous school-related studies have been based on Atkinson's (1957) risk-taking theory. In the empirically oriented approach motivational variables are selected for study from a variety of theoretical models on the basis of phenomenological analyses or plausible assumptions. The data are then analyzed for interrelationships (e.g. by factor analysis). For example, Chiu (1967) identified and interpreted five motivational factors relevant to school learning: Positive orientation toward school learning, need for social recognition, curiosity, failure avoidance, and conformity (for a new comparative study and a recent discussion of this approach, see Entwistle & Kozeki, 1988).

Clearly, each strategy has certain advantages and disadvantages. Results from the empirically oriented approach reflect the variety of motivational factors that are relevant to school learning. In addition to the multidimensional structure of the individual's motivation to learn, there is also variability in motivational tendencies that becomes evident when different classrooms and school systems are compared. However, the scientific status of empirically derived motivational factors is conceptually vague and theoretically controversial. Also, with this approach it is not possible to specify what mechanisms produce interactions among motivational variables nor what mechanisms underlie the impact of motivational variables on learning.

In the theoretically oriented approach, the advantages and disadvantages are just the inverse. In this approach a motivational construct and its hypothesized impact on learning are explicitly conceptualized. However, it is often not specified how the motivational concept should interact with other needs, goals, and preferences in the full context of motivation and learning. This dilemma can only be resolved by combining theoretically and empirically oriented approaches. On the one hand, the highly complex and multifaceted phenomena of learning and motivation must be studied without theoretical restrictions. On the other hand, the fundamental mechanisms of motivated learning require a precise theoretical clarification and definition. A precondition for developing research strategies to fulfill such contradictory demands is the resolution of at least three conceptual deficits, which are described in the following.

### What should motivational constructs explain?

Most theoretical models and empirical studies concerned with learning and motivation fail to indicate precisely which set of dependent variables is to be predicted and explained, and fail to justify the choice of a particular set of variables. Thus, as a rule, it is not clear whether an analysis concerns different motivational determinants of the willingness to learn (approach versus avoidance tendencies, formation of learning intentions, state versus action orientation etc.), characteristics of learning processes (choice of task difficulty, effort investment, persistence), or the quantity and quality of learning performance (episodic versus cumulative achievement, speed versus power tests, etc.).

A good example of the atheoretical approach to dealing with dependent variables is again Atkinson's (1957) risk-taking theory. Originally conceptualized to explain choice of task difficulty, the theory was soon used to explain the intensity and persistence of learning activities, and was finally expanded to predict achievement differences. Thus, it is no surprise that the results from studies based on this model in school-related contexts were often disappointing. Atkinson's model provides no theoretical basis for predicting scholastic achievement; nor does it take account of the constraints encountered when it is applied to a school setting. For example, in a classroom, students would rarely have an opportunity to choose between levels of task difficulty. Quite the contrary: "Classrooms are work settings in which students must cope with activities that are compulsory and subject to public evaluation" (Brophy, 1983, p. 201). Hence, theoretical models of learning motivation must not only explicitly define motivational factors and mechanisms, but they must also specify how motivational processes work under the constraints, processes and outcomes of learning under classroom conditions.

### What is the theoretical meaning of "motivated learning behavior"?

For cumulative learning to occur, one must assume that various conditions and mechanisms have a reciprocal influence. This gives rise to questions as to: whether and how latent motives are activated through positive and negative incentives; whether and how motivation leads to learning activities through the formation of intentions and the processes of action initiation; whether and how learning activities lead to scholastic achievement through internal routines of action control and the use of relevant cognitive resources.

Many theories concerning the motivation to learn have in the past continued to naively assume that motives and motivational tendencies alone determine learning activities and achievements. However, this assumption is wrong. Nuttin (1984) pointed out the need to better understand how nebulous and occasionally unconscious motives are transformed into very personal and concrete intentions and plans. Heckhausen and Kuhl (1985) have tried to conceptualize the "long journey from wishes to actions" within a theoretical model of their own. This model connects motivational and volitional components, and represents an important step in reconceptualizing learning paradigms in the school setting (cf. Halisch & Kuhl, 1987; Heckhausen 1987; Rheinberg, 1988).

### What are the "essential" motivational variables?

Research on learning and achievement is inflated with different motivational concepts. It is difficult and in many cases impossible to recognize the theoretical relationships, parallels, and distinctions among these concepts. Therefore, it is also difficult to compare the theoretical postulates and empirical support for different models of motivation. This situation often leads to rather meaningless discussions which attempt to determine the "real" motivational variables.

It appears more promising to attempt to classify the many motivational concepts according to their generality and stability as internal determinants of individual behavior. At first glance, at least four hierarchical levels can be distinguished in such a classification system:

A abstract, general and stable dispositional motives and self-concepts (e.g., achievement motive, affiliation motive, power motive, trait anxiety, general self-concept);

B stable but malleable personal belief-value systems (e.g., domain-specific self-concepts, special attitudes, current concerns, life tasks);

C more or less stable expectancies with respect to different classes of situations (e.g., self-efficacy, hopes, fears, threats); and

D concrete goals, wishes, intentions, and expectations in given situational contexts.

Stability (versus variability) and specificity (versus globality) are the two dimensions of the proposed hierarchical classification model.

In order to explain how situation-specific wishes, intentions and expectations influence actual behavior, different hypothetical mechanisms are postulated: Anticipation of affective reactions, activation of cognitive goal representations, means-end relationships, and action-initiation routines (Dweck & Elliott, 1983; Kuhl, 1985).

This proposed conceptual classification of motivational variables is not meant as the basis for a theory, but is instead a heuristic model which allows motivational concepts to be described at many levels of generalizability and stability. In addition, it provides a basis for developing and testing hypotheses regarding whether and how variables at a higher level of abstraction determine motivational processes at a more concrete level.

### Methodological deficits

Questionnaires are the primary tool for measuring motivational variables in educational research. Sometimes this poses a serious problem when one wants to compare subjects' thoughts and biases with structures and processes assumed by motivational theories. It is in principle difficult to distinguish motives, belief-value systems, expectancies, and concrete motivational tendencies on the basis of questionnaire data. Relatively high correlations between questionnaire scores and scholastic achievement often result from a mixture of different motivational indicators, as well as from the overlap of predictor and criterion in single items. A typical example is Hermans' (1976) questionnaire assessing different aspects of achievement motivation (cf. Petermann & Zielinski, 1979).

Considering the problems involved in questionnaire studies, it is not surprising that researchers testing theoretically derived hypotheses frequently find differences between questionnaire data and data from projective measures of motivation (McClelland, 1980). Projective tests often have another type of construct validity than questionnaires (Halisch, 1986; Heckhausen & Halisch, 1986). Unfortunately, projective measures are not easy to use as group tests in the classroom, and other methods, including those categorized somewhere between questionnaires and projective measures (e.g., grid-techniques, cf. Schmalt, 1976), behavioral indices of motivational factors, and psychophysiological measures have not yet proved adequate in school-related motivational research. In contrast, teacher ratings of motivational differences among students often demonstrate surprisingly high validity (cf. Fincham et al., 1989). In any case there are many options in choosing adequate measures of motivational tendencies, depending on the theoretical approach of the study under consideration. Nonetheless, one of the most important goals of future research is to improve the assessment of various motivational constructs and processes.

## A new look at motivation in school learning and some future research proposals

It is both tedious and difficult to predict or recommend future research perspectives in a review focussing on the current state of the art. Fresh ideas, new concepts and the development of better measures are the heart of scientific progress, and these neither can nor should be fully predictable from past experience. Therefore in this section only a few recent developments in the domain of motivation to learn will be discussed. These are developments that seem particularly fruitful with respect to theoretical progress and that may provide important perspectives for future research.

### Motivation in a developmental perspective

As mentioned above, many motivational models are appropriate only for predicting behavior during brief learning or achievement episodes. Yet, as in the case of Atkinson's (1957) risk-taking theory, situation-invariant motivational dispositions must also be postulated. It is true that school learning consists of single episodes, but it is also a cumulative process which can only be understood in the context of long-term developmental changes and stabilities. The individual's self-concept of ability and the expectations as well as the causal attributions related to this self-concept seem to play an important role in this respect.

This expectation is supported by the results of Helmke's (in press, b) longitudinal study, which investigated the interplay between self-concept of ability and math achievement in the fifth and sixth grades. The data were analyzed using causal modeling techniques and yielded an interesting pattern of results showing the dynamic interaction between the self- concept and math achievement (see Figure 2).

"Neither a pure self-enhancement nor a pure skill development interpretation is supported by these results. Rather, the pattern changes after one school year: Whereas achievement was clearly causally dominant during the fifth grade, the relationship between these constructs was reciprocal during the sixth grade" (Helmke, in press, b). Of particular theoretical interest is the finding that the achievement fostering effects of a high self-

Figure 2. Dynamics of interactions between self-concept and academic achievement: results of the PLS-causal modeling analysis (from Helmke, 1988c, p.44).

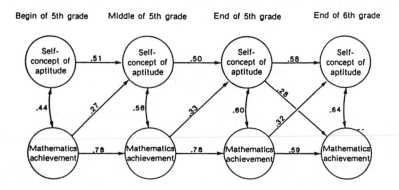

concept of ability are mediated by the quality of school-related effort (preparatory work for school, students' involvement in classroom learning).

Helmke's findings are consistent with the results of studies investigating the influence of academic success on a positive self-concept (Eccles, 1983; Harter, 1982, 1985), with the established relationship between low academic achievement and a decrease in the self-concept of ability (Kifer, 1975), and affirm the long-term predictability of school achievement through measures of learned helplessness and test anxiety (Fincham et al., 1989).

In interpreting these data, it is important to consider that the overall self-concept is not a uniform construct, but is a collection of more or less general, stable, and ego-relevant self-representations, while "the working self-concept is the subset of representations which is accessible at a given moment" (Markus & Wurf, 1987, p. 314). The degree to which the working self-concept and the dispositional self-concept can be influenced by personal experiences and social contexts varies, depending on a person's individual learning history. A developmental frame of reference and the consideration of individual differences are, therefore, essential to theories of learning motivation. It is especially important to take a developmental perspective when considering the elementary school years: In the course of cognitive development attributional concepts (especially ability and effort) are still being differentiated, and the ability to infer a single causal factor from a whole constellation of conditions improves considerably (Heckhausen, 1980; Nicholls, 1978). Special attention should be devoted to the conceptualization of two aspects of effort: as the socially desired involvement in learning activities, and as a possible compensation for low ability in mastering learning tasks (Meyer, 1984).

*Motivation as both a determinant and a consequence of learning activities*
Future research based on a developmental frame of reference must investigate how learning-related changes in motivation, goals, and attitudes change as a function of individual achievement, classroom instruction, the classroom situation, and incentives outside the classroom. Ever since the Enlightenment, educational philosophers have viewed motivation not only as a condition, but also as an important goal of school learning (Herbart, 1806). Weinert and Helmke's (1988) results graphically illustrate that the course of development for different components of motivation to learn under the same instructional conditions can be quite variable. This study investigated short- and long-term effects of direct instruction on cognitive and motivational learning outcomes. Although the positive correlations between different indicators of direct instruction (classroom management, use of time, individualized support) and math achievement remained relatively stable over a two year period, correlations with some motivation measures were considerably less stable (see Table 1).
These results demonstrate that direct instruction does lead to both short-term and long-term enhancement of performance and to a corresponding improvement in the self-concept of ability, but that attitudes toward school and mathematics significantly deteriorated over one and a half years as a consequence of this type of instruction. Does this mean that instruction that owes its success to external control of students' learning activities serves to reduce the value components of motivation (i.e., enjoyment of classroom activities and intrinsic interests)? Although the results are consistent with such an interpretation, the empirical basis is yet too small to give a satisfactory answer. However, because of the theoretical and practical importance of this issue, additional research is urgently needed.

Table 1: Zero-order correlations between observational measures
of direct instructions (classroom management) and motivational outcomes
after six months (short-term) and eighteen months (long-term) of previous
instruction; N = 39 classrooms.

| Motivational outcome | short-term | long-term |
|---|---|---|
| Self-concept of ability | .43 | .19 |
| Test anxiety | -.55 | .03 |
| Positive attitudes toward school | .12 | -.39 |
| Positive attitudes toward math | .01 | -.27 |

(from: Weinert & Helmke, 1988, p. 237)


*Motivation, metacognition, and the processing of self-related information*
Does the ability to learn improve as a student acquires knowledge about
how to learn? Does cognitive performance depend on knowledge about
how the cognitive system functions? Does intelligent learning depend on
expertise in learning? Is the level of performance dependent on the veridi-
cality of one's achievement-related concepts? Such issues are the concern
of metacognitive research, an area that has greatly expanded over the last
20 years.
Generally, metacognition refers to declarative knowledge about learning
abilities, learning tasks, and appropriate learning strategies, and to proce-
dural skills that allow effective organization of one's own learning activities (Weinert & Kluwe, 1987). Metacognitive knowledge is frequently characterized as a naive theory about (one's own) cognitive structures, processes and functions, which makes its relationship to the concept of learning
motivation obvious. It is therefore not surprising that the theoretical constructs and empirical indicators, especially in cognitive theories of motivation, are highly similar to those employed in metacognitive research
(Weinert, 1987). As a result, two previously distinct research approaches
are gradually converging: The acquisition and use of (naive) knowledge
about cognitive abilities, "laws" of learning, and evaluation standards
serve both as the basis for "learning to learn" (Baron & Sternberg, 1987),
and as part of the essential cognitive prerequisites for processing self-related information. This naive knowledge is, however, also a central component in almost all modern models of learning motivation. An increase in

systematic studies on the relations between metacognitive knowledge and beliefs, cognitive resources, and motivational variables can contribute to a better understanding of the important but perhaps limited role of metacognitive knowledge in learning motivation.

*Motivation, volition and the control of goal-directed learning behavior*
The problem of inferring dispositional motives or current wishes from learning behavior and learning outcomes has already been mentioned in the description of some conceptual deficits in current motivational research. To predict and explain differences in learning and achievement more precisely traditional motivational models must be supplemented with volitional components such as intention formation, action initiation, motivational versus volitional states of mind, action control, and so on. In his Rubicon model, Heckhausen (1987) posited that individuals are reality-oriented and open-minded with respect to new information before deciding upon a specific action (motivational state of mind), but are realization-oriented and closed-minded after making the decision (volitional state of mind). Several hypotheses about differences in information processing in the two states of mind have been empirically confirmed (Heckhausen & Gollwitzer, 1987). Of course it is unlikely that everyday action and school learning require continual conscious, specific decisions. Study habits, behavioral routines, automatized mechanisms of action control, and teacher control of learning behavior undoubtedly play an essential role. However, the incorporation of these action regulation processes in theories of learning motivation must be supplemented with investigation of the more or less conscious, motivational and volitional processes involved in the internal control of learning.

*Motivation, instruction, and some compensatory mechanisms
in controlling learning behavior*
As discussed above, the correlations between motivational variables and levels of achievement vary, while differences in classroom instruction remain stable. To analyze this phenomenon we conducted a study (Weinert & Helmke, 1987) based on the following assumptions: The achievement-fostering effect of direct instruction is due to the fact that external direction and control of student learning activities provide all students with behavior patterns that are typically found only in highly motivated students in less structured classrooms. According to this view, as the effectiveness of the method of direct instruction increases, the causal role of individual levels of motivation in determining performance levels may decrease. Conversely, we hypothesized that when students have greater freedom during instruction and are less controlled in their learning activi-

ties, the impact of individual levels of motivation on achievement will increase.

These hypotheses concerning a possible functional compensation between motivation and instruction in determining students' learning and achievement have been empirically supported. Considerably more variance ($R^2$ = .34) could be explained by measures of direct instruction (individualized support) in students with a low self-concept of ability than in students with a high self-concept ($R^2$ =.13). In line with our theoretical expectations, no such difference was found for test anxiety. The functional compensation between student self-concept (as a valid indicator of learning motivation) and instructional variables was shown not only in its determining influence on math achievement, but also in its effect on the attained achievement level. However, the threshold levels for such functional compensation between motivation and instruction are presently unclear. On the basis of statistical meta-analyses, Walberg (1984) concludes that the essential determinants of academic achievement "appear to substitute, compensate or trade-off for one another at diminishing rates of returns" (p.22).

As mentioned earlier, Helmke (1988) found that the achievement-impairing effects of test anxiety depend on how intensely instructional time was used, the degree to which the teacher structured information, and the incentive value of success and failure in the classroom. The discovery and analysis of compensatory relations between motivation and instruction is especially important for educational practice, because it is probably easier to implement changes in instruction than to alter stable student motives and self-concept.

*The social context of students' learning motivation*

Many models of learning motivation are limited to a consideration of conditions and processes within the individual and ignore the classroom context. Yet there are numerous empirical findings that confirm the importance of the classroom as a frame of reference (as perceived by the student) for making social comparisons and for setting normative standards. Achievement expectations and performance evaluations by teachers, peers, and parents play a significant role in how the student processes success and failure. The long-term negative consequences of a series of failures on the self-concept of ability can be reinforced or mitigated by social punishment or social support (Kifer, 1975; Pekrun, 1985). However, the influence of social context arises not just from personal interactions, but also from the classroom climate, classroom norms, social atmosphere, and from internalized group standards. Because the impact of social context on the relations between motivation, learning, achievement, and reactions to success and failure differs greatly across individuals, theories of learning motivation would benefit from a systematic study of the interplay between universal mechanisms of motivation, the effects of social context, and the influences of individual differences.

## Concluding remarks

The recognizable problems in existing approaches to motivational research in an educational context offer little prospect for a rapid or fundamental improvement in theories of motivation and learning. Moreover, a general model that would integrate motivational constructs and mechanisms arising from different traditions cannot be expected in the near future. Indeed, the empirical possibilities and theoretical underpinnings for a large and homogenous research program in this area are limited.

A more interesting and more promising approach would be to use a heuristic model of learning motivation to combine and integrate the information generated by diverse lines of research. Such a model would need to take into account large-scale, comprehensive empirical studies to analyze the phenomenon of learning motivation, as well as more narrowly conceived theoretical work to elucidate single mechanisms of learning motivation. Because learning at a given point of time can only be understood in relation to many individual and social factors, relations between motivational constructs and cognitive, metacognitive, instructional, and social variables deserve special attention. There is a need to link together experimental and field studies, cross-sectional and longitudinal investigations, and theoretically and empirically oriented research. Ultimately, however, theoretical advancement is not only dependent on good ideas, but also on the development of improved methods for assessing motivational constructs and processes as determinants and consequences of school learning.

## References

Abramson, L.Y., M.E.P. Seligman & J.D. Teasdale (1978) Learned helplessness in humans: Critique and reformulation. *Journal of Abnormal Psychology*, Vol. 87, pp. 49-74.

Allen, G.J. (1980)  The behavioral treatment of test anxiety:Therapeutic innovation and emerging conceptual challenges. *Progress in Behavior Modification*, Vol. 9, pp. 81-127.

Atkinson, J.W. (1957)  Motivational determinants of  risk-taking behavior.

*Psychological Review*, Vol. 64, pp. 359-376.

Atkinson, J.W. & W. Lens (1980) Fähigkeit und Motivation alsDeterminanten momentaner und kumulativer Leistungen. In: H. Heckhausen (ed.) *Fähigkeit und Motivation in erwartungswidriger Schulleistung.* Göttingen: Verlag für Psychologie.

Atkinson, J.W. & J.D. Raynor (1974) *Motivation and Achievement.* Washington, D.C.: Winston.

Baron, J.B. & R.J. Sternberg (1987) *Teaching Thinking Skills: Theory and Practice.* New York: Freeman.

Boekaerts, M. (1988a) Introduction to "Emotion, motivationand learning". *International Journal of Educational Research*, Vol. 12, pp. 229-234.

Boekaerts, M. (1988b) Motivated learning: Bias in appraisals.*International Journal of Educational Research*, Vol. 12, pp. 267-280.

Brophy, J. (1983) Conceptualizing student motivation. *Educational Psychology*, Vol. 18, pp. 200-215.

Chiu, L.H. (1967) *A factorial study of academic motivation.* Unpubl. doctoral dissertation. Teachers College, Columbia University.

DeCharms, R. (1968) *Personal Causation.* New York: Academic Press.

DeCharms, R. (1976) *Enhancing motivation. Change in the Classroom.* New York: Irvington Publisher.

Deci, E. & Ryan, R.M. (1985) *Instrinsic Motivation and Self Determination in Human Behavior.* New York: Plenum Press.

Dweck, C.S. (1983) Children's theories of intelligence: Consequences for learning. In: S.G. Paris, G.M. Olson & H.W. Stevenson (eds.) *Learning and Motivation in the Classroom.* Hillsdale, N.J.: Erlbaum.

Dweck, C.S. (1986) Motivational processes affecting learning. *American Psychologist*, Vol. 41, pp. 1040-1048.

Dweck, C.S. & E.S. Elliott (1983) Achievement motivation. In: P.H. Mussen (ed.) *Handbook of child psychology. Vol. IV: Sozialization, Personality, and Social Development.* New York: Wiley.

Dweck, C.S. & E.L. Leggett (1988) A social-cognitive approach to motivation and personality. *Psychological Review*, Vol. 95, pp. 256-273.

Eccles, J. (1983) Expectancies, values, and academic behaviors. In: J.T. Spence (ed.), *Achievement and achievement motives.* San Francisco: Freeman.

Elliott, E. S. & C.S. Dweck (1988) Goals: An approach to motivation and achievement. *Journal of Personality and Social Psychology*, Vol. 54, pp. 5-12.

Entwistle, N. & B. Kozeki (1988) Dimensions of motivation and approaches to learning in British and Hungarian secondary schools. *International Journal of Educational Research*, Vol. 12, pp. 243-255.

Eysenck, M.W. (1985) Anxiety and cognitive-task performance.*Personality and Individual Differences*, Vol. 6, pp. 579-586.

Fincham, F.D., A. Hokoda & R. Sanders jr. (1989) Learned helplessness, test anxiety, and academic achievement: A longitudinal analysis. *Child Development*, Vol. 60, pp. 138-145.

Fraser, B. J., H.J. Walberg, W.W. Welch & J.A. Hattie (1987) Syntheses of educational productivity research. *International Journal of Educational Research*, Vol. 11, pp. 145-252.

Gagné, R.M. & W. Dick (1983) Instructional psychology. *Annual Review of Psychology*, Vol. 34, pp. 261-295.

Haertel, G.D., H.J. Walberg & T. Weinstein (1983) Psychological models of educational performance: A theoretical synthesis of constructs. *Review of Educational Research*, Vol. 53, pp. 75-91.

Halisch, F. (1986). Elaborieren und Initiieren einer Handlung als respondente versus operante Reaktion. Vortrag gehalten im Rahmen des Symposiums "*Wiederaufbereitung des Wollens*" auf dem 35. Kongress der Deutschen Gesellschaft für Psychologie, Heidelberg 1986.

Halisch, F. & J. Kuhl (eds.)(1987) *Motivation, intention, and volition*. Berlin: Springer-Verlag.

Halisch, F. & H. Heckhausen (in press) Motive-dependent versus ability-dependent valence functions for success and failure. In: F. Halisch & J.H.L. van den Bercken (eds., in collaboration with S. Hazlett) *International perspectives on achievement and task motivation*. Lisse: Swets & Zeitlinger.

Hansford, B.C. & J.A. Hattie (1982) The relationship of self-concept and achievement/performance measures. *Review of Educational Research*, Vol. 52, pp. 123-142.

Harter, S. (1982) A developmental perspective on some parameters of self-regulation in children. In: P. Karoly & F.H. Kanfer (eds.) *Self management and behavior changes: From theory to practice*. New York: Pergamon Press.

Harter, S. (1985) Processes underlying self-concept formation in children. In: J. Suls & A. Greenwald (eds.) *Psychological perspectives on the self*. Hillsdale, N.J.: Erlbaum.

Heckhausen, H. (1977) Achievement motivation and its constructs: A cognitive model, *Motivation and Emotion*, volume 1. pp. 283-329.

Heckhausen, H. (1980) *Motivation und Handeln*. Berlin: Springer Verlag.

Heckhausen, H. (1987) Wünschen - Wählen - Wollen. In: H. Heckhausen, P.M. Gollwitze, & F. E. Weinert (eds.) *Jenseits des Rubikon: Der Wille in den Humanwissenschaften*. Berlin, Heidelberg, New York: Springer-Verlag.

Heckhausen, H. & P.M. Gollwitzer (1987) Thought contents andcognitive functioning in motivational and volitional states of mind. *Motivation and Emotion*, Vol. 11, pp. 101-120.

Heckhausen, H. & F. Halisch (1986) "Operant" versus "respondent" motive measures: A problem of validity or of construct? Paper presented on the

*"Symposium on Achievement Motive: Its definition and assessment"* at the 21th International Congress of Applied Psychology in Jerusalem, 13-18 July.

Heckhausen, H. & S. Krug (1982) Motive modification. In: A.J. Stewart (ed.) *Motivation and Society.* San Francisco: Jossey-Bass.

Heckhausen, H. & J. Kuhl (1985) From wish to action: The dead ends and short cuts on the long way to action. In: M. Frese & J. Sabini (eds.) *Goal directed behavior: Psychological theory and research on action.* Hillsdale, N.J.: Erlbaum.

Heckhausen, H. & F. Rheinberg (1980) Lernmotivation im Unterricht, erneut betrachtet. *Unterrichtswissenschaft,* Vol. 8, pp. 7-47.

Helmke, A. (1983) Prüfungsangst - Ein Ueberblick über neuere theoretische Entwicklungen. *Psychologische Rundschau,* Vol. 34, pp. 193-211.

Helmke, A. (1988a) The role of classroom context factors forthe achievement-impairing effect of test anxiety. *Anxiety Research,* Vol. 1, pp. 37-52.

Helmke, A. (1988b) A longitudinal analysis of the dynamicsof interaction of self-concept of math aptitude and math achievement in elementary school children. *European Journal of Psychology of Education. Special Issue "The child's functioning at school",* pp. 43-44.

Helmke, A. (in press,a) Mediating processes between children's self-concept of ability and mathematics achievement: A longitudinal study. In: E. de Corte, H. Lodewijks & H. Mandl (eds.) *Learning and instruction in an international context.* Oxford: Pergamon Press.

Helmke, A. (in press,b) On the role of incentive value of school-related success and failure for academic achievement. In: F. Halisch & J.H.L. van den Bercken (eds. in collaboration with S. Hazlett) *International perspectives on achievement and task motivation.* Lisse: Swets & Zeitlinger.

Herbart, J.F. (1806) *Pädagogische Schriften.* Düsseldorf: Küpper (new edition 1965).

Hermans, H.J.M. (1976) *Prestatie motivatie test* (2nd ed.). Amsterdam: Swets & Zeitlinger.

Kifer, E. (1975) Relationships between academic achievementand personality characteristics: A quasi-longitudinal study. *American Educational Research Journal,* Vol. 12, pp. 191-210.

Krohne, H.W. (1978) Individual differences in coping with stress and anxiety. In: C.D. Spielberger & J.G. Sarason (eds.) *Stress and Anxiety,* volume 5. Washington: Hemisphere.

Krug, S. (1983) Motivförderungsprogramme: Möglichkeiten und Grenzen. *Zeitschrift für Entwicklungspsychologie und Pädagogische Psychologie,* Vol. 15, pp.317-346.

Kuhl, J. (1985) Volitional determinants of cognition-behavior consistency: Self-regulatory processes and action versus state orientation. In: J. Kuhl

& J. Beckmann (eds.) *Action control: From cognition to behavior.* Berlin: Springer.

Licht, B.G. & C.S. Dweck (1984) Determinants of academic achievement: The interaction of children's achievement orientations with skill area. *Developmental Psychology*, Vol. 20, pp. 628-636.

Markus, H. & E. Wurf (1987) The dynamic self concept: A socialpsychological perspective. *Annual Review of Psychology*, Vol. 38, pp. 299-337.

Maruyama, G. & H.J. Walberg (1984) Educational productivity in a social psychological context. In: H. Oosthoek & P. van den Eeden (eds.) *Education from the Multi-Level Perspective: Models, Methodology and Empirical Findings.* New York: Gordon and Breach.

McClelland, D.C. (1980) Motive dispositions: The merits ofoperant and respondent measures. In: L. Wheeler (ed.) *Review of personality and social psychology*, volume 1. Beverly Hills: Sage.

McClelland, D.C., R. Koestner & J. Weinberger (in press) How do self-attributed and implicit motives differ? In: F. Halisch & J.H.L. van den Bercken (eds., in collaboration with S. Hazlett) *International perspectives on achievement and task motivation.* Lisse: Swets & Zeitlinger.

Meyer, W.U. (1984). *Das Konzept von der eigenen Begabung.* Bern: Huber.

Meyer, W.U. (in press) Attributionale Analysen der Lernmotivation. In: H.S. Skowronek & W.-U. Meyer (eds.) *Motivation in Lernprozessen.* Weinheim: Beltz.

Nicholls, J.G. (1978) The development of the concepts of effort and ability, perception of own attainment and understanding that difficult tasks require more ability. *Child Development*, Vol. 49, pp. 800-814.

Nicholls, J.G. (1984) Conceptions of ability and achievement motivation. In: R.E. Ames & C.A. Ames (eds.) *Research on Motivation in Education, volume 1. Student Motivation.* Orlando: Academic Press.

Nicholls, J.G., M. Patashnick, P. Chung Cheung, T.A. Thorkildsen & J. Lauer (in press) Can achievement motivation theory succeed with only one conception of success? In: F. Halisch & J.H.L. van den Bercken (eds., in collaboration with S. Hazlett) *International perspectives on achievement and task motivation.* Lisse: Swets & Zeitlinger.

Nuttin, J. (1984) *Motivation, planning, and action: A relational theory of behavior dynamics.* Hillsdale, N.J.: Erlbaum.

Paris, S.G. & D.R. Cross (1983) Ordinary learning: Pragmatic connections among children's beliefs, motives, and actions. In: J. Bisanz, G. Bisanz & J. Kail (eds.) *Learning in children.* New York: Springer-Verlag.

Pekrun, R. (1985) Classroom climate and test anxiety: Developmental validity of expectancy - value theory of anxiety. *Advance in Test Anxiety Research*, Vol. 4, pp. 147-158.

Petermann, F. & W. Zielinski (1979). Der L-M-T; ein Verfahren zur Erfassung der Leistungsmotivation. *Diagnostica*, Vol. 25, pp. 351-364.

Pintrich, P.R., D.R. Cross, R.B. Kozma, & W.J. McKeachie (1986) Instructional psychology. *Annual Review of Psychology*, Vol. 37, pp. 611-651.

Rand, P. (1987) Research on achievement motivation in school and college. In: F. Halisch & J. Kuhl (eds.) *Motivation, intention, and volition.* Berlin: Springer.

Rheinberg, F. (1988) Motivation and learning activities: How research could proceed. *International Journal of Educational Research*, Vol. 12, pp. 299-306.

Sarason, J.G. (1980) *Test Anxiety.* Hillsdale, N.J.: Erlbaum.

Sarason, J.G. & B.R. Sarason (1986) Cognitive interferenceas a component of anxiety: Measurement of its state and trait aspect. *Advances in Test Anxiety Research*, Vol. 5, pp. 3-14.

Schmalt, H.D. (1976) *Die Messung des Leistungsmotivs.* Göttingen: Hogrefe.

Shulman, L.S. (1982) Educational psychology returns to school. In: A. G. Kraut (ed.) *The G. Stanley Hall Lecture Series*, volume 2. Washington, D.C.: American Psychological Association.

Uguroglu, M.E. & H.J. Walberg (1979) Motivation and achievement: A quantitative synthesis. *American Educational Research Journal*, Vol. 16, pp. 375-389.

Walberg, H.J. (1984) Improving the productivity of America's schools. *Educational Leadership*, Vol. 41, pp. 19-30.

Weiner, B. (1984) Principles for a theory of student motivation and their application within an attributional framework. In: R. Ames & C. Ames (eds.) *Research on Motivation in Education, volume 1: Student Motivation.* Orlando: Academic Press.

Weiner, B. (1986) *An Attributional Theory of Motivation and Emotion.* New York: Springer-Verlag.

Weinert, F.E. (1987) Introduction and Overview: Metacognition and motivation as determinants of effective learning and understanding. In: F.E. Weinert & R. H. Kluwe (eds.) *Metacognition, motivation and understanding.* Hillsdale, N.J.: Erlbaum.

Weinert, F.E. & A. Helmke (1987) Compensatory effects of student self-concept and instructional quality on academic achievement. In: F. Halisch & J. Kuhl (eds.) *Motivation, intention, and volition.* Berlin: Springer.

Weinert, F.E. & A. Helmke (1988). Individual differences incognitive development: Does instruction make a difference? In: M. Heatherington, R. Lerner & M.\Perlmutter (eds.) *Child development in life span perspective.* Hillsdale, N.J.: Erlbaum.

Weinert, F.E. & R.H. Kluwe (1987). *Metacognition, motivation and understanding.* Hillsdale, N.J.: Erlbaum.

# Multilingual and Multicultural Education, What For? Confronting Ends and Means

Miguel Siguan
University of Barcelona
Spain

### A controversial question

The educational systems of many countries, particularly the most developed ones, seem to take it for granted that the population is monolingual. In reality, however, the opposite tends to be the case, and in the world as a whole bilingualism predominates in education, either because the educational system is explicitly bilingual, making use of two or more languages, or implicitly, because the language used in teaching is different from the first language of the pupils. This phenomenon is becoming more rather than less widespread. Even in Europe, educationally bilingual situations are on the increase, due on the one hand to progressive European integration, and on the other to increasing immigration from outside Europe. These situations are on the way to becoming the principal pedagogical problem in the near future.

As is well-known, the first attempts to evaluate the results of bilingual education by scientific criteria date from Saers' studies in Welsh schools in the 1920s, and from his discussion in the Luxembourg Seminar in 1928. This seminar ended with a formal condemnation of bilingualism in education, and recommended delaying the introduction of a second language in the curriculum as long as possible. However, many studies carried out after World War II have shown contrary results, favorable to bilingualism in education. Among these, the best-known are those by Balkan, analyzing the results achieved in Geneva with French-speaking children receiving education in French and English, as well as the classic studies of Lambert in Montreal, where children from English families were taught in French, and various studies along the same lines inspired or carried out by Cummins. The agreement between the results of these different studies has generated an optimistic vision with regard to bilingual education and the possibilities of "immersion" as a method. In contrast with this vision, bilingual education in most countries is still problematic and a source of conflict, and its results are turning out to be far from satisfactory.

Although literature on bilingualism was relatively scanty thirty years ago, it is now abundant. However, most of it is limited to descriptions of specific situations judged from within their own parameters, so that the results are difficult to compare. Theoretical reflection on the processes underlying bilingual education has, on the other hand, been rather restricted. This has had a negative influence on research and its possible applications, since, as has often been said, there is nothing so practical as a good theory.

Theoretical work on the foundations of bilingual education needs to proceed in two directions: one which we might call psycholinguistic and another which we might call sociocultural. We might add a third, more complex question, that of the inter-relation between the two. In the psycholinguistic dimension we should start by clarifying the relationship between verbal development and intellectual development, and between these two and academic success. On this basis we may see how the introduction of a language can be geared to these developments, and under what conditions it reinforces or hinders them. The second type of reflection should be concerned with showing how with the acquisition of language the child is integrated into a society and a culture; to what extent the acquisition of another language involves participation in another society and culture, and under what conditions this dual integration may lead to synthesis or conflict.

Fortunately, the progress of psycholinguistics in recent years, as well as the analysis of some experiences with positive bilingualism, provide us with a relatively coherent theory on the first subject. The present volume includes a paper by Cummins, who has done much to clarify the theoretical bases of bilingualism in education (Cummins, 1984), but I do not consider it out of place to set out my own ideas on the subject here. These ideas justify my later comments on the sociological and cultural aspects of bilingual education, where unfortunately conceptual reflection is still far from adequate.

## Introducing a second language

Soon after birth the child begins to communicate somehow with the people around it, and during its second year it starts to do so verbally. All children in the world, whatever the language they begin to speak, follow the same stages in the acquisition and development of language at approximately the same ages, which seems to imply the presence of an organic basis for this development. At the same time, however, the language in which the child starts to speak is a specific language, the language of the people around it, and with this language the child assimilates a particular cultural heritage. In other words, the basis for a child's linguistic development is both biological and sociocultural. In the course of its linguistic development the child increases its vocabulary and its repertoire of grammatical structures. This development takes place in the context of dialogue, and along with these developing linguistic skills the child perfects his ability to engage in dialogue. It learns to use language for different functions. At first these will be purely pragmatic, but later also informative. In this informative function different forms of discourse can soon be distinguished: description, narration, argumentation. As the evolution of its language progresses, the child becomes increasingly able to express more general and abstract meanings.

The school, at least the school as we understand it in Western society, takes the child when its ability to exchange information has already begun. The school develops this ability systematically in the direction of decontextualization and generalization, in the service of abstract knowledge, and at the same time introduces the child to the code of written language. Given the close relationship between knowledge and its verbal expression, it is not surprising that we should discover strong correlations between measures of linguistic development and measures of intellectual development, and between both of these and academic results.

It is important to bear in mind that school programs assume that a child has already reached a certain level of linguistic development at school entry, so that a continuity can be established between this level of development and the "treatment" given in school. This continuity is never at all complete: the teacher's dialogue - often monologue - with the child is very different from the child's dialogue with its parents or friends, and the functions of language to which the school gives priority are different. However, although this difference between the language of the family and the language of school is always present, it is greater for some children than for others. There are of course individual differences, but there are also sociocultural differences. There are families where the adults speak to the children in a way similar to that of the teacher in school, not so much because they use a similar vocabulary or an "upper class code", but because they use language in a similar way, stimulating the more strictly informative and discursive functions. In other family environments an affective or pragmatic use of language will predominate, and when children from these environments go to school, they find themselves required to make an effort of linguistic adaptation that may become a permanent handicap.

So far I have been referring to a child who enters a school where the language is the same as that of its own family. Obviously, if a different language is used for communication and teaching at school, wholly or in part, an additional complication enters the process. This complication may become an obstacle to the continuity of linguistic development, and may therefore have negative effects on later learning and on academic results.

Of course, such an introduction to a second language does not always or necessarily have a negative effect. Just as there are children who grow up in a family environment where two languages are used, and who have no difficulty in learning both of them, becoming perfect bilinguals, there are also children who become familiar with a second language at school, and who become able to communicate and be taught in it with no negative effects on their learning. The effort required may even turn out to have a stimulating effect on their intellectual development, so that we can speak of positive or additive bilingual education. However, this obviously only occurs under certain conditions, and what we have to do is to define these conditions. In my view, the conditions under which the introduction and use of a second language can produce favorable results are the following:

1  At the moment of introduction, the level of knowledge and use of the L2 which is aimed at for the pupil should not be higher than the level of knowledge and use which he has reached in his L1. On the other hand, the pupil's development in the L2 should follow a similar path to that of the L1, which makes it advisable to introduce the L2 through a pragmatic dialogue linked to action and immediate reality. Taking these two principles into account, it would seem that the most suitable moment to introduce the L2, if teaching is going to be wholly or partially in this language, is in the pre-school period, when the child is already able to communicate in its first language and when a pragmatic dialogue linked to action (in games) can easily be achieved.

2  When the pupil is already able to communicate in the L2, and can understand and produce messages without difficulty, instruction in reading and writing in this language can begin, and the L2 can start to be used for strictly informative functions with a moderate level of abstraction. At this stage, then, it can be used as a medium of teaching. It should not begin earlier.

3 Even when the child is able to communicate in the L2, and can read and write and be taught in this language, the L1 still continues, at least for some time, to be its principal language, and therefore his intellectual activity continues to be based on the L1. It is therefore necessary to make sure that the development of this language as an instrument of thinking proceeds at the same rate as the knowledge and use of the L2. Only if such a parallel development takes place can we expect that acquisitions in either one of the languages will be shared and will reinforce each other. If the pupil's family environment is sufficiently stimulating to ensure this parallel development, the school needs to pay little attention to this question, but if not, the school must take responsibility for ensuring this development, by maintaining the teaching and use of the pupil's L1 to some extent.

4 In addition to the psycholinguistic or strictly linguistic conditions mentioned above, there are others which are more directly psychological. For the early introduction of a second language to have favorable results, the child has to feel a positive motivation to acquire it. This motivation has to come in the first instance from the family environment; in other words, the parents have to agree with the introduction of the L2. In some cases the child gets its principal motivation from friends, when it needs to learn their language in order to join in their games. However, the most decisive factor is usually the teacher's attitude. A pupil should not experience the teacher's use of the L2 as a rejection of his L1, which would mean a rejection of his own person, of his family and of his social world. Instead, he should feel himself accepted by the teacher. The teacher should not only show this acceptance in an affective way, but should also understand the pupil when he speaks in his own language. It is a good thing, therefore, if the teacher is bilingual himself.

The preceding description presents a set of conditions that must be met if the early introduction of a second language in education is to produce positive results. Obviously, in many cases these conditions cannot be fulfilled, and the natural conclusion seems to be that in these cases the early stages of schooling should be based on the mother tongue, and that the introduction of the L2 should be delayed and take a slower, more gradual form.

The positive experiences with bilingual education mentioned at the beginning of this article seem to confirm this point of view, since in all of them the minimum recommended conditions are fulfilled to a greater or lesser extent. Conversely, it is easy to see that in the large number of cases where bilingual education leads to problems and conflict, these minimum conditions are not met. From this it might be concluded that compliance with these conditions would be sufficient to produce positive results. This is not true, however. It is true that the examples of bilingual education mentioned above, which are more or less familiar to everybody, do meet the psycholinguistic conditions which I have set out. In addition, however, they have taken place in certain political and cultural conditions which have made them possible, while the numerous examples of problematic and conflictive bilingual education with negative results take place in different political and cultural circumstances. It is these differing circumstances which in the first instance explain the difference in the results. What we need is a coherent theory of the role played by sociopolitical and cultural factors which affect languages and the societies who speak them, as well as of the psycholinguistic and intellectual development of pupils in a bilingual educational system. For the moment, a theory of this type scarcely exists, although we can outline the problems which it ought to address.

## Bilingual education in diglossic situations

Let us first look at the situation of the Welsh children studied by Saers in the 1920s, who were being educated exclusively in English. In their case, obviously, the introduction of English as a second language fulfilled none of the conditions which I have previously cited as necessary, and the results could therefore only be negative.

Why were the necessary conditions not met? We could find many answers to this question, but they all come down to one thing: because the necessary political will did not exist. The government and the educational authorities were preoccupied with the prestige and promotion of the English language, and could not see what interest the presence of Welsh might have for them, while the Welsh-speaking families did not have enough confidence in the value and usefulness of their language to demand its presence.

Sixty years later, the situation has changed completely. There are now groups and movements in Wales who are demanding the inclusion of their language in the educational system, and the authorities are showing some sympathy for this point of view. In principle, it is no problem to take account of the fact that Welsh is the family language of a certain proportion of schoolchildren, to give it a place in the educational system, and to introduce English in a non-traumatic way which meets the psycholinguistic requirements given above. However, when looking at this in practice, we soon come to realize that the problem is much more complicated.

It is not enough to choose the most suitable and pedagogically most efficient way of making the pupil familiar with the second language. It also has to be decided how much importance is going to be given to the child's first language once the second has been introduced - in this case what role Welsh is going to have in the curriculum when the pupil has learned to communicate in English.

As we know, there are basically three possibilities, although there are many intermediate variants. The mother tongue can be used simply to introduce the second language, disappearing from the curriculum once this has been acquired. The first language can be used to introduce the second and then knowledge and use of it can be maintained to some extent within the school. Finally, the first language, having been used to introduce the second language, can continue alongside it as a teaching language throughout the curriculum, with relatively equal status within the educational system. Choosing between these three possibilities is obviously a political decision that will depend on the relative weight of the different forces involved, but what I want to point out here are the educational consequences of this choice.

The explanation for the negative results of the Welsh children whom Saers studied, and for those of any child in a diglossic situation, is not merely that certain psycholinguistic rules have not been held to in the introduction of the second language. It is something much more serious and much more difficult to correct. For these children, the fact that they have to acquire and use English (or whatever is the dominant language) at school means that their family language is shown to be inferior, unsuitable for being used in important situations or for talking about important subjects. The difficulty they have in using English, compared to other children, therefore seems to show that they themselves are inferior. In this situation, with this attitude, their chances of linguistic and academic failure are evidently greater than if they were taught in their own language. Furthermore, it is not only possible but probable that they will end up choosing either to achieve mastery of English at any cost, ignoring their own language, or conversely, convincing themselves that they will never learn English and taking refuge in their own language. The so-called "seesaw" effect, which leads in some cases to a full command of the second language, forgetting the first, but which in most cases produces an inadequate level in both languages, justifies the label "semi-bilingualism".

If the dominant language is introduced "gently", through the language used at home, and if the first language continues to be developed to some extent, then the change of language will be less of a shock, and the negative effects will not be so great. However, the children's feelings that their languageis inferior and that they are inferior to their classmates who have always spoken the strong language will remain, and will continue to have negative effects. Only if the two languages are both used for teaching, under conditions of relative equality, can this impression be overcome, and only then will simultaneous and balanced development in both languages be possible. However, in a society that is not linguistically balanced, in which there is a clear distinction between a strong and a weak language, it is difficult to imagine a political decision being taken to set up bilingual education with equal conditions for both languages. Even if such a decision were taken, it is difficult to imagine how it could work in schools, in clear contradiction to the social reality all around.

The same conclusion can be reached from another perspective. Genuine bilingual education, giving equal weight to the strong and the weak language, means not only that the speakers of the weak language have to acquire the strong language quickly at school, but also that the speakers of the strong language must quickly acquire the weak language. Only in this way can the former lose their feeling of inferiority relative to the latter. However, in a linguistically unbalanced society, it is difficult to imagine this happening, except under very special circumstances. It is hard to imagine parents who speak the strong language voluntarily accepting that their children should spend time and effort acquiring the weak language when in later life they will have no pressing need to use it.

I have given as an example the situation of a linguistic minority in a developed country. If we now turn our attention to bilingual education in underdeveloped countries, we will find the same problems in a much more severe form.

## Diglossia and underdevelopment

Almost everywhere in the Americas there are indigenous populations, and in some Central American countries these make up more than 50%, in some cases 70% of the inhabitants. Most of these indigenous populations have a lower level of economic and social development than that of the country as a whole, living in marginalized and isolated conditions. Most of these populations also maintain languages of their own, which are different from the language of the State which surrounds them. This linguistic difference can be seen as simultaneously a cause and a consequence of their isolation, which a not very effective system of public education in Spanish has not succeeded to break down. Only bilingual education can achieve this, and for some years there have been increasing efforts in this direction (Herrera, 1987; Morren, 1988).

We can illustrate the difficulties these efforts have met with by taking a recent plan, exemplary in terms of the way it was carried out, to establish a system of bilingual education in a region of Guatemala. The first difficulty the organizers encountered was the great variety of languages and dialects spoken in the region, most of which had not been codified. It was thus necessary to start by hastily fixing a vocabulary, grammar and orthographic rules for each language. On the basis of this work, some minimal pedagogical materials had to be produced in each of the languages, and only then was it possible to tackle the main difficulty, the lack of teachers able to take on the task of bilingual education. There were practically no teachers who knew the languages of the region, and although a start was made with training these, it would be years before they were available in sufficient numbers. It was necessary, therefore, to resort to local people who had no training as teachers, but who knew some Spanish. These people acted as auxiliary teachers, to give the indigenous children a start with initial schooling in their own language and to ease the way for the Spanish-speaking teachers. In terms of the seriousness of the project and the quantity of resources put at its disposal, this attempt to confront one of the most typical and serious problems of Central America deserves nothing but praise. However, the current limitations - lack of previous use of the language and lack of teachers - make it obvious that only limited results can be achieved. Only if the effort is maintained over a long time, and a sufficient quantity of teachers becomes available, and some written use of the indigenous language is achieved, will it be possible to speak of real bilingual education.

Needless to say that these limitations are not exclusive to Guatemala, but are common to all indigenous languages in underdeveloped countries (Amadio, 1987).

However, even if the language of the indigenous people can be brought into the educational system, teachers and texts being available, the results may still be ambiguous. In Peru, the attempt to establish bilingual education has been made for much longer and more consistently than in Guatemala. It is also easier, since the Quechua language has greater linguistic uniformity and even some tradition of literary and pedagogical use. To the extent that these attempts have been successful, isolated monolingual Quechua-speaking populations have acquired a certain level of education, and have supplemented their improved knowledge of Quechua with a knowledge of Spanish, which they did not possess previously. With this knowledge, they have a better chance to emigrate to the slum areas of the cities, where opportunities for progress, or even just for subsistence are greater than in the places from which they come. However, these opportunities for progress are within a diglossic society, and are linked to a command of Spanish. The risk of losing or devaluing their Quechua is therefore much greater than in the places from which they come. We know that in many African countries this unwanted consequence of bilingual education has taken an even more acute form. Efforts to educate inhabitants of remote regions in their own language have included among other things offering to the most promising students the possibility of continuing with teacher training in an urban environment. This means acquiring a more widely-spoken language, in most cases English or French. A significant proportion of these aspiring teachers do not go back to their regions to take up teaching once they have finished their studies, but prefer to remain in the city, making use of their recently acquired knowledge in any way they can. These cases are not just casual anecdotes, but strike at the heart of the subject I am addressing.

A disequilibrium between two languages in any society, a diglossic situation, is very often the expression of a social and economic disequilibrium between the groups who speak the two languages. In these conditions, bilingual education projects are unlikely to be proposed, and if they are, there will be many difficulties in putting them into practice. If they are put into practice they will not succeed if the original disequilibrium has not changed in the meantime - something which bilingual education in itself cannot change. I am not trying to dispute the value of any attempt at bilingual education; I merely want to caution against the excessive expectations which are frequently voiced. Bilingual education can only work if it is the expression of a collective will for coexistence between the languages and the social groups who speak them (Siguan & Mackey, 1987).

From this, one can work out a recommendation for researchers in bilingual education, or those simply interested in the subject. When describing or evaluating an experiment in bilingual education, it is not enough just to analyze its internal aspects or to evaluate its pedagogical results. The experiment has to be considered within the framework of the linguistic policy and the general political reality of the country, and its objectives have to be defined as a function of these factors. Only in relation to these factors does it make sense to talk of the success or failure of the experiment.

## Social factors and cultural factors in bilingual education

The large number of people in the United States whose first language is not English, and who are therefore potential subjects of a bilingual education, has caused initiatives in this direction to multiply. There is a great diversity among these, both in their pedagogical foundations and in the ways they have been organized. However, taking into account what was said in the previous section, what ultimately characterizes bilingual education in the United States is the lack of agreement about its ultimate objectives. Up to four different positions can be distinguished.

In the first place, there are those who defend to the death the "American Way of Life" on the Anglo-Saxon model. They believe that the best possibility for speakers of other languages, in particular Hispanics, to integrate themselves into American society is to learn English as soon as possible, and to abandon their own language or relegate it to strictly domestic use. From this point of view, the school should only be concerned with English.

In the second place, there are those who, while pursuing the same ultimate objective, claim that the best way to learn English is through a "gentle" transition from the mother tongue, arguing that the school should use the mother tongue (Spanish in the case of the Hispanics) to make the transition easier.

In the third place, especially among the Hispanics themselves, there are those who, while accepting that their destiny is to become integrated into American society with English as the common language, consider that the school should not just use Spanish to introduce English, but should encourage the pupils to develop their Spanish so that they can go on using it both inside and outside the school.

Finally, a fourth position is taken by those for whom the school should not just ensure the maintenance of Spanish but should offer a genuinely bilingual education, with Spanish having an equal place with English as a teaching language. Obviously, this position is taken by those who defend a model of a multilingual and multicultural society for the United States.

There is, therefore, no general agreement about the ultimate objectives of bilingual education and, at a deeper level, no agreement about the type of society which should be aspired to from a linguistic point of view. It is probably this lack of agreement which explains the poor results shown so far of much bilingual education among Hispanics. For many of them, the "seesaw" effect seems to apply, causing those who make most progress in one language to pay less attention to the other, i.e., causing those who make most progress in English to lose interest in Spanish.

Nevertheless, it is curious that in the numerous discussions of this subject and the vast amount of literature which has arisen, there should have been so little attention given to the Hispanics in Florida. These, who have mostly emigrated from Castro's Cuba at different times, constitute an important minority, and like all immigrants they have had to make an effort to integrate themselves into their new society. In the first place they have had to acquire a new language, and their children have had an education which is to some extent bilingual (Garcia & Otheguy, 1986, 1987).

However, this does not seem to have caused them special difficulties or interfered with their academic results. Most remarkable is the fact that in most of the schools supported by the Hispanic community in Florida no special measures have been adopted to institute bilingual education: instead, most of the teaching is in English right from the beginning. It is true, though, that most of the teachers are bilingual and are immigrants themselves, so it is natural for the pupils to speak to them in Spanish when they cannot manage to do so in English (Garcia & Otheguy, 1987).

How can one explain the fact that these schoolchildren achieve notably better results than those in other Hispanic groups? Two different explanations can be found, one based on socio-economic factors, the other on cultural factors.

At the beginning of this article, in the description of the child's linguistic evolution and acquisition of a second language, reference was made to the relationship between the socio-economic level of the families and the development of the different functions of language. We saw that the effect of this is detrimental to children from disadvantaged socio-economic backgrounds, and leads to a difficult reception of the second language if this is used only in the school context. In this light, the fact that most Hispanics in the USA live at a lower socio-economic level than the Anglo population should be sufficient to explain their inferior results at school, even when some form of bilingual education is offered. On the other hand, among the Hispanics of Florida, as opposed to the Puerto Ricans of New York or the Chicanos of Arizona and California, there are large numbers of professionals and middle-class white collar workers. Children from these families get a "correct" model of the language, since their parents insist from the beginning on correct speech, but they also get used to using language in ways similar to those in which it will be used at school, even though at school another language, English rather than Spanish, is used for these purposes. Besides training them in certain uses of language, these families inculcate certain attitudes in their children towards languages: the importance of mastering English quickly, but at the same time a satisfaction and pride in continuing to use Spanish, and these attitudes are shared by the teachers. For these children, being educated bilingually or even exclusively in English does not imply a devaluation of their own language nor the risk of abandoning it once they have mastered English.

This is the socio-economic explanation, which has many supporters and many arguments in its favor, but it is not the only possible one. It is becoming common to explain failure at school of certain non-Anglo-Saxon populations in the USA, especially Amerindian populations (Swisher & Deyhle, 1987) by reference to the contrast between the style and educational practices of the ethnic family environment and that of the school institutions. Thus it is said that children who are taught within the family to participate in collective activities, to conform strictly to the norms of the group, and repress any attempt to stand out as an individual, are encouraged when they get to school to compete with others and to show off their own abilities and successes. And they have to do this in competition with classmates whose family environment does prepare them for this rivalry. The greater success at school of the Florida Hispanics can be explained equally easily from this perspective. Although they arrive at school with a different language from that spoken there, their value system and motivation are the same as those of the school - the ethic of competition and success - and in this sense they are no different from their Anglo classmates.

Of course, these two explanations are not incompatible: in many cases they can be combined. It is common for speakers of a minority language to form a socially disadvantaged and marginalized population, and in addition to be culturally distinct. However, even if we accept that these are two facets of the same situation, recognition of the role of cultural factors means that we should be more cautious in proposing solutions and in making predictions about their viability. If there are merely differences of language within a society, a multilingual ideal can be envisaged, guaranteeing a minimum of legal and political equality for the languages involved, and with a system of bilingual education aiming at a good command of both languages. However, if underlying the linguistic differences there are differences of culture, then the ideal solution would have to involve not just acceptance of different languages, but also the peaceful coexistence of different cultures, an altogether more complex matter.

For many years, educators in France have been pointing to the poor results achieved in French schools by immigrant children, in particular Arabs coming from the Maghreb countries - Morocco, Algeria and Tunisia - and demanding that attention should be paid to the difficulty these children have in handling the French language compared to French schoolchildren. These demands have had some effect in the form of various measures for compensatory education, but the results have remained unsatisfactory. Recently, therefore, more radical solutions have been proposed: bilingual and bicultural schools where Arab children could come into contact with French culture without abandoning contact with their own culture, and where at the same time French children could come into contact with Arab culture, without ceasing to cultivate their own (Dichy, 1988). An experiment of this kind requires many conditions which are difficult to fulfil - including staff who are proficient in both languages and familiar with both cultures. However, even if these conditions can be met, and the experiment is successful in itself, the multicultural ideal which inspires the experiment and its promoters can in no way be said to be the objective of French society at large or its educational system.

In the Maghreb countries - Morocco, Algeria and Tunisia - education is also largely bilingual, in French and Arabic, but although the languages involved are the same ones as in the previous case, they have a totally different meaning for the objectives of the educational system (Fitouri, 1983; Bentahila, 1988). In these countries, Arabic is both the language spoken at home by the pupils and the national language of the country, even though a significant distance exists between the dialectal Arabic of everyday life and the literary Arabic used in schools. More even than a national language, Arabic unites these three and other Arab countries, as the expression of the highly differentiated Arab culture. French on the other hand, once the language of the colonialists, is no longer linked to political power but has become the vehicle of the culture of science and technology, and of international contacts. Its important presence in the educational system, where in some subjects it is the medium of teaching, shows that the political and spiritual leaders of these countries believe that islamic tradition can incorporate the results of science and modern technology through French.

The role played by the old colonial languages in the ex-colonies and in some Asian countries after the consolidation of their independence can be viewed as a response to the same demand: that of constructing a society which, while maintaining its cultural traditions expressed in its own languages, can absorb the values and the techniques which characterize developed societies. Such attempts, however, are not without risk. The richness and the power of the Islamic tradition are undeniable, but African local traditions are very fragile, and can easily become devalued and disappear on coming into contact with Western ways of life and thinking. This may be the reason why the role in education of the languages of many of these countries seems to have been diminishing in recent years, in favor of the former colonial languages.

## Possibilities and limitations of a bilingual and bicultural education

We have now reached the heart of the matter. Any system of bilingual education implies a collective political project for the harmonious coexistence of different languages. However, to the extent that the languages represent cultural differences, a system of bilingual education also implies a collective project for the coexistence or synthesis of different cultures. Some traditional societies, especially in Asia, have shown that it is possible to establish stable societies based on bilingualism and the coexistence of cultures - India is still making an effort to keep to this model (Ward, 1985;

Pattanayak, 1981). Nevertheless, it seems that where one of these cultures is Western culture, supported by technology in the service of economic success, coexistence becomes difficult. In the underdeveloped countries this is because their own languages and traditions become devalued by comparison. In developed countries, the languages and cultures of immigrants from the Third World are devalued even more strongly. In these situations, to propose cultural pluralism and the equality of all cultures as the objective of the political system is in danger of remaining nothing but an expression of a worthy intention (Watson, 1984).

We can now return to the theme with which I began. We have a relatively coherent theory about the linguistic development of children and the acquisition of a second language. On the basis of this theory we can deduce the rules which the introduction of a second language at school should follow so as not to endanger school learning, and even to enhance it. We also know, and have many convincing examples thereof, that bilingual education can have positive results when it is based on two prestige languages; when the greater role is given to the weaker of the two languages; and when the cultures they express are mutually compatible or variants of the same cultural system. On the other hand, however, we know very little about the effects of differences in socio-economic status between the language groups and of conflicts of prestige and power on the acquisition and development of the second language and the results of bilingual education. We know even less about the effects of differences and conflicts between the cultures expressed by the two languages. The potential field for research is enormous. I will confine myself to one example.

In discussions of bilingual education there are frequent debates over whether learning to read and write should begin in the first or the second language, and to what extent skills related to the written language are transferable from one language to another. Almost all these studies concern languages which use an alphabetic script, mostly the Latin alphabet. Even going from the Latin alphabet to the Cyrillic raises additional difficulties which have been little studied. However, the biggest problems appear when we consider languages whose writing systems have totally different foundations, as is the case for example with bilingual education in French and Arabic, or English and Chinese. It is logical to suppose that differences in the writing system affect cognitive processes, and that the possibilities and limitations of bilingual education are different in these cases from those which we are used to thinking about, and would require a deeper analysis.

As a case in point one might compare English written language with Chinese written language. In cases where the differences are this complex one cannot actually speak of two simultaneous learning processes or mutually dependent learning processes, as they may involve different developmental stages and temporal sequences. One might even suppose that the learning of each language requires different intellectual abilities and different ways of representing reality.

There is something more important to consider, however. The differences we have mentioned between the writing systems of different cultures cannot be reduced to differences in techniques for transcribing the oral language, which may be more or less straightforward and require more or less intellectual effort. Over and above these differences is the fact that the very operations of reading and writing have considerably different meanings in different cultures, and these in turn have effects on the educational process. As an example, think of what learning to read means in a Koranic school where reading the Koran is confused with becoming able to recite it from memory; or of what learning to write means in the tradition of the mandarins of the "Celestial Empire", for whom writing was an artesanal activity with a high aesthetic content which even a lifetime was not long enough fully to master. No more examples are necessary to make us aware of the extraordinary complications which may lie hidden behind any proposal for multicultural education.

### A general orientation towards research in multicultural and multilingual education

In the preceding pages I have stressed more than once the importance of particular topics that need further investigation in experiments, possibly under field conditions. I have pointed out, for instance, that in most studies on bilingual education the two languages that are examined have the same graphic representation system and use the same alphabet. On a global scale, however, bilingual situations are not always that simple. It is evident that the use of different types of script does affect the implementation (process) and the results of bilingual education. In such a situation the knowledge and skills acquired in one of the languages may not be easily-transferable to situations in which one has to use the other language.

This topic, which has been little studied, deserves thorough investigation. However, I think that it is more important to propose a general orientation towards research in this field than to suggest specific, isolated research themes.

First of all, I would like to remind the reader that there exist many reports on studies in multilingual and multicultural education, but unfortunately these contain few theoretical reflections, particularly where the multicultural nature of the situations under study is concerned. This makes it difficult to understand and explain the research findings and, worse, to draw up useful guidelines for ways to tackle conflict situations. In my view, the disappointing outcome of so many studies is caused by their being too specific. They usually deal with one particular situation, set in one particular educational system and they are often mainly concerned with linguistic data. For investigators who are working in other situations and in a context with a different language policy, such information offers no links with their own situation and is therefore of little significance to them. In other words, the majority of studies in multilingual and multicultural education, due to the lack of common points of reference, seem to be entities without interrelations, like a collection of anecdotes which, although interesting in itself, cannot be integrated into one whole. To overcome this, I would like to put forward two propositions.

First, I would like to recommend that when an investigation is planned, one gives an account of the educational system and the role that the two languages play in it. On completion of the research, the findings should be evaluated in linguistic as well as in academic terms. Furthermore, the findings should be evaluated in the light of the socio-linguistic and socio-political factors by which the bilingual education is characterized. This is not all, however. Other points for consideration should be the role played by the bilingual educational systems in current language policy as well as the relationship between the educational system and the goals that are set in language policy concerning the integration of languages and cultures that play a role in the education of students. Of course, there is the posssibility that policy is not formally specified or that what is officially formulated differs from actual practice. It might be the case that policy instead of being directed at the integration of the various ethnic groups, actually manifests itself in a confrontation between ethnic groups and their different cultures, including their various language policies. Again, in such a complicated situation it should be tried to describe and evaluate the role that formal education plays in respect of the various policies. And last but not least the investigator himself should express his own opinion about and his attitude towards the total situation, including the political reality and the bilingual educational setting that is explored.

The advantage of planning and presenting studies in such a manner is that it will be possible to compare the results. This will enable us to draw conclusions and to formulate hypotheses that are well-founded. It is, however, not very probable that all this will come about spontaneously. This is where I come to my second proposition.

It is desirable to promote the realization of research programs in multilingual and multicultural education in different countries and different situations, but the researchers should aim at a common focus on all the factors mentioned earlier, as well as on the research method, the data analysis and the presentation of results. In order to avoid setting too extensive research problems or tasks that are impossible to execute we should agree that these research programs should be concerned with distinct situations - distinct, but at the same time referring to a similar fundamental type of intercultural contact or confrontation. A fine example of such an undertaking is a program that was recently initiated and promoted by the OECD. This program is aimed at the evaluation of comparable educational innovations in various European countries that are directed at the linguistic and cultural integration of immigrants. The participants have agreed on using a common method for data collection and data analysis.

It will not be difficult to set up similar programs in Europe that focus on situations that are of a more intercultural nature or that are more homogeneous.

It is more important, however, that this type of program is initiated outside Europe. One could think for example of a program in which various representative cases of bilingual education for the indigenous population of Latin America are simultaneously explored. As I stated earlier, a number of important studies have already been conducted in Latin America, but these were set up in isolation of each other and that makes it difficult to compare the results.

The same can be said about the African countries, where since their independence the native languages and the traditional colonial language are both used in the educational system. Each of these countries, however, has its own system of linguistic coexistence in which changes take place as time progresses without there being a possibility to objectively evaluate the total process.

It will be no less important to compare the linguistic and cultural dualism in the educational institutions in Arabic countries. Using the common cultural tradition as a basis, these institutions are trying in various ways to integrate tradition with the products of modern technology.

The list of possible research programs can easily be extended. Probably one of the first tasks will be to identify situations that are sufficiently general to justify a venture on such a scale.

# References

Amadio, M. (1987) *Educacion y pueblos indigenas en Centro America. Un balance critico*. Santiago de Chile: UNESCO/OREAL.

Bentahila, A. (1988) Aspects of Bilingualism in Morocco. In:C.B. Paulston (ed.) *International handbook of bilingualism and bilingual education*. New

York: Greenwood Press.

Cummins. J. (1984) *Bilingualism and special education. Issues in assessment and pedagogics*. Clevedon, England: Multilingual Matters.

Dichy, J. (1988) Arabic as a second language in France in the context of immigration. The case-study of Lyon and the Lyon university. *Paper presented at the 7th conference on minority language rights and minority education*. Ithaca N.Y.: Cornell University.

Fitouri, C. (1983) *Biculturalisme, bilinguisme et education*. Neuchatel: Delachaux et Niestle.

Garcia, O. & R. Otheguy (1986) The masters of survival send their children to school. *Bilingual Review/Revista Bilingua*, nr. 1, pp. 3-19.

Garcia, O. & R. Otheguy (1987) American children in Dade County's ethnic schools. *Language and Education*, Vol. 1, nr. 2, pp. 83-95.

Herrera, G. (1987) *Estado del arte sobre educacion bilingue en Guatemala*. Guatemala: Centro de informacion y Documentacion Educativa de la Universidad de Guatemala.

H.M.S.O. (1985) *Education for all, The report of the Comittee of Inquiry into the Education of Children of Ethnic Minority Groups*. (The Swann report). London: HMSO.

Morren, R.C. (1988) Bilingual education curriculum in Guatemala. *Journal of Multilingual and Multicultural Development*. Vol. 9, pp. 353-370.

Pattanayak, D.P. (1981) *Multilingualism and mother tongue education*. Delhi: Oxford University Press.

Siguan, M. & W.F. Mackey (1987) *Education and bilingualism*. London: Kogan Page/UNESCO.

Swisher, K. & D. Deyhle (1987) Styles of learning and learning of styles. Educational conflicts for American Indian-Alaskan Native youths. *Journal of Multilingual and Multicultural Development*. Vol. 8, pp. 345-360.

Ward, C. & M. Hewstone (1985) Ethnicity, language and intergroup relations in Malaysia and Singapore: A social psychological analysis. *Journal of Multilingual and Multicultural Development*. Vol. 6, pp. 271-296.

Watson, K. (1984) Training teachers in the United Kingdom for multicultural society: The rhetoric and the reality. *Journal of Multilingual and Multicultural Development*. Vol. 5, pp. 385-400.

# Multilingual/Multicultural Education: Evaluation of Underlying Theoretical Constructs and Consequences for Curriculum Development

Jim Cummins
Ontario Institute for Studies in Education
Canada

The goal of this paper is to evaluate theoretical constructs and research findings in the area of multilingual/multicultural education; in other words, to identify the knowledge base that exists to guide policy decisions regarding bilingual and multilingual education programs in general and the education of cultural and/or linguistic minority students in particular. Prior to examining the research and theory in the area of multilingual/multicultural education, it is necessary to clarify the scope of multilingual/multicultural education and to outline the social and policy contexts within which research is conducted and interpreted.

## The scope of bilingual and multilingual education

The terms "bilingual education" and "multilingual education" have been used in various ways in the literature. In some situations, terms like "multilingual" (or multicultural, multiethnic, multiracial) education have been used in a general sense to refer to the schooling of children who come from linguistically and culturally diverse backgrounds with no implications as to the kind of school program provided for these students. In other words, the focus is on characteristics of the school population rather than on specific types of interventions. Frequently, however, the terms are used to refer to educational practices that have been specifically designed to address the learning needs of students from culturally diverse backgrounds. The terms "intercultural" and "anti-racist" education are also used in this sense to refer to specific types of interventions aimed at promoting goals such as inter-ethnic tolerance and minority student academic development. In the present paper the terms "multilingual" and "multicultural" education are being used in a general sense to refer to the education of students in a linguistically- and culturally-diverse milieu. Within this rubric, the primary programmatic response that will be analyzed is bilingual education.

"Bilingual education" usually refers to the use of two (or more) languages of instruction at some point in the student's school career. In other words, it is generally defined in terms of the means through which particular educational goals are achieved. When used in this sense, proficiency in two languages is not necessarily a goal of bilingual education. For example, in some contexts bilingual instruction is employed as a temporary measure to help students from linguistic minority groups make a transition between the language of the home and the language of the school without falling behind in mastery of subject matter. When it is assumed that students have attained sufficient proficiency in the school language to follow instruction in that language, home language instruction is discontinued. However, the term "bilingual education" is sometimes defined in terms of goals, to refer to educational programs that are designed to promote bilingual skills among students. When used in this broader sense, "bilingual education" may entail instruction primarily or exclusively through only one language, as for example, when instruction is delivered through a minority language in order to provide students with the maximum opportunity to learn that language. Second language "immersion" programs of this type are implemented widely in certain countries (e.g. Canada's French immersion programs).

A variety of typologies of bilingual education have been proposed, the most elaborate of which is Mackey's (1972) which distinguishes 90 different potential varieties depending on the intersection of home language(s), curricular organization of languages, and language(s) of the neighborhood and country.

Perhaps the most useful typology for understanding the intersections between educational and sociopolitical factors in bilingual/multilingual education for both minority and majority students is that developed by Skutnabb-Kangas (1984). According to this typology, the medium of instruction can be either primarily the majority language, the minority language or both; the program can be designed for the majority (dominant) group, the minority (subordinate) group or both together (a "two-way" or integrated program); societal goals of bilingual education can include direct assimilation of minority students, segregation (possibly with a view to repatriation) of minority students, equality for minority students, or enrichment and/or instrumental benefits (e.g. jobs) for both minority and majority students; finally, the linguistic aims include monolingual (or strongly dominant) in the majority language (e.g. transitional bilingual programs in the United States), monolingual (or strongly dominant) in the minority language (e.g. some primarily L1 programs for guest-worker children), and bilingualism.

This typology is useful in considering some of the current controversies about bilingual education insofar as it captures the direct relationship between inter-ethnic power relations and program organization. The scope of the typology could be broadened by elaborating the "societal goals" category into "educational goals", "sociolinguistic goals" and "sociopolitical goals". Educational goals include "equity" (vis-a-vis academic achievement) and "enrichment" (access to two languages and cultures); sociolinguistic goals refer to promoting access to a language of wider communication (usually a language of economic or political power) versus promoting access to a lesser used language (usually a "heritage" language whose survival is threatened); finally, sociopolitical goals refer to the status and modes of participation envisaged for students upon graduation into the wider society; for example, total assimilation into the mainstream culture, integration that permits maintenance of some bicultural allegiance, or segregation.

In summary, the terms "multilingual" and "multicultural" education will be used in a general sense to refer to the education of children from linguistically- and culturally-diverse backgrounds while the term "bilingual education" will refer to specific programs for either majority or minority students that use two or more languages as media of instruction at some point in the students' school career.

## The social context of multilingual/multicultural education

In most of the western industrialized countries the proportions of students from linguistically- and culturally-diverse backgrounds have increased rapidly during the past 20 years. The increased proportions result both from continued high rates of immigration in many countries together with declining birthrates among the native-born populations of these countries. Data from several OECD (Organization for Economic Cooperation and Development) countries reveal a clear pattern.

The OECD's Centre for Educational Research and Innovation (CERI) (1987), for example, recently reported data regarding the numbers and educational performance of school children of foreign nationality in seven European countries. The average foreign enrolment levels at the Primary level varied from 4.8 per cent in The Netherlands to 18 per cent in Switzerland and 38 per cent in Luxembourg. The proportions for Belgium (13.5%), France (10.1%), Germany (11.9%) and Sweden (8.7%) were also substantial (table 8, p. 18)[1]. The profound changes that are taking place in the schools of these countries can be illustrated by the fact that between schoolyear 1974/75 and1981/82, the number of students in German schools (excluding the pre-primary level) fell by 700,000, the net result of a loss of 1.1 million German children and a gain of 400,000 foreign children. Other countries showed similar patterns.

With respect to foreign student placement, two clear patterns were observed in the OECD data: first, the overrepresentation of foreign students in special education classes, and second, the overrepresentation of foreign students in low academic streams at the secondary level. The report notes that the disproportionate placement of foreign children in special education classes "persists over the years without any apparent significant improvement (and) affects primarily certain of the nationalities that are more recent arrivals and/or whose cultural values are further removed from those of the host country" (1987, p. 32).

The report notes that these children find themselves relegated to special classes, not because their condition warrants this, but because they are for the moment unable to follow a normal course of education as a result of insufficient command of the language of instruction. This approach may provide a convenient solution over the short term but, according to CERI (1987, p. 33) "over the longer term seriously jeopardizes the school careers of the children concerned".

With respect to streaming at the secondary level the data show that "when there are a number of alternative streams available, the enrolment rate of foreign children is always higher than that of nationals in those streams or cycles which either require only minimal qualifications or provide only a short course of instruction" (1987, p. 33). Lack of minimal school qualifications, according to CERI, is closely associated with long-term unemployment and the social consequences of these trends are significant; specifically, "it is clear that exclusion from the education system constitutes the first stage in a process of marginalization, culminating in exclusion from the system of production and - since social integration depends on integration within the labour force - in exclusion from society itself" (1987, p. 35).

In the United States, it is estimated that documented and undocumented immigrant children represent about six per cent of the American school population (National Coalition of Advocates for Students (NCAS), 1988). However, geographic concentration of immigration has resulted in major influxes in several States and urban centers. For example, in the year 2001, the NCAS report estimates that minority enrolment levels will range from 70 to 96 per cent in the nation's 15 largest school systems. In California, by that time, minority groups (e.g. Hispanics, Blacks, Asians) will represent a greater proportion of the school population than Anglo students.

Many minority groups in the United States experience a much higher secondary school drop-out rate than Anglo students and are frequently streamed into low ability groups. According to the NCAS report, "inflexible assessment practices can lead to very low expectations of immigrant students by school personnel. Many young newcomers are placed in low expectation tracks or ability groups, where inadequate educational experiences may result in alienation from school, dropping out, and the impossibility of attaining higher education" (1988, p. 48).

Similar patterns have emerged from reports in Canada (Wright & Tsuji, 1984) and Britain (Swann, 1985). Canadian immigration projections illustrate the long-term nature of the educational issues that must be addressed in many western countries in that it is estimated that the rate of immigration will need to almost double just to prevent the Canadian population from declining (Ashworth, Cummins & Handscombe, 1989).

In conclusion, linguistic and cultural diversity is the norm in many western school systems and will continue to be so for the forseeable future. From the data sketched above, it is clear that school systems are still struggling to adapt to this changing multilingual/multicultural educational reality, with varying degrees of success. There are still no universally accepted models for the education of minority students and no consensus regarding the fundamental knowledge base that might guide programmatic intervention. This is partly a result of the volatile sociopolitical context within which issues related to immigrants and minority groups are analyzed. For example, the fact that particular interventions (e.g. bilingual education) involve the institutionalization of minority languages and confer status and power on previously subordinated minority groups means that research findings and theoretical interpretations are not neutral with respect to the societal power structure. Thus, while advocates for very different forms of educational provision almost invariably proclaim that their primary concern is the right of minority children to a quality and equitable education, the suggested interventions and their rationales vary widely.

Within this context, it becomes even more important to rationally evaluate the research and theoretical constructs that should guide policy decisions in the area of multilingual/multicultural education. However, in order for research and theory to be applied appropriately to policy, the relationship between research, theory and policy must be understood. This issue is examined in the next section.

## The relation between research, theory and policy

In the United States, controversy has raged for almost twenty years on appropriate ways of educating minority language children. Bilingual programs were virtually mandated by the Office of Civil Rights in their interpretation of the Supreme Court's Lau versus Nichols decision in 1974 but there still exists no consensus regarding the effectiveness of such programs and many educators and policy-makers have expressed fears that bilingual education is "unAmerican" and will balkanize the country.

A major reason why many policy-makers and educators in the United States regard the research basis for bilingual education as minimal or even non-existent is that they have failed to realize that data or "facts" from bilingual programs become interpretable for policy purposes only within the context of a coherent theory. It is the theory rather than the individual research findings that permits the generation of predictions about program outcomes under different conditions. Research findings themselves cannot be directly applied across contexts. For example, the fact that kindergarten and grade 1 Punjabi-background students in a bilingual program in Bradford, England, learned English just as successfully as a control group in a traditional English-only program (Rees, 1981) tells us very little about what might happen in the case of Greek-background students in Bradford or Hispanic students in the United States. Similarly, the findings of French immersion programs for majority students in Canada cannot be directly applied to policy-decisions regarding programs for minority students in the United States. Yet clearly the accumulation of research findings does have relevance for policy. This relevance is achieved by means of the integration of the findings within a coherent theory from which predictions regarding program outcomes under different conditions can be generated.

In short, although research findings cannot be applied directly across contexts, theories are almost by definition applicable across contexts in that the validity of any theoretical principle is assessed precisely by how well it can account for the research findings in a variety of contexts. If a theory cannot account for a particular set of research findings, then it is an inadequate or incomplete theory.

However, in assessing the relation between policy and both theory and research, it is clear that the sociological context, i.e. the power relations between dominant and subordinate groups in the society, plays a major role in determining the choice of issues to investigate, the conduct of the research, the interpretation of findings, and the relevance they assume for policy. In other words, the power relations within the society will strongly influence what policy-makers regard as "legitimate knowledge". This will be illustrated below by contrasting the application of theory to policy in the United States and Canada with respect to bilingual education and psychological assessment of minorities. First, however, it is important to clarify what theoretical constructs are supported by the research data related to the academic development of bilingual students. It is possible to distinguish four psychoeducational principles that appear to be supported by data from a wide variety of sociopolitical contexts and thus have some claim to generalizability, i.e. to represent a fundamental knowledge base.

## Principles of language development and bilingual academic achievement

### The additive bilingualism enrichment principle

In the past many students from minority backgrounds have experienced difficulties in school and have performed worse than monolingual children on verbal I.Q. tests and on measures of literacy development. These findings led researchers in the period between 1920 and 1960 to speculate that bilingualism caused language handicaps and cognitive confusion among children. Some research studies also reported that bilingual children suffered emotional conflicts more frequently than monolingual children. Thus, in the early part of this century bilingualism acquired a doubtful reputation among educators, and many schools redoubled their efforts to eradicate minority children's first language on the grounds that this language was the source of children's academic difficulties.

However, virtually all of the early research involved minority students who were in the process of replacing their L1 with the majority language, usually with strong encouragement from the school. Many minority students were physically punished for speaking their L1 in school. It appears more reasonable to attribute the academic difficulties of minority students to the treatment they received in schools rather than to their bilingualism.

Consistent with this interpretation are the results of more recent studies which suggest that bilingualism can positively affect both intellectual and linguistic progress. A large number of studies have reported that bilingual children exhibit a greater sensitivity to linguistic meanings and may be more flexible in their thinking than are monolingual children (Bialystok, 1984; Cummins & Swain, 1986; Diaz, 1986; Hakuta & Diaz, 1985). Most of these studies have investigated aspects of children's metalinguistic development; in other words, children's explicit knowledge about the structure and functions of language itself.

In general, it is not surprising that bilingual children should be more adept at certain aspects of linguistic processing. In gaining control over two languages, the bilingual child has had to decipher much more language input than the monolingual child who has been exposed to only one language system. Thus, the bilingual child has had considerably more practice in analyzing meanings than the monolingual child.

The evidence is not conclusive as to whether this linguistic advantage transfers to more general cognitive skills; McLaughlin's review of the literature, for example, concludes that: "It seems clear that the child who has mastered two languages has a linguistic advantage over the the monolingual child. Bilingual children become aware that there are two ways of saying the same thing. But does this sensitivity to the lexical and formal aspects of language generalize to cognitive functioning? There is no conclusive answer to this question - mainly because it has proven so difficult to apply the necessary controls in research" (1984, p. 44).

An important characteristic of the bilingual children in the more recent studies (conducted since the early 1960s) is that, for the most part, they were developing what has been termed an *additive* form of bilingualism (Lambert, 1975); in other words, they were adding a second language to their repertory of skills at no cost to the development of their first language. Consequently, these children were in the process of attaining a relatively high level of both fluency and literacy in their two languages. The children in these studies tended to come either from majority language groups whose first language was strongly reinforced in the society (e.g. English-speakers in French immersion programs) or from minority groups whose first languages were reinforced by bilingual programs in the school. Minority children who lack this educational support for literacy development in L1 frequently develop a *subtractive* form of bilingualism in which L1 skills are replaced by L2.

This pattern of findings suggests that the level of proficiency attained by bilingual students in their two languages may be an important influence on their academic and intellectual development (Cummins, 1979). Specifically, there may be a threshold level of proficiency in both languages which students must attain in order to avoid any negative academic consequences and a second, higher, threshold necessary to reap the linguistic and intellectual benefits of bilingualism and biliteracy.

Diaz (1986) has questioned the threshold hypothesis on the grounds that the effects of bilingualism on cognitive abilities in his data were stronger for children of relatively low L2 proficiency (non-balanced bilinguals). This suggests that the positive effects are related to the initial struggles and experiences of the beginning second-language learner. This interpretation does not appear to be incompatible with the threshold hypothesis since the major point of this hypothesis is that for positive effects to manifest themselves, children must be in the process of developing high levels of bilingual skills. If beginning L2 learners do not continue to develop both their languages, any initial positive effects are likely to be counteracted by the negative consequences of subtractive bilingualism.

In summary, the conclusion that emerges from the research on the academic, linguistic and intellectual effects of bilingualism can be stated thus: The development of additive bilingual and biliteracy skills entails no negative consequences for children's academic, linguistic, or intellectual development. On the contrary, although not conclusive, the evidence points in the direction of subtle metalinguistic, academic and intellectual benefits for bilingual children.

### The conversational/academic language proficiency principle

A considerable number of investigators have argued that it is necessary to distinguish between the processing of language in informal face-to-face situations and the language processing required in most academic situations. Face-to-face interaction relies on "here-and-now" contextual and paralinguistic cues in addition to specifically linguistic cues for communicating meaning whereas this is much less the case in many academic situations (e.g. writing an essay, reading a text, etc). Among these distinctions are Bruner's (1975) distinction between communicative and analytic competence, Olson's (1977) distinction between utterance and text, Donaldson's (1978) embedded and disembedded thought and language, Bereiter and Scardamelia's (1981) distinction between conversation and composition, and Snow's (1983) distinction between contextualized and decontextualized language.

The importance of this type of distinction is reinforced by a considerable amount of research from both Europe and North America which suggests that very different time periods are required for minority students to achieve peer-appropriate levels in conversational as compared to academic second language proficiency. (Collier, 1987; Cummins 1984; Skutnabb-Kangas & Toukomaa, 1976). Specifically, conversational skills often approach native-like levels within about two years of exposure to the target language whereas the research suggests that for academic aspects of language proficiency, a period of five years or more may be required for minority students to achieve as well as native speakers (Collier, 1987; Cummins, 1981).

This pattern can be attributed to the fact that native speakers of the school language continue to make significant progress in academic skills (e.g. reading and writing skills) year after year. They do not stand still waiting for the minority student to catch up. In conversational skills, on the other hand, after the first six years of life, changes tend to be more subtle. In addition, in face-to-face conversation the meaning is supported by a range of contextual cues (e.g. the concrete situation, gestures, intonation, facial expression, etc.) whereas this is seldom the case for academic uses of language (e.g. reading a text).

Cummins (1984) reported that psychologists often failed to take account of the difference between these two aspects of proficiency when they tested minority students. Because students often appeared to be fluent in English, psychologists tended to assume that they had overcome all problems in learning English and consequently IQ tests administered in English were valid. The data clearly showed that this assumption was unfounded. Students were frequently labelled as "learning disabled" or "retarded" on the basis of tests administered within one or two years of the students' exposure to English in school. The data show that even students who had been instructed through English for three years in school were performing at the equivalent of 15 IQ points below the grade norm as a direct result of insufficient time to catch up with their native English-speaking peers.

In short, the research evidence suggests that although there are large individual differences between children in the rapidity with which they acquire different aspects of proficiency in the school language, verbal psychological tests tend to underestimate minority students' academic potential until they have been learning this language for at least five years. Another implication of these findings is that for students who have been learning the school language for less than this period, it becomes extremely problematic to attempt any diagnosis of categories such as "learning disability" since any genuine learning problems are likely to be masked by as yet inadequately developed proficiency in the school language. The unresolved problems inherent in disentangling the assessment of language and academic skills among minority students can be seen in the fact that in Texas Hispanic students are still over-represented by a factor of 300% in the "learning disabilities" category. However, a first step in addressing the complexities of non-discriminatory assessment and placement of minority students is to acknowledge that students' surface fluency in English cannot be taken as indicative of their overall proficiency in English.

### The linguistic interdependence principle
Evaluations of bilingual programs for both majority and minority students consistently show that students instructed for all or part of the day through a minority language experience no long-term academic retardation in the majority language (for reviews of these data see Appel & Muysken, 1987; Cummins & Swain, 1986; Krashen & Biber, 1988). The fact

that there is little relationship between amount of instructional time through the majority language and academic achievement in that language strongly suggests that first and second language academic skills are interdependent, i.e., manifestations of a common underlying proficiency. The interdependence principle has been stated formally as follows (Cummins, 1981, p. 29): "To the extent that instruction in Lx is effective in promoting proficiency in Lx, transfer of this proficiency to Ly will occur provided there is adequate exposure to Ly (either in school or environment) and adequate motivation to learn Ly."

In concrete terms, what this principle means is that in, for example, a Basque-Spanish bilingual program in the Basque country of Spain, Basque instruction that develops Basque reading and writing skills (for either Basque L1 or L2 speakers) is not just developing <u>Basque</u> skills, it is also developing a deeper conceptual and linguistic proficiency that is strongly related to the development of literacy in the majority language (Spanish) (see EIFE, 1986.) In other words, although the surface aspects (e.g. pronunciation, fluency, etc.) of different languages are clearly separate, there is an underlying cognitive/academic proficiency which is common across languages. This "common underlying proficiency" makes possible the transfer of cognitive/academic or literacy-related skills across languages. Transfer is much more likely to occur from minority to majority language because of the greater exposure to literacy in the majority language outside of school and the strong social pressure to learn it.

The results of virtually all evaluations of bilingual programs for both majority and minority students are consistent with predictions derived from the interdependence principle (see Cummins, 1983, 1989). The interdependence principle is also capable of accounting for data on immigrant students' L2 acquisition (e.g. Cummins, 1981; Skutnabb-Kangas & Toukomaa, 1976) as well as from studies of bilingual language use in the home (e.g. Bhatnagar, 1980; Dolson, 1985). Correlational studies also consistently reveal a strong degree of cognitive/academic interdependence across languages.

Recent studies continue to support the interdependence principle. Kemp (1984), for example, reported that Hebrew (L1) cognitive/academic abilities accounted for 48% of the variance in English (L2) academic skills among 196 seventh grade Israeli students. In a longitudinal study conducted in Newark, New Jersey, Ramirez (1985) followed 75 Hispanic elementary school students enrolled in bilingual programs for three years. It was found that Spanish and English academic language scores loaded on one single factor over the three years of data collection. Hakuta & Diaz (1985), with a similar sample of Hispanic students, found an increasing correlation between English and Spanish academic skills over time.

Between Kindergarten and third grade the correlation between English and Spanish went from 0 to .68. The low cross-lingual relationship at the Kindergarten level is likely due to the varied length of residence of the students and their parents in the United States which would result in varying levels of English proficiency at the start of school.

A case study of five schools attempting to implement the theoretical framework for the education of language minority students developed by the California State Department of Education showed consistently higher correlations between English and Spanish reading skills (range r = .60 - .74) than between English reading and oral language skills (range r = .36 - .59) (California State Department of Education, 1985). In these analyses scores were broken down by months in the program (1 - 12 months through 73 - 84 months). It was also found that the relation between L1 and L2 reading became stronger as English oral communicative skills grew stronger (r = .71, N = 190 for students in the highest category of English oral skills).

In conclusion, the research evidence shows consistent support for the principle of linguistic interdependence in studies investigating a variety of issues (e.g. bilingual education, memory functioning of bilinguals, age and second language learning, bilingual reading skills, etc.) and using different methodologies. The research has also been carried out in a wide variety of sociopolitical contexts. The consistency and strength of support indicates that highly reliable policy predictions can be made on the basis of this principle.

### The interactive pedagogy principle

The relative success of bilingual instruction in comparison to formal teaching of second languages is usually attributed in part to the fact that the target language is used for genuine communicative purposes rather than being taught only as a subject (e.g. Swain & Lapkin, 1982). The acquisition process is similar to that of first language learning in that students focus on meaning rather than on language itself. Most second language theorists (e.g. Krashen, 1981, 1982; Long, 1983; Schachter, 1983; Wong Fillmore, 1983) currently endorse some form of the "input" hypothesis which essentially states that acquisition of a second language depends not just on exposure to the language but on access to second language input which is modified in various ways to make it comprehensible.

The notion that comprehensible input is sufficient in itself to account for most aspects of L2 acquisition (Krashen, 1982) has been criticized on several counts. First, the term "comprehensible input" focuses only on the receptive or "input" aspects of interaction whereas both receptive and expressive aspects appear to be important (Swain, 1986). Swain and Wong Fillmore (1984) have expressed the importance of meaningful interaction for second language learning by synthesizing the views of leading researchers in the field in the form of an "interactionist" theory whose major proposition is that "interaction between learner and target language users is the major causal variable in second language acquisition" (p. 18).[2] A second criticism of theories that place the major emphasis on the notion of "comprehensible input" is that they underestimate the role of formal L2 instruction in contributing to proficiency. Several studies (e.g. Harley et al, in press) have shown that a focus on form within the context of meaningful communicative interaction does promote mastery of the target language. Swain (1986) has attributed the failure of students in Canadian French immersion programs to attain native-like expressive abilities in French both to the lack of ample opportunities to use the language either within or outside the classroom and to the unsystematic attention paid to formal features of the target language by teachers. Thus, meaningful active use of the target language by students together with systematic attention to form are important adjuncts to comprehensible input as contributors to L2 acquisition.

Recent research on effective teaching strategies for handicapped bilingual students supports the adoption of interactive models of pedagogy (Swedo, 1987; Willig, Swedo & Ortiz, 1987). The goal of the study was to identify instructional strategies that address both language status and learning problems, result in high task engagement and lead to improved second language and academic performance. Data from videotaping four special education classes serving Hispanic students in grades four to six were analyzed to assess which instructional strategies resulted in highest levels of task engagement. Swedo summarizes the results as follows:

"Academic activities associated with the most intensive and prolonged levels of task engagement drew heavily upon, and encouraged expression of, students' experiences, language background and interests. They also fostered feelings of success and pride in accomplishment, gave children a sense of control over their own learning, and included peer collaboration or peer aproval. Furthermore they were holistic in nature in that they did not involve learning or drilling of isolated, decontextualized segments of information. ... On the other hand, activities that presented decontextualized information in drill format were among those producing the lowest rate of task engagement and low success rates" (1987, pp. 3-4).

In short, interactive pedagogy that promotes motivated and non-trivial communication in the classroom appears to be a major factor in stimulating student task engagement. Interactive pedagogy in L2 teaching entails:

A  the provision of ample comprehensible input to learners;

B  promotion of active student use of the target language in both oral and written modalities; and

C development of students' awareness of and ability to manipulate the more formal aspects of the target language (e.g. discourse and grammatical features) in the service of more effective communication.

Formal instruction in the absence of meaningful interaction will seldom result in communicative proficiency.

One important link between the notion of comprehensible input and the common underlying proficiency principle is that knowledge (e.g. subject matter content, literacy skills etc.) acquired through linguistic interaction in one language plays a major role in making input in the other language comprehensible (Cummins, 1984; Krashen, 1982). For example, an immigrant student who already has the concept of "justice" in his or her first language will require considerably less input in the second language containing the term to acquire its meaning than will a student who does not already know the concept. In the same way the first language conceptual knowledge developed by minority students in bilingual programs greatly facilitates their acquisition of L2 literacy and subject matter content.

## Conclusion

This review of psychoeducational data regarding bilingual academic development shows that, contrary to the opinions of some researchers and educators, a theoretical basis for at least some policy decisions regarding minority students' education does exist. In other words, policy-makers can predict with considerable confidence the probable effects of bilingual programs for majority and minority students implemented in very different sociopolitical contexts.

First, they can be confident that if the program is effective in continuing to develop students' academic skills in both languages, no cognitive confusion or handicap will result; in fact, students may benefit in subtle ways from access to two linguistic systems.

Second, they can predict that when minority students have access to the target language in the environment, they are likely to take considerably longer to develop grade-appropriate levels of L2 academic or conceptual skills in comparison to how long it takes to acquire peer-appropriate levels of L2 conversational skills.

Third, they can be confident that for both majority and minority students, spending instructional time through the minority language will not result in lower levels of academic performance in the majority language, provided of course the instructional program is effective in developing academic skills in the minority language. This is because at deeper levels of conceptual and academic functioning, there is considerable overlap or interdependence across languages. Conceptual knowledge developed in one language helps to make input in the other language comprehensible.

Finally, the research suggests that conceptual and linguistic growth are dependent upon opportunities for meaningful interaction in both the target language and in the L1. Exposure to the target language itself and/or formal decontextualized teaching of the language are insufficient to ensure either language acquisition or conceptual growth.

*Controversial theoretical constructs: language deficit and semilingualism*

Theorists on both sides of the Atlantic have spent considerable energy debating the extent to which minority students may experience cognitive and/or linguistic deficits and, if so, to what extent such deficits may be regarded as a causal factor in explaining their poor academic performance (Brent-Palmer, 1979; Cummins & Swain, 1983; Edelsky, Hudelson, Flores, Barkin, Altwerger & Jilbert, 1983; Hansegard, 1968; Martin-Jones & Romaine, 1986; Ouvinen-Birgerstam & Wigforss, 1978; Paulston, 1982; Skutnabb-Kangas, 1984; Stroud, 1978). In many respects the controversy parallels the debate regarding whether or not working-class children are characterized by language deficits that contribute to their difficulties in schools (Bernstein, 1971; Labov, 1970).

According to Skutnabb-Kangas (1984), Hansegard (1972) has provided the most complete description of the construct of "double semilingualism" based on his observations among Finnish and Sami communities in Northern Sweden. The six characteristics outlined by Hansegard are as follows:

1 size of the repertoire of words, phrases, etc. understood or actively available in speech;
2 correctness with respect to syntactic, phonemic and discoursal aspects of language use;
3 degree of automatism in use of the language;
4 ability to create or neologize in the language;
5 mastery of the cognitive, emotive and volitional function of language;
6 degree of richness in the semantic networks available to the individual through the language.

Edelsky et al. (1983) characterize this description of the construct as "a confused grab-bag of prescriptive and descriptive components" and argue that to attribute minority students' academic difficulties to "semilingualism" even as one link in a causal chain constitutes a deficit theory that "blames the victim". Paulston (1982) similarly argues that there is no empirical evidence for the construct and deplores its use (primarily by Skutnabb-Kangas) in the Swedish debate as an argument for Finnish home language classes.

Skutnabb-Kangas (1984), in response to criticism of the construct, makes the point that most of the studies that claim not to have found evidence for inadequate command of two languages have focused on syntax whereas many of those that support the construct have focused on range of vocabulary. She furthermore argues that semilingualism cannot be regarded as a deficiency inherent in the individual but should be treated as one result of the societal and educational discrimination to which minority groups are subjected. Semilingualism can be avoided when minority children receive intensive L1 instruction through "language shelter" (i.e. L1 immersion) programs.

Several authors have adopted an intermediate position with respect to this debate. McLaughlin (1985), for example, suggests that "Semilingualism may be a useful way of describing those cases where, through extreme social deprivation, bilingual children do not learn to function well in either language. At issue here, however, is whether it is a useful concept when talking about bilingual children in general. If the concept of semilingualism is defined as meaning that bilingual children do not perform as well as native speakers in either language, then there is some agreement that in fact this may be the case at certain points in the development of their languages" (1985, p. 33).

McLaughlin goes on to cite Magiste's (1979) findings that German-speaking children learning Swedish required four to five years to reach native-like proficiency (as defined by performance on a reaction-time test) on comprehension skills, and about six years on production skills in the second language. Furthermore, as reaction times improved on the L2 tasks they declined on the L1 tasks. According to McLaughlin, this research suggests that there may be points during the L2 acquisition phase when neither language is at native-like levels.

Appel & Muysken (1987) make the point that the bilingual's verbal repertoire can be viewed as different and not deficient even though at some point in their development they may know less of each of their languages than monolingual children. For example, bilinguals' code-switching abilities give them the opportunity to convey messages in subtle and sophisticated ways not available to monolinguals. Appel and Muysken also point out that comparisons with monolinguals may not be justified since bilinguals use their two languages in different domains and for different purposes. In other words, from a sociolinguistic perspective the two languages of the bilingual can be viewed as one linguistic repertoire that is adequate in a wide variety of situations.

The issues in this debate appear to be less complex than might be indicated by the heated controversy that surrounds the use of the term. In the first place, if one admits that variation in language and literacy abilities exists among monolingual populations, then there is no reason to deny the existence of such variation among bilingual populations in their two languages. It is clear that there are major individual differences in both literacy skills and in certain aspects of oral language skills among the general population in their L1's. Everybody is not capable of reading and writing at the same level nor does everybody have identical oral repertoires (e.g. oratorical skills). In the same way, bilingual children and adults vary in their degree of mastery of different aspects of their two languages. Even Edelsky et al. (1983) admit that "semilingualism might mean something more substantial (e.g. an inability to use language in its ideational or representational function...)" (p. 11).

If we allow that variation exists then it appears that certain bilinguals will have relatively low levels of literacy in both their L1 and L2 while others will have relatively high levels of literacy in both languages. Certainly among some minority children born in the host country who do not receive sufficient L1 instruction at school, their L1 oral and literacy skills develop to a much lower level than those of equivalent monolingual children in the home country (Harley, Allen, Cummins & Swain, in press). These children will also vary in the degree of L2 academic skills that they develop at school.

In short, the issue does not seem to revolve around the existence of variation in language and literacy skills among bilingual (and monolingual) populations. The issue is rather whether it is appropriate or theoretically useful to label some of these bilingual children "semilingual" or "double semilingual" or "deficient" as a means of characterizing their relatively lower levels of proficiency in certain aspects of their languages.

There appear to be compelling scientific and sociopolitical reasons to avoid using such labels. First, as the debate clearly shows, there has been no precise linguistic or cognitive operationalization of the term "semilingualism". In other words, there is no scientific rationale for choosing one arbitrary cut-off point over another as the level below which it is appropriate to label an individual "semilingual". Thus, the term has no explanatory or predictive value but is rather a restatement of the vague notion of "relatively low levels of proficiency in two languages". At a sociopolitical level the term is pejorative and may be misinterpreted as suggesting that linguistic deficits are a primary cause of minority students' academic difficulties, despite denials to the contrary. Furthermore, the futile debates to which use of the term has given rise suggest that its continued use is counterproductive.

In summary, there appears to be little justification for continued use of the term "semilingualism" in that it has no theoretical value and confuses rather than clarifies the issues. However, those who claim that "semilingualism does not exist", appear to be endorsing the untenable positions that (a) variation in educationally-relevant aspects of language does not exist and (b) there are no bilinguals whose literacy skills are inadequately developed in both L1 and L2. Just as there as monolinguals whose literacy skills are inadequately developed, there are bilinguals whose literacy skills are inadequately developed.

## The application of theory to policy in multilingual/ multicultural education in the United States and Canada

Although initially implemented during the same period of time (the late 1960s and 1970s), Canadian and United States (U.S.) bilingual education programs differ in many respects, most notably in the major client groups for the programs; Canadian French immersion programs were implemented to promote the learning of French by the English-speaking majority group and have tended to attract middle-class students whose parents want better job opportunities and an enriched educational experience for their children. By contrast, bilingual education in the United States was implemented in the context of policies designed to promote educational equity and the major client groups are minority students who tend to come from low socio-economic backgrounds. This difference in whose interests are being served by the programs appears to play a major role in the extent of successful implementation of bilingual education and in the way research is conducted and interpreted in the two contexts.

### Theoretical rationales for the bilingual programs

In both Canadian and U.S. situations the general perceived problem was similar, namely, lack of student proficiency in a socially-valued language (French in Canada and English in the United States). With respect to causes of this problem, sociopolitical considerations have been largely ignored in the policy debates. However, as Paulston (1980) has frequently pointed out, the major causes of most language planning problems are sociopolitical in nature with psychoeducational and linguistic factors acting as intervening variables. By the same token, the effects of educational interventions aimed at resolving such problems can usually be understood only in terms of their interaction with sociopolitical factors. In other words, interventions based on linguistic or psychoeducational hypotheses in isolation from the context of inter-ethnic group relations will frequently fail to produce the predicted outcomes (see Cummins, 1989, for discussion of the interactions between psychoeducational and sociopolicial factors).

In the Canadian situation, the writings of the Montreal neurosurgeon

Wilbur Penfield were influential. Penfield (1965) had speculated (partly on the basis of neuropsychological evidence) that there is an optimal prepubertal period for acquiring an L2 and our language learning capacity declines after this period; he also suggested that second languages should be taught by what he called "the mother's method" by which he meant used as a medium of communication in the classroom to permit children to acquire their L2 in much the same way as they acquired their L1. It is not difficult to see how these hypotheses gave rise to early French immersion programs.

Subsequent research and theory have tended to refute Penfield's "optimal age" hypothesis in that older learners appear to acquire most aspects of the L2 more efficiently than younger learners (e.g. Harley, Allen, Cummins & Swain, in press). However, his notion of the "mother's method" is entirely compatible with the current emphasis on interaction as a basis for language learning, as discussed above.

In the United States situation, two opposing theoretical assumptions have dominated the policy debate regarding the causes of minority students' academic difficulties and the effectiveness of bilingual education in reversing these difficulties. Each of these assumptions is associated with a particular form of educational intervention designed to reverse this failure. In support of transitional bilingual education where some initial instruction is given in students' L1, it is argued that students cannot learn in a language they do not understand; thus, a home-school language switch will almost inevitably result in academic retardation unless initial content is taught through L1 while students are acquiring English. In other words, minority students' academic difficulties are attributed to a "linguistic mismatch" between home and school.

The opposing argument is that if minority students are deficient in English, then they need as much exposure to English as possible. Students' academic difficulties are attributed to insufficient exposure to English in the home and environment. Thus, bilingual programs that reduce this exposure to English even further appear illogical and counterproductive in that they seem to imply that less exposure to English will lead to more English achievement.

Viewed as theoretical principles from which predictions regarding program outcomes can be derived, the "linguistic mismatch" and "insufficient exposure" hypotheses are each patently inadequate. The former is refuted by the French immersion data which clearly demonstrate that for English-background students in Canada a home-school language switch results in no academic retardation. The success of a considerable number of minority students under home-school language switch conditions similarly refutes the linguistic mismatch hypothesis.

The "insufficient exposure" hypothesis fares no better. As outlined above, virtually every bilingual program that has ever been evaluated (including French immersion programs) shows that students instructed through a minority language for all or part of the school day perform, over time, at least as well in the majority language (e.g. English in North America) as students instructed exclusively through the majority language.

Since neither of these theoretical assumptions is capable of accounting for the research data, it is not surprising that programs implemented on the basis of these assumptions have not been particularly successful.

### The goals of bilingual education programs

The goals of Canadian immersion programs and means of achieving these goal were clearly defined and non-problematic. They served the interests of the dominant group and there was general consensus regarding the appropriateness of these goals and means. This, however, was not the case with bilingual education in the United States. All parties agreed with the goal of improved English academic skills but many minority advocates also desired bilingual programs to further the development of a pluralistic society through an emphasis on native culture and language maintenance. This goal was vehemently resisted by many "mainstream" educators and policy-makers. During the late 1970s, the suspicion grew that bilingual programs were in reality intended only to promote Hispanic political and economic goals (even Hispanic separatism following the Quebec model) under the guise of developing students' English language skills. Thus, lack of consensus on goals and means compounded difficulties created by questionable psychoeducational assumptions used to justify bilingual education.

Problems of implementation followed naturally from the confused psychoeducational rationale and disputed goals of bilingual education in the United States. An enormous variety of programs resulted, ranging from considerable use of L1 in the early grades to virtually no use of L1. Some programs appeared to work extremely well, others no better than English-only programs. By contrast, immersion programs started off on a very small scale with the St. Lambert program in the Montreal area (Lambert & Tucker, 1972) and no further implementation was carried out until the initial results of this evaluation were available.

### The role of evaluative research

In both the United States and Canadian contexts, a considerable amount of evaluative research has been carried out to assess the effects of the bilingual programs. In the case of the immersion programs, the initial St. Lambert program was thoroughly evaluated over a period of seven years

(Lambert & Tucker, 1972) and students were also followed through high school and beyond. As the immersion program spread to other areas, large-scale evaluations were also carried out to assess the consistency of findings with those of the St. Lambert program (e.g. Swain & Lapkin, 1982). One of the reasons for this was continued doubts among educators and parents that children could spend so much instructional time through French with no negative consequences for their English academic skills. Although some problematic issues have emerged, the weight of research evidence has overwhelmingly confirmed the initial St. Lambert findings and the results were interpreted within the context of the interdependence notion (Cummins, 1979).

The story has been very different in the evaluations of bilingual programs in the United States. Much of the research carried out was poorly designed (Baker & De Kanter, 1981), in part because of the much more complicated sociopolitical and educational context. For example, students were frequently exited from bilingual programs at very early stages (e.g. after one year) with the result that if students continued to perform poorly in English academic skills it was unclear whether this was due to premature exit to an all-English program or to the lack of effectiveness of bilingual education. Evaluations also tended to be atheoretical in that theory-based predictions regarding outcomes were seldom generated and tested. Thus, evaluators attempted to assess the "effectiveness" of bilingual education without any well-articulated hypotheses regarding how long it would take minority students to acquire age-appropriate levels of English academic skills and under what sociopolitical and instructional conditions (e.g. length and intensity of L1 instruction). Thus, research suggesting that very different time periods are required for minority students to acquire peer-appropriate conversational as opposed to academic L2 skills (as reviewed above) was ignored in the design and interpretation of research.

The overall conclusion of immersion program evaluations is that the programs have been a resounding success and this has been effectively communicated to policy-makers, parents and educators. The result has been a huge increase in parental demand for French immersion programs which now have an enrolment of about 230,000 students and are offered in every Canadian province. Sociopolitical and administrative problems have emerged as a result of the increased demand for immersion programs (e.g. concerns by minority francophones of increased competition for bilingual jobs, layoff of teachers who do not speak French, etc). However, these problems have not significantly slowed the momentum of immersion.

By contrast, bilingual programs in the United States are perceived much more equivocally by policy-makers and educators. This perception was reinforced by the research review conducted by Baker & De Kanter (1981) which concluded that transitional bilingual programs overall were not much more successful than English-only programs in promoting minority students' achievement. This review reflects the major problems of transitional bilingual education in that it is almost completely atheoretical and consequently ignores the consistent patterns that do emerge in the research data regarding interdependence of cognitive/academic skills across languages. A subsequent meta-analysis of the same data base did report more positive outcomes from bilingual as opposed to English-only programs (Willig, 1985) but the huge variation in program design and implementation together with the lack of a unified theoretical framework remains an obstacle to clear interpretation of the results.

The extent to which sociopolitical considerations dominate the interpretation of research in the U.S. context can be seen in the frequent argument that the success of French immersion programs in Canada constitutes an argument for "English immersion" programs for minority students in the U.S. (e.g. Baker & De Kanter, 1981). The logic here is to argue for a monolingual English-only program, taught largely by monolingual teachers, and aimed at producing monolingualism, on the basis of the success of a program involving full bilingual instruction, taught by bilingual teachers, whose explicit goal is to produce additive bilingualism and biliteracy.

In summary, two broad conclusions emerge from this comparative case study of the relation between research, theory and policy in the area of bilingual education: first, the central role of theory is minimally understood by many policy-makers. "Theory" is frequently dismissed as idle speculation ("it's just theory") by policy-makers who fail to appreciate that "facts" become interpretable only in the context of a coherent theory. For policy, theory is essentially the means of predicting outcomes under divergent conditions, and as such, is inseparable from the policy making process. The comparison of the Canadian and U.S. situations illustrate how policy makers often operate with implicit theoretical assumptions that become immune from critical scrutiny as a result of the absence of a systematic process of validating/revising these theoretical assumptions in relation to research data.

The second general conclusion is that sociopolitical factors related to power and status relations between dominant and subordinate groups play a major role in the importance assigned to particular issues, the initiatives taken by policy-makers, the resources assigned to carry out research on particular topics, the conduct and interpretation of research, and the application of research to policy. There is no such thing as "pure research" on issues that reflect the power conflicts within society.

The contrast between the general acceptance and application of immersion program findings in Canada compared to the lack of acceptance of similar findings supporting exactly the same theoretical principles (i.e. the four principles outlined above) in the case of bilingual education in the United States illustrates the importance of inter-group power relations in research interpretation. Immersion programs are implemented by and serve the interests of the dominant group in Canada whereas bilingual programs in the United States confer power and status (e.g. through jobs) on previously dominated minorities and serve the interests of minorities rather than those of the dominant group.[3] The demographic changes occuring in the United States with respect to the huge increase in the Hispanic population add to the urgency felt by many within the dominant group to restrict as much as possible the expanding power base of the minorities. This has been done by emasculating bilingual programs as much as possible by reducing the use of L1 and denying the value of these programs regardless of any research pointing to the contrary (see Cummins, 1989, and Hakuta, 1986 for detailed analyses of the U.S. debate).

Both language and education have traditionally served to stratify societal groups along class and ethnic lines and, in the past, research has legitimized this stratification; for example, by attributing school failure to inherent deficiencies of the minorities themselves, such as genetic inferiority, bilingualism, and cultural deprivation (see Hakuta, 1986, for a review). Given the societal commitment to preserve the power relations between dominant and subordinate groups, funded research will naturally tend to serve the interests of the dominant group, as documented above. Researchers (and policy-makers) concerned to contribute to societal equity are faced with the delicate task of persuading representatives of the dominant group to fund research whose results are likely to challenge the power of the dominant group.

## Future directions for theory and research

The previous analysis suggests that advances in scientific knowledge with respect to multilingual/multicultural education are likely to come from research that is theoretically motivated and takes explicit account of the societal context within which minority (and majority) students develop. In other words, the research design (and theoretical framework) should attempt to elucidate the potential interactions between psychoeducational and sociopolitical factors.

One theoretical framework which could be used to generate such research questions is presented in Figure 1 (see next page). The framework presents both a causal analysis of minority students' academic difficulties and an intervention model for reversing these difficulties. Although the framework is empirically-based in that there is research support for its independent propositions, further research is required to assess the adequacy and specific applications of these propositions and to evaluate the interactions among the propositions in different sociopolitical situations.

A considerable amount of data shows that power and status relations between minority and majority groups exert a major influence on school performance (Cummins, 1984; Ogbu, 1978; Ogbu & Matute-Bianchi, 1986). Minority groups that tend to experience academic difficulty (e.g. Finns in Sweden, Hispanic, Black, and Indian groups in the U.S., Franco-Ontarian, Black and Indian groups in Canada) appear to have developed an insecurity and ambivalence about the value of their own cultural identity as a result of their interactions with the dominant group. A central proposition of the theoretical framework is that minority students are disempowered educationally in very much the same way that their communities are disempowered by interactions with societal institutions.

Figure 1. Empowerment of Minority Students: A framework for
          Intervention.

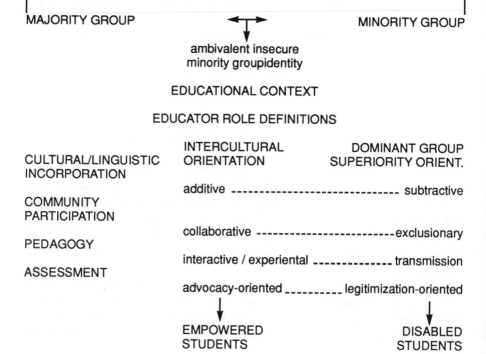

The converse of this is that minority students will succeed educationally to the extent that the patterns of interaction in school reverse those that prevail in the society at large. In short, minority students are "empowered" or "disabled" as a direct result of their interactions with educators in the schools. These interactions are mediated by the implicit or explicit role definitions that educators assume in relation to four institutional characteristics of schools. These characteristics reflect the extent to which: (1) minority students' language and culture are incorporated into the school program; (2) minority community participation is encouraged as an integral component of children's education; (3) the pedagogy promotes intrinsic motivation on the part of students to use language actively in order to generate their own knowledge; and (4) professionals involved in assessment become advocates for minority students by focusing primarily on the ways in which students' academic difficulty is a function of interactions within the school context rather than legitimizing the location of the "problem" within students.

Each dimension can be analyzed along a continuum, with one end reflecting an intercultural (or anti-racist) orientation (role definition) and the other reflecting the traditional dominant-group-superiority orientation. The overall hypothesis is that this latter orientation will tend to result in the personal and/or academic disabling of minority students while anti-racist orientations (as operationally defined with respect to the framework) will result in minority student empowerment, a concept that, in the present context, implies the development of the ability, confidence and motivation to succeed academically.

At least three of the dimensions analyzed (cultural/linguistic incorporation, community participation, and assessment) are integral to most statements of "multicultural education" policy. Although policy with respect to linguistic (as compared to cultural) incorporation has tended to be vague and ambivalent, the linguistic component is regarded as central to the present framework on the grounds that a multicultural education policy that ignores linguistic diversity is vacuous and there is considerable research evidence showing the importance of the linguistic component for minority students' academic achievement. The inclusion of "pedagogy" as a central dimension of a framework for analyzing anti-racist education may appear unusual; its relevance, however, derives from the fact that genuine incorporation of students' experiences (cultures) into the school program requires that educators abandon pedagogical assumptions that focus primarily on transmission of pre-determined knowledge and skills.

### Cultural/Linguistic Incorporation

Considerable research data suggest that for minority groups who experience disproportionate levels of academic failure, the extent to which students' language and culture are incorporated into the school program constitutes a significant predictor of academic success (see Appel & Muysken, 1988; Cummins, 1989; Hakuta, 1986). In programs where minority students' L1 skills are strongly reinforced, their school success appears to reflect both the more solid cognitive/academic foundation developed through intensive L1 instruction and also the reinforcement of their cultural identity.

With respect to the incorporation of minority students' language and culture, educators' role definitions can be characterized along an "additive-subtractive" dimension. Educators who see their role as adding a second language and cultural affiliation to students' repertoire are likely to empower students more than those who see their role as replacing or subtracting students' primary language and culture in the process of assimilating them to the dominant culture. As noted above, cognitive and linguistic benefits (e.g. enhanced metalinguistic development) have been frequently reported in association with continued development of skills in two languages.

### Community Participation.

It has been argued (Cummins, 1989) that minority students will be empowered in the school context to the extent that the communities themselves are empowered through their interactions with the school. When educators involve minority parents as partners in their children's education, parents appear to develop a sense of efficacy that communicates itself to children with positive academic consequences (see, for example, Ada, 1988; Tizard, Schofield & Hewison, 1982).

The educator role definitions associated with community participation can be characterized along a collaborative-exclusionary dimension. Teachers operating at the collaborative end of the continuum actively encourage minority parents to participate in promoting their children's academic progress both in the home and through involvement in classroom activities. Teachers with an exclusionary orientation, on the other hand, tend to regard teaching as their job and are likely to view collaboration with minority parents as either irrelevant or actually detrimental to children's progress. Often parents are viewed as part of the problem since they interact through their L1 with their children at home.

### Pedagogy.

As outlined above, two major orientations can be distinguished with respect to pedagogy. These differ in the extent to which the teacher retains exclusive control over classroom interaction as opposed to sharing some of this control with students. The dominant teacher-centered instructional model in most western industrial societies has been termed a "trans-mission" model (Barnes 1976; Wells, 1986) or a "direct instruction" model (e.g. Becker, 1977). This can be contrasted with "interactive/experiential" or "whole language" models of pedagogy that focus on promoting active student use of both oral and written language for genuine communication.

The relevance of these two pedagogical models for multicultural education derives from the fact that empowerment of minority students is likely to be considerably more difficult within a transmission model of pedagogy. To be sure, content about other cultural groups can be transmitted but appreciation of other cultural groups can come about only through interaction where experiences are being shared. Transmission models exclude, and therefore effectively suppress minority students' experiences and consequently do not allow for validation of minority students' cultural and linguistic background in the classroom.

In short, pedagogical approaches that empower students encourage them to assume greater control over setting their own learning goals and to collaborate actively with each other in achieving these goals. The approaches reflect what cognitive psychologists such as Piaget and Vygotsky have emphasized about children's learning for more than half a century. Learning is viewed as an active process that is enhanced through interaction. The stress on action (Piaget) and interaction (Vygotsky) contrasts with behavioristic pedagogical models that focus on passive and isolated reception of knowledge. As reviewed above, there is evidence that for minority students who are "at risk" educationally, interactive pedagogy is more appropriate than transmission pedagogy (Swedo, 1988).

## Assessment

Historically, in many western countries, psychological assessment has served to legitimize the educational disabling of minority students by locating the academic "problem" within the students themselves. This has had the effect of screening from critical scrutiny the subtractive nature of the school program, the exclusionary orientation of teachers towards minority communities, and transmission models of teaching that inhibit students from active participation in learning.

This process is virtually inevitable when the conceptual base for the assessment process is purely psychoeducational. If the psychologist's task (or role definition) is to discover the causes of a minority student's academic difficulties and the only available tools are psychological tests (in either L1 or L2), then it is hardly surprising that the child's difficulties are attributed to psychological dysfunctions. The myth of bilingual handicaps that still influences educational policy and practice was generated in exactly this way during the 1920s and 1930s.

The alternative role definition that is required to reverse the traditional "legitimizing" function of assessment can be termed an "advocacy" role. This implies that the conceptual basis for assessment should be broadened so that it goes beyond psychoeducational considerations to take account of the child's entire learning environment. The primary focus should be on remediating the educational interactions that minority children have experienced rather than focusing exclusively on "deficient" characteristics of the children themselves. The type of research that appears most likely to elucidate the operation and interactions of the factors highlighted in this framework is case study research that does not attempt to isolate specific variables from their context. Many of the central variables are likely to be difficult to measure quantitatively (e.g. amount and effectiveness of community participation) but are amenable to qualitative description and analysis. Since the academic difficulties of minority students are attributed primarily to the ways in which the school as an institution, and educators within the school, relate to minority students and their communities, the school itself must be the major unit of analysis.

This emphasis does not imply that other forms of research are not valuable in contributing to the scientific basis for policy in multilingual/multicultural education. Evaluative research, for example, has clearly contributed substantially to the generation of the theoretical principles discussed above and statistical research (e.g. Centre for Educational Research and Innovation, 1987) has pointed to patterns that require explanation. The point is that within the context of the theoretical framework presented above, minority students' academic difficulties are a function of both sociopolitical and educational factors that interact with each other. Thus, this complexity needs to be built into the design of research aimed at fully understanding the nature of minority students' school progress. Within the context of case studies, cross-case analysis can, in many cases, elucidate the operation of fundamental causal factors. Research that focuses on more limited issues or variables in particular educational and sociopolitical contexts can contribute important information but investigation of the operation of these variables in a variety of contexts and in interaction with other relevant variables is necessary before confident generalization about their effects can be made.

## References

Ada, A.F. (1988) The pajaro Valley experience: Working with Spanish-speaking parents to develop children's reading and writing skills in the home through the use of children's literature. In: T. Skutnabb-Kangas & J. Cummins (eds.) *Minority education: From shame to struggle*. Clevedon: Multilingual Matters.

Appel, R. & P. Muysken (1987) *Language contact and bilingualism*. London: Edward Arnold.

Ashworth, M., J. Cummins & J. Handscombe (1989) *Report of the external review team on the Vancouver School Board's ESL programs*. Vancouver: Report submitted to the Vancouver School.

Baetens Beardsmore, H. & J. Kohls (1988) Immediate pertinence in the acquisition of multilingual proficiency: The European schools. *The Canadian Modern Language Review*, Vol. 44, pp. 680-701.

Baker, K.A. & A.A. de Kanter (1981) *Effectiveness of bilingual education: A review of the literature*. Washington, D.C.: Office of Planning and Budget, U.S. Department of Education, 1981.

Barnes, D. (1976) *From communication to curriculum*. Harmondsworth: Penguin, 1976.

Becker, W.C. (1977) Teaching reading and language to the disadvantaged: What we have learned from field research. *Harvard Educational Review*, Vol. 47, pp. 518-543.

Bereiter, C. & M. Scardamelia (1982) From conversation to composition: The role of instruction in a developmental process. In R. Glasser (ed.) *Advances in instructional psychology*, volume 2. Hillsdale, NJ: Lawrence Erlbaum Associates.

Bernstein, B. (1971) *Class, codes, and control*, volume 1. London: Routledge & Kegan Paul.

Bhatnagar, J. (1980) Linguistic behaviour and adjustment of immigrant children in French and English schools in Montreal. *International Review of applied Psychology*, Vol. 29, pp. 141-149.

Bialystok, E. (1984) *Influences of bilingualism on metalinguistic development*. Paper presented at the symposium "Language awareness/reading development: Cause? Effect? Concomitance?" at the National Reading Conference Meeting, St. Petersburg Florida.

Brent-Palmer, C. (1979) A sociolinguistic assessment of the notion "immigrant semilingualism" from a social conflict perspective. *Working Papers on Bilingualism*, Vol. 19, pp. 137-180.

Bruner, J.S. (1975) Language as an instrument of thought. In: A. Davies (ed.) *Problems of language and learning*. London: Heinemann.

California State Department of Education (1985) *Case studies in bilingual education*: First Year Report. Sacramento: California State Department of Education.

Centre for Educational Research and Innovation (1987) *Immigrants' children at school*. Paris: OECD.

Collier, V.P. (1987) Age and rate of acquisition of second language for academic purposes. *TESOL Quarterly*, Vol. 21, pp. 617-641.

Cummins, J. (1979) Linguistic interdependence and the educational development of bilingual children. *Review of Educational Research*, 49, 222-251.

Cummins, J. (1981) Age on arrival and immigrant second language learning in Canada: A reassessment. *Applied Linguistics*, Vol. 2, pp. 132-149.

Cummins, J. (1983) *Heritage language education: A literature review.* Toronto: Ministry of Education, Ontario.

Cummins J. (1984) *Bilingualism and special education: Issues in assessment and pedagogy.* Clevedon: Multilingual Matters.

Cummins, J. (1989) *Empowering minority students.* Sacramento: California Association for Bilingual Education.

Cummins, J. & M. Swain (1983) Analysis-by-rhetoric: Reading the text or the reader's own projections? A reply to Edelsky et al. *Applied Linguistics*, Vol. 4, pp. 23-41.

Cummins, J. & M. Swain, (1986) *Bilingualism in education: Aspects of theory, research and practice.* London: Longman.

Harley, B., P.A. Allen, J. Cummins & M. Swain *Second language development: A multifaceted study of school-aged learners.* Cambridge: Cambridge University Press, in press.

Diaz, R.M. (1986) Bilingual cognitive development: Addressing three gaps in current research. *Child Development*, Vol. 56, pp. 1376-1388.

Dolson, D. (1985) The effects of Spanish home language use on the scholastic performance of Hispanic pupils. *Journal of Multilingual and Multicultural Development*, Vol. 6, pp. 135-156.

Donaldson, M. (1978) *Children's minds.* Glasgow: Collins.

Edelsky, C., S. Hudelson, B. Flores, F. Barkin, B. Altwerger & K. Jilbert (1983) Semilingualism and language deficit. *Applied Linguistics*, Vol. 4, pp. 1-22.

E.I.F.E. (1986) *Influence of factors on the learning of Basque.* Victoria-Gasteiz: Department of Education, Universities and Research and Secretariat for Language Policy.

Hakuta, K. (1986) Mirror of language: The debate on bilingualism. New York: Basic Books.

Hakuta, K. & R.M. Diaz (1985) The relationship between degree of bilingualism and cognitive ability: A critical discussion and some new longitudinal data. In: K.E. Nelson (ed.) *Children's language*, volume 5. Hillsdale, N.J.: Erlbaum.

Hansegard, N.E. (1972) *Tvasprakighet eller halvsprakighet?* Stockholm: Aldus series 253.

Kemp, J. (1984) *Native language knowledge as a predictor of success in learning a foreign language with special reference to a disadvantaged population.* Thesis submitted for the M.A. Degree, Tel-Aviv University.

Krashen, S.D. (1981) Bilingual education and second language acquisition theory. In: California State Department of Education, Schooling and Language Minority Students: *A theoretical framework*. Los Angeles: Evaluation, Dissemination and Assessment Center.

Krashen, S. (1982) *Principles and practice in second language acquisition*. New York: Pergamon Press.

Krashen, S. & D. Biber (1988) *On course: Bilingual education's success in California*. Sacramento: California Association for Bilingual Education.

Labov, W. (1970) *The study of nonstandard English*. Champaign, Illinois: National Council of Teachers of English.

Lambert, W.E. (1975) Culture and language as factors in learning and education. In: A. Wolfgang (ed.), *Education of immigrant students*. Toronto: OISE.

Lambert, W.E. & G.R. Tucker (1972) *Bilingual education of children: The St. Lambert Experiment*. Rowley, Mass.: Newbury House.

Long, M.H. (1983) Native speaker/non-native speaker conversation in the second language classroom. In: M.A. Clarke & J. Handscombe (eds.) *On TESOL '82: Pacific perspectives on language learning and teaching*. Washington D.C.: TESOL.

Mackey, W. (1972) A typology of bilingual education. In: J. Fishman (ed.) *Advances in the sociology of language, volume 2: Selected studies and applications*. Den Haag: Mouton.

Magiste, E. (1979) The competing language systems of the multilingual. A developmental study of decoding and encoding processes. *Journal of Verbal Learning and Verbal Behavior*, Vol. 18, pp. 79-89.

Martin-Jones, M. & S. Romaine (1986) Semilingualism: A half-baked theory of communicative competence. *Applied Linguistics*, Vol. 7, pp. 26-38.

McLaughlin, B. (1984) Early bilingualism: Methodological and theoretical issues. In: M. Paradis & Y. Lebrun (eds.) *Early bilingualism and child development*. Lisse: Swets & Zeitlinger.

McLaughlin, B. (1985) *Second-language acquisition in childhood*, volume 2. Hillsdale, N.J.: Lawrence Erlbaum Associates.

National Coalition of Advocates for Students (1988) *New voices: Immigrant students in U.S. public schools*. Boston: National Coalition of Advocates for Students.

Ogbu, J.U. (1978) *Minority education and caste*. New York: Academic Press.

Ogbu, J.U. & M.E. Matute-Bianchi (1986) Understanding sociocultural factors: Knowledge, identity and school adjustment. In: California State Department of Education (ed.) *Sociocultural factors and minority student achievement*. Sacramento: California State Department of Education.

Olson, D.R. (1977) From utterance to text: The bias of language in speech and thought. *Harvard Educational Review*, Vol. 47, pp. 90-108.

Ortiz, A.A. & J.R. Yates (1983) Incidence of exceptionality among Hispanics: Implications for manpower planning. *NABE Journal*, Vol. 7, pp. 41-54.

Ouvinen-Birgerstam, P. & E. Wigforss (1978) A critical study of Toukomaa's investigation of the bilingual development of Finnish immigrant children in Sweden. *Pedagogical Bulletin* (No. 6). University of Lund, Department of Education, Lund, Sweden.

Paulston, C.B. (1980) *Bilingual education: Theories and issues*. Rowley, Mass: Newbury House.

Paulston, C.B. (1982) *Swedish research and debate about bilingualism*. Stockholm: Swedish National Board of Education.

Penfield, W. (1965) Conditioning the uncommitted cortex for language learning. *Brain*, Vol. 88, pp. 787-798.

Ramirez, C.M. (1985) *Bilingual education and language interdependence: Cummins and beyond*. Doctoral dissertation, Yeshiva University.

Rees, O. (1981) Mother tongue and English Project. In: Commission for Racial Equality (ed.) *Mother Tongue Teaching Conference Report*. Bradford: Bradford College.

Schachter, J. (1983) Nutritional needs of language learners. In: M.A. Clarke & J. Handscombe (eds.) *On TESOL '82: Pacific perspectives on language learning and teaching*. Washington D.C.: TESOL.

Skutnabb-Kangas, T. (1984) *Bilingualism or not: The education of minorities*. Clevedon: Multilingual Matters.

Snow, C. (1983) Literacy and language: Relationships during the preschool years. *Harvard Educational Review*, Vol. 53, pp. 165-189.

Stroud, C. (1978) The concept of semilingualism. *Working Papers*, Lund University, Department of General Linguistics, Vol. 16, pp. 153-172.

Swann Report (1985) *Education for all*. London: HMSO.

Swain, M. (1986) Communicative competence: Some roles of comprehensible input and comprehensible output in its development. In: J. Cummins & M. Swain, *Bilingualism in education: Aspects of theory, research and practice*. London: Longman.

Swain, M. & S. Lapkin (1982) *Evaluating bilingual education*. Clevedon: Multilingual Matters.

Swain, M. & L.W. Wong Fillmore (1984) *Child second language development: Views from the field on theory and research*. Paper presented at the 18th Annual TESOL Conference, Houston Texas, March.

Swedo, J. (1987) Effective teaching strategies for handicapped limited English proficient students. *Bilingual Special Education Newsletter*, Vol. 6, pp. 1-5.

Tizard, J., W.N. Schofield & J. Hewison (1982) Collaboration between teachers and parents in assisting children's reading. *British Journal of Educational Psychology*, Vol. 52, pp. 1-15.

Wells, G. (1986) *The meaning makers*. Portsmouth, NH: Heinemann.

Willig, A.C. (1985) A meta-analysis of selected studies on the effectiveness of bilingual education. *Review of Educational Research*, Vol. 55, pp. 269-317.

Willig, A.C., J.J. Swedo & A.A. Ortiz (1987) *Characteristics of teaching strategies which result in high task engagement for exceptional limited English proficient Hispanic students*. Austin, TX: University of Texas, Handicapped Minority Research Institute on Language Proficiency.

Wong Fillmore, L. (1983) The language learner as an individual: Implications of research on individual differences for the ESL teacher. In: M.A. Clarke & J. Handscombe (eds.) *On TESOL '82: Pacific perspectives on language learning and teaching*. Washington, D.C.: TESOL.

Wright, E.N. & G.K. Tsuji (1984) *The grade nine student survey: Fall 1983*. Toronto: Toronto Board of Education.

# Notes

1 These figures do not take account of the substantial number of students who, although of foreign origin, have acquired the nationality of the host country. Thus, they underestimate the real extent of linguistic and cultural diversity in the school systems of these countries.

2 The relatively better performance of students learning French as an L2 in the European schools in comparison to those in Canadian French immersion programs has also been attributed to the greater opportunities for out-of-school interaction in the medium of French in the European schools context (see Baetens Beardsmore & Kohls, 1988).

3 It is noteworthy that attempts to implement bilingual programs for non-official (i.e. non-French, non-English L1) language groups in Canada have been strongly resisted in most parts of the country and the debate has been very similar to that in the U.S. with the most prominent arguments focusing on balkanization of the educational system and the need for minorities to learn English.

# Teaching for Learning: Retrospect and Prospect

Noel Entwistle
University of Edinburgh
Scotland

This chapter addresses learner differences in the processes of learning from the standpoint of the teacher. It considers the research that has been done, and could be done, to decide how teaching and differentiation activities can be best attuned to those learner characteristics which are most influential in affecting learning outcomes.

The focus is on "fundamental studies" - those which necessarily precede subsequent development work or interventions, those which represent the growth points for future research, and those which have broad generality and applicability, being independent of the current state of an educational system and the present policies of its government and managers. The ultimate question to be addressed is which specific fundamental studies in educational research might be pursued in this particular area, bearing in mind the requirement that the focus should not be constrained by the reductionist tendencies of individual academic disciplines.

To reach the point where proposals for future directions in fundamental studies can be made, it will be necessary to review a range of studies in which the effects of individual differences among students have been examined in relation to the activities of the teachers. To do this it will be necessary, initially, to provide brief descriptions of a range of important concepts which describe those learner characteristics considered most influential in relation to learning. The concepts chosen for this purpose are: intellectual ability, concepts and conceptions, learning style and personality, motivation, approach to learning, and study skill. It will then be necessary to consider how these individual differences are influenced by the learning environment and how they have been utilized in trying to improve levels of academic performance, either by particular teaching methods or by grouping policies.

The particular choice of concepts has been guided by relevance of each of the concepts to the topic, but also by the need to develop a coherent theoretical framework from which to generate ideas for future research. This particular set of concepts leads to the development of a model which emphasizes the interactions between the person, the task, and the learning environment - of which the most important components are teaching and assessment procedures.

It is argued that all of the work described in the following sections is fundamental, in all three senses used in this book. It has originated in the research community rather than with policy makers, although it is attuned to the concerns of the teacher. It has broad applicability and generality. Although much of the work originates in higher education, it addresses issues which affect all levels of education, and the model which has been derived from the findings has been successfully used in school-level research. As several of the concepts are relatively recent, there are many areas which represent growth points for future research, and the work represents necessary preliminaries for subsequent interventions.

## Characteristics of the learner

### Intellectual ability

When teachers are asked to explain differences in the levels of attainment reached by students, the most frequent concepts used are ability and effort. Apparently, academic achievement is often seen as a simple consequence of the combined effects of ability and effort (Entwistle & Percy, 1974). For many years, psychologists focused their research on the effects of ability on learning outcomes, and were able to show that there were substantial correlations. At first it was considered that ability was a relatively fixed characteristic of the individual, but gradually the influence of environment was admitted, although the relative strength of hereditary and environmental effects are a matter of continuing dispute (Eysenck & Kamin, 1981). From the teacher's point of view it is important to establish that ability can be improved through effective teaching, but it is also important to establish whether different educational "treatments" should be used for students with differing levels of ability.

A crucial first step is to decide whether there is such a thing as "general ability", and that has proved just as divisive a topic as the debate about the relative effects of heredity and environment. The early work of Spearman, Thomson, Thurstone, and subsequently Vernon and Guilford, left the impression that, depending on the form of analysis and the ages of the samples used, intelligence could be described either as a general ability or as a series of specific abilities. For a while it seemed that the idea of general ability was no longer accepted, but it has become re-established (Snow & Lohman, 1984; Gustafsson, 1987) along with continuing arguments about its inadequacy (Sternberg & Detterman, 1987).

For some purposes it seems more useful to identify separate components of intellectual ability, either in terms of information processing, as Jenson (1970) and Sternberg (1985) have done, or as distinct categories or multiple intelligences (Gardner, 1984). The Jenson approach has the advantage of simplicity, identifying the main processing skills as associative and analytical. This dichotomy has the advantage of mapping directly on to the dichotomy in learning or memory processes described as rote and meaningful learning (Ausubel, Novak & Hanesian, 1987), but ignores additional intellectual skills such as imaginative thinking (Entwistle, 1981).

The classification by Gardner (1984) into multiple intelligences - linguistic, musical, logical-mathematical, spatial, bodily-kinaestheitic, inter-personal, and intro-personal - offers more immediate relevance to teachers through links with identifiable subject areas, but the theory will need further development before its educational implications become clear (Gardner, 1985).

In deciding how to group students in order to teach most effectively, clearly the decision on whether a general ability, or a specific ability is to be used, is crucial and will affect the type of grouping procedure and the teaching methods considered appropriate. It is also important to know whether learning in school is thought to depend mainly on the use of associative ability through rote learning, or the establishment of firm conceptual structures through active meaningful learning. There is considerable evidence that much school learning encourages a rote approach, and so much of the recent research effort has been directed towards reversing that tendency.

## Concepts and conceptions

Effective learning of academic subject matter depends on, not only the storage and recall of information, but also the formation and appropriate use of abstract concepts. A good deal of effort has been put into describing the differing conceptions held by students, particularly of scientific concepts. The starting point was in schools, where many pupils were found to have naive concepts of physics which interfered with their understanding of the scientific concepts they were supposed to be acquiring (Driver & Erickson, 1983; Pfundt & Duit, 1985). In a recent review of this work, West (1988) has pointed out that this research differs from earlier studies by adopting mainly a qualitative approach, asking students to give explanations for everyday experiences, drawing on their scientific knowledge. It appears that many students keep their scientific knowledge compartmentalized. They do not seek to interrelate topics within or between school subjects, and they keep their experiences of everyday life even more separate from academic learning. The utility of knowledge learned in school, or rather the lack of it, becomes all too clear from the interviews reported in these studies. It seems that for any topic taught in school or college, students will develop a range of "alternative conceptions" which are used to make sense of the material to be learned. In many cases those conceptions are totally at variance to the conception held by the teacher, and because, in science at least, many alternative conceptions have their origins in explanations of everyday experiences which have been used for many years, they are very resistant to change. Thus teaching is not so much a question of providing new concepts, as of helping students to readjust their existing conceptions along lines which will allow easier subsequent progression in that subject.

Marton has been developing a distinctive research methodology - phenomenography - which describes in terms of a few distinctive categories the range of conceptions held by students (Marton, 1981). In this research, knowledge and understanding are seen as being reconstructed and adapted as new information is acquired or problems solved (Marton, 1988). Using a phenomenographic procedure, Svensson (1989) has argued that, in trying to solve problems designed to test physical principles, students seem to draw not on a well-organized body of abstract concepts and theories, but rather use a haphazard procedure in which naive conceptions from everyday experience are intermixed with scientific concepts to produce explanations which show little evidence for consistent conceptions. It is as if the conception emerges from the attempt to solve the individual problem. From this study, and other studies using the phenomenographic procedures (Marton, 1988), doubt is thrown upon the whole idea of there being firmly established concepts held in cognitive structure, at least in any fixed form. It is interesting to see how recent ideas in cognitive psychology have begun to move in a similar direction, with Greeno (1989) arguing that children elaborate and reorganize their knowledge in relation to experiences of the social and material world, so that understanding is reconstructed anew in relation to specific situations or problems. He attacks the conventional view of understanding involving simply the acquisition and application of concepts and procedures. Suggestions for ways of extending this important new area of research will be made in a later section.

Important though the development of sound conceptual structures must be for academic learning, a good deal of that learning still necessarily involves, at least in the initial stages of learning a subject, the ability to absorb and retain substantial bodies of information. This type of learning is neither rote learning in its laboratory form, nor meaningful learning in its generally accepted sense, but is of an intermediate kind. It is similar to what Ausubel has described as "meaningful reception learning" (Ausubel et al., 1978), in which information is conveyed in a lecture or a book and "directly" absorbed by incorporation into cognitive structure with little if any conscious effort. Of course, subsequent reorganization and systemization occurs, particularly during revision, but the initial process has neither the rehearsal properties of rote learning nor the active establishment of linkages which is the characteristics of other forms of meaningful learning. This type of learning, although prevalent, has been rather ignored by researchers. We need to know more about how students manage to impose meaningful frameworks on such bodies of knowledge, and how those frameworks relate to the development of concepts.

### Learning style and personality

The term learning style is usually employed to describe differences in the ways in which students prefer to learn. In itself a style will not be generally more effective for learning, but matched to an equivalent style in the presentation of information it will be, and if mismatched, interference with learning can become severe. As it appears that many teachers develop styles of teaching which reflect their own learning style (they teach as they prefer to learn), the problems of matching can become serious (Entwistle, 1981).

Witkin's research on cognitive styles pointed up the potential importance of taking this student characteristic into account (Witkin et al., 1977). He described global and articulated styles as the cognitive processing equivalents of field-dependence and field-independence. The articulated style involved creating a clear logical structure within which to learn. He suggested that students with global styles required teachers who could provide clear structure, but he found that they preferred teachers of their own style.

The work of Pask (1976, 1988) has introduced the distinction between students with holist and serialist styles, which have a descriptive similarity to Witkin's categories. The holist style involves a preference for starting with a broad view of the topic to be learned, looking for connections between ideas and developing a personal stance in relation to them, and making wide use of illustrative material and concrete examples in developing understanding. The serialist style shows a preference for a narrow focus on the step-by-step learning of the component parts of the material presented. The stance is cautious and impersonal with considerable emphasis on evidence and logical progression, and shows a reluctance to reach personal interpretations.

The great advantage of these categories, over those describing cognitive styles, is that they emerged from analyses of the way students tackled learning materials similar to those used in classrooms. Thus these learning styles relate more closely to differences which are likely to be found in everyday studying. Pask (1976) was, in fact, able to demonstrate quite clearly the effects of matching and mismatching learning materials to the students' own styles: the differences in learning outcomes were substantial, particularly in the mismatched condition. Whereas earlier learning theories had expected all students to benefit from material arranged within a tight logical structure and progressing by small steps, Pask's findings showed clearly that only students who preferred a serialist style of learning found this material congenial and progressed rapidly: students who preferred a holist style learned slowly and ineffectively with it. Pask went on to demonstrate that students could be trained to use their own style more effectively in their studying (Pask, 1988).

The particular style of learning preferred by a student may reflect earlier experiences in school, but there is some evidence that these preferences may be more fundamental and enduring. A holist style is related to personality characteristics such as thinking introversion, readiness to act on impulse, and emotionality or a lack of personal integration (Entwistle & Ramsden, 1983). It has also been suggested that learning styles reflect hemisperical dominance and that these are largely genetically determined (Sperry, 1983; Cohen, 1983). If this is correct then we shall have to pay more attention to matching learning materials to students' preferences than in providing training programs to change those styles.

It appears that some of the preferences that, for example, field-dependent students have been shown to have for informal teaching (Witkin et al., 1977) may be as much a reflection of their sociability as of their cognitive style as such. Other research has shown more direct relationships between personality characteristics and learning outcomes, although the most recent work makes it clear that the nature of instruction interacts strongly with these relationships. For example, children have been shown to develop stronger motivation in unstructured learning situations, but also to show rises in anxiety (Bennett, 1976). Anxious children have been shown to learn better with structured materials rather than when encouraged to use discovery learning (Trown & Leith, 1975), while pairs of children matched on extraversion, but with contrasting anxiety levels, worked most productively together (Leith, 1974). All in all, it may be safe to assume that the strongest effects are not so much in terms of particular teaching methods, but in terms of interactions between students and teachers. There can be little doubt that the nature of the relationship between teacher and student influences learning substantially. It is not, however, in the straightforward manner implied by writers such as Rogers (1969), where "unconditional regard" is the single essential ingredient. It must be accepted that some teachers are able to communicate enthusiasm and show empathy with the students in ways which are probably generally perceived to be beneficial, but it is also evident that it is through an appropriate match in learning style and personality between the teacher and an individual student that the strongest interpersonal influences on learning seem to be generated (Entwistle, 1981).

## Motivation

As we have seen already, teachers have tended to rely on ability and effort as the twin cornerstones of the conceptual edifice constructed to explain differences in students' academic attainment. And both teachers and psychologists tend to see the amount of effort as depending on the level of motivation. The sources of motivation can be found in the home, where parents' attitudes and reward systems have been found to influence the form and the level of school motivation in their children (Kozeki, 1985). And the recent impact of unemployment on the motivation of secondary school pupils has been marked (Entwistle, 1988). Even though many sources of motivation are beyond the teacher's control, there are still ways of influencing general levels of motivation in the classroom, and these will be discussed in a subsequent section.

Another set of concepts used to explain differences in the amount of effort put into academic work has emerged from attribution theory. When people are asked to explain the reasons for success or failure in a task they have undertaken, they tend to make either internal or external attributions. Internal attributions point to ability, effort, or strategy as accounting for their performance, while external attributions deny personal responsibility and use luck, task difficulty or easiness, and the generosity or unfairness of the assessor, to explain the outcomes. Researchers (Ames & Ames, 1984) have argued that it is important to help students to move away from external towards internal attributions. It seems that, unless students are prepared to take responsibility for their own learning, little improvement in their work can be expected. And teachers, recognizing the effects of ability and effort, regularly encourage students to put more effort into their work. Covington (1983), however, has pointed out the "double-edged sword" involved in encouraging students to make internal attributions and then stressing effort. If students put more effort into their work and it is still judged to be unsatisfactory, they will come to the conclusion that they lack ability, and that diminishes their feelings of self-worth, undermines their self-confidence, and so leads to "effort-avoidance" (Rollett, 1987).

There is, however, an alternative attribution that teachers could encourage and support, namely strategy (Entwistle, 1987a). One important reason for not performing well is that the task has been tackled in the wrong way. Weiner (1984) pointed out the crucial difference between ability and effort as attributions. Ability is considered by non-psychologists as being immutable: you either have it or you have not got it. In contrast the individual chooses the amount of effort to be invested in a task. Strategy, like effort, is perceived to be modifiable but, unlike effort, strategies can be taught. Thus teachers can help students to develop more effective skills and strategies to tackle their academic work. Often this is done in a way which can be linked to training in "learning how to learn", as we shall see.

### Approaches to learning

Cognitive psychologists, in their descriptions of academic learning, have often lost sight of one particularly important aspect of it. Although recognizing the distinction between intentional and incidental learning, they have given little recognition to the fact that, in academic settings, learning is also purposeful. Thus the learning strategies adopted by students depend on their specific intentions in tackling that particular academic task. Academic learning is generally goal-orientated, and that goal usually involves not just acquiring knowledge, but also the passing of examinations which will lead to qualifications. It was Marton who identified the important differences in approaches to learning which were found when students were asked to read an academic article and to be ready to answer questions on it afterwards (Marton & Saljö, 1984). Students were found to adopt either a deep or a surface approach to the reading.

The crucial difference lay in the contrasting intentions shown by students. In a deep approach an intention to reach a personal understanding led to the student interacting critically with the content, relating it to previous knowledge and experience, examining evidence, and evaluating the logical steps by which conclusions have been reached. In contrast, a surface approach was found to involve an intention merely to satisfy task or course requirements, seen as external impositions largely remote from personal interests, and this led to mainly rote memorization. The surface approach could still be active, but it relied on identifying the elements within the task most likely to be assessed, and then memorizing those details.

Marton and his colleagues were able to show that only by adopting a deep approach to reading an article were students able te demonstrate a deep level of understanding of the author's arguments and conclusion. Moreover, after five weeks, students who had used a deep approach were more likely to be able to recall factual details from the article than those who had relied on a surface approach (Marton & Saljö, 1976). Combining a deep approach with effective study methods was found to be strongly related to examination success, while a surface approach seemed to lead to a lack of interest in studying and poor examination performance (Svennson, 1977).

Prosser and Millar (1989) have developed this research further by showing a relationship between approach to learning and conceptual development. They have shown, in an undergraduate physics course, that students who do not have a deep approach to learning show no evidence of having changed their conceptions in relation to specific physical concepts and theories taught in that course. Most of the students adopting a deep approach, either had an appropriate conception initially or developed it during the course. Here we see the necessity for bringing together research on the processes of developing understanding of a specific subject area with more general conclusions about how students tackle their studying.

Marton's original work, and indeed much of the subsequent work which maps alternative conceptions, has been carried out as naturalistic experiments. That situation has, of course, important advantages but it fails to take account of the crucial influence that assessment procedures play in the real learning context in school or college. Ramsden (1981) asked students about their way of tackling their everyday academic work. Again the deep and surface approaches represented important distinctions, but it was also necessary to add a third, strategic approach, which related to studying as well as to learning. In this approach the student adopts deep and surface approaches in a combination designed to achieve the highest possible marks. The approach involves using well-organized study methods and careful time management (Entwistle & Waterston, 1988), but above all there is an alertness to any cues given by tutors about what they are looking for in deciding grades or marks, or what questions they are going to set in the examinations (Ramsden, 1981). Students appear to have two distinct foci of attention - the content and the teacher's reward system. While lecturers expect the students to focus on the former, assessment demands shift attention to the latter (Entwistle, 1987; Laurillard, 1984).

## Study skill

Attempts to operationalize the concepts derived from the interviews led to the Approaches to Studying Inventory (Entwistle & Ramsden, 1983), which also contained scales describing motivation and study attitudes and methods. Factor analyses of the items showed that each approach was associated with a different form of motivation - deep approach correlated closely with intrinsic motivation, surface was linked with fear of failure and instrumental motivation, while strategic was associated with need for achievement. These combinations of scales held together so consistently that they have been referred to as study orientations - meaning, reproducing, and achieving. A final non-academic orientation was found to be characterized by low levels of motivation, negative attitudes to studying, and disorganized study methods. A similar pattern linking motive to strategy has been reported independently by Biggs (1975, 1987) using a different theoretical framework and a different inventory, while four similar descriptive categories have also been used by Schmeck (1983) from factor analyses of an inventory derived from ideas from cognitive psychology. The similarity between the concepts underlying the three inventories, and their validity, have been amply demonstrated (Biggs, 1987; Entwistle & Waterston, 1988; Speth & Brown, 1988; Watkins, 1983).

From a pedagogical standpoint, it is important to take account of the link between motivation and approach to learning reflected in the study orientations described above. Different forms of motivation are associated with different approaches to learning, and so with qualitatively different learning outcomes. Thus, it will be important in considering how to promote student motivation, to ask what kinds of motivation are being encouraged, and whether these are likely to facilitate the required learning outcomes.

Biggs (1987) has gone on to relate the use of his inventory to attempts to improve the study skills of students. He argues that there is a developmental sequence through which students progress. Initially students need to be taught specific study skills in a fairly directive way, then progressively they can be weaned off reliance on the teacher and shown how to develop effective strategies adapted to the demands of different subject areas or topics, and to their own purposes. The techniques used for developing study skills, and their relative effectiveness, will be discussed in a later section. Here it is sufficient to note that the measurement of study orientations provides a basis for interventions designed to improve learning. These orientations can be seen to be relatively stable, being built up from earlier educational experiences, and yet the approach to learning cannot be simply acharacteristic of the student. As we shall see, approach is markedly affected by the students' perceptions of their learning environment.

Svensson (1984) has argued that rather than emphasizing "study skills" we should consider "skill in learning", and this idea helpfully brings together work on studying and learning. Svensson views them as essentialy complementary activities. Students vary in their ability to extract the essence of what they have to learn, and this seems to depend on how well they are able to organize incoming information, relate it to previous knowledge, and reconstruct ideas in relation to examination questions or problems set (Svensson, 1989). The formation and reorganization of concepts in relation to factual information depends on an active process of organization designed to promote understanding and retention. Very similar organizational skills are found to be central to effective study strategies, and so attempts to improve the effectiveness of learning will have to promote organizational skills of these different kinds. And strategy also proves to be important when it comes to encouraging students to put more effort into their learning activities.

### Interventions related to learner characteristics

Much of the work designed to improve the effectiveness of teaching has tended to suggest methods which overcome the need to take account of the characteristics of the learner, except in rather general ways. For example, the model of learning suggested by Carroll (1963) and developed by Bloom (1977) and others in the form of "mastery learning", rejects the need to consider the separate characteristics of the learner. The theory is based on a form of behaviorism, in that the outcomes of learning are seen as depending more on the conditions provided for learning than on the activities and abilities of the individual learner. There can be little doubt that these ideas have been influential, and indeed have contributed to the improvement of teaching, but they do not come within the remit of this paper. It will be necessary, nevertheless, to keep in mind the fact that learning does indeed depend on the time spent "on task", and that one important facet of teaching is the management of attention and time to keep students orientated towards the most important learning goals established for that course (Westbury, 1977).

Here, however, we shall concentrate more on the learner's characteristics by taking each of the main concepts introduced above and considering what interventions, or grouping arrangements, are suggested by the various research findings, to provide indications for future work.

#### Taking account of intellectual differences

When Cronbach (1967) first introduced the idea of aptitude-treatment interaction (ati), intellectual ability was the aptitude most commonly

investigated. The continuing debate about the nature of ability or intelligence makes it somewhat difficult from a research point of view to decide
how to operationalize it, but in fact rather similar conclusions seem to
emerge. For example, Jensen (1970) has argued that associative ability is in
a hierarchical relationship with analytic ability. It is a necessary prerequisite for analytic reasoning. Students low in analytic ability may still have
substantial rote learning skills, and Jensen argues that it is necessary to
capitalize on those skills rather than seek to use the weaker analytic ability.
This argument should not, of course, be taken to extremes, as most teachers would want to help students to develop their weaker skills as well as
capitalizing on their existing strengths, but Jensen's ideas do sound a
warning against assuming that a reliance on analytic skills will be best for
all students.

A recent review by Snow and Lohman (1984) fills out the ideas of Jensen.
Investigating the interactions between general ability and treatment in
relation to academic performance from a variety of studies, they came to
the conclusion that low ability pupils progress more satisfactorily with
instruction which is explicit, direct, and carefully structured, whereas high
ability pupils tend to benefit from being provided with a greater variety of
material with freedom to explore it and to form their own structures
through which to develop meaning. In devising programs of study, however, it will be crucial to take into account, within the system adopted, the
very real dangers of labeling and of students becoming reliant on learning
strategies which inevitably lead to a ceiling in possible progression as
work becomes more advanced conceptually and more analytic in its
requirements.

This brings us to the central argument about grouping procedures, as
these are generally based either on measures of general ability or on the
academic aptitude already shown for school work. In Britain, until 1964,
the use of "streaming" was wide-spread, and the practice persisted for
many years thereafter, although gradually being modified into a less
extreme form. In primary schools, streaming was widely used to assign
pupils to homogeneous ability groups, and then at transfer to secondary
school at age eleven or twelve they were allocated either to an academic
grammar school or to a "secondary modern" school, which covered the
remaining, say, 80% of the school population. (The actual percentage varied regionally quite markedly.) Thereafter, the pupils were often placed in
classes on the basis of the same mixture of intelligence test scores and
teachers' estimates which determined their allocation of school. Thus, ability groupings of various kinds could be found throughout the British
school system.

One of the best known evaluations of this practice was conducted by the

National Foundation for Educational Research in England. Its conclusion was that there was no detectable difference at primary school level between pupils taught in streamed or unstreamed classes (Barker Lunn, 1970). A recent review by Slavin (1987) of a range of studies from various countries came to the same conclusion. It appears that keeping students in the same class based on ability grouping does not produce all-round advantages, however Slavin did suggest that advantages did occur where "setting" was used. In that arrangement students have a "home"class of heterogeneous ability but are assigned to ability groups for work in, say, mathematics and reading in the elementary school classes. The consistency of the findings reviewed by Slavin suggests that this advantage occurs irrespective of the teaching that is given to the separate ability levels, which is rather surprising. If the work described by Snow and Lohman (1984) was used to ensure that the teaching methods provided were effectively geared to the requirements of each ability group, then even more substantial improvements in performance might be anticipated.

The main argument against ability grouping is that the attitudes and motivation of pupils in the lower streams are adversely affected but this problem seems to be largely overcome where students spend only a proportion of their time in ability groups, and where there is opportunity to move between groups as performance changes. In a sense, the use of mastery learning, by allowing students as much time as they require to complete work satisfactorily, provides a form of ability grouping, but with the rate of progress being the responsibility of the individual pupil.

Arguments against Slavin's conclusions (Hiebert, 1987) rest on the fact that the better teachers are often allocated to the higher ability groupings, and that the quality of work is mainly dependent on the quality of teaching provided. Moreover, the survey designs of much of the research fail to put sufficient emphasis on the effect of different teaching methods (Gamoran, 1987). In fact, Slavin (1987) does recognize the weaknesses in much of the older research and argues for future studies to combine quantitative and qualitative methods to provide a fuller picture of the relative merits and demerits of ability grouping. The pattern of findings does, however, seem to support his contention about the general advantages of specific forms of ability grouping.

### Trying to produce more adequate conceptions

The ideas of Ausubel (Ausubel et al., 1978) indicate the importance of providing firmly established anchoring ideas in any topic area, and then the advantage of providing some preliminary "ideational scaffolding" in the form of advance organizers. Ausubel argues that the careful organization and spacing of important concepts within a course, and the systematic teaching of those concepts in a thorough way with many practical examples is likely to be effective in both secondary and higher education. Helping students to think with concepts is one way that has been suggested for strengthening meaningful learning and the use of concept maps has been shown to have some important effects with children of a wide range of ages and abilities (Novak & Gowin, 1984).

The researchers who have been concerned with students' alternative conceptions have emphasized the importance of not just providing time to teach the anchoring ideas more thoroughly than is commonly done, but also to provide opportunities for discussion to explore the reasons why the naive conceptions are inadequate ways of describing the phenomena that have been observed. Some of these discussions should emerge naturally in the course of teaching where the teacher deals with queries or asks questions designed to test understanding, but there is also scope for using peer tutoring. Very often having to explain an idea to another student both tests the level of understanding and leads to productive disagreements about the nature of the concept (West, 1988; Svensson, 1989). It is also clear that textbooks have to be designed to emphasize the development of understanding, rather than providing simply a cataloguing of information. And students need guidance about how to use even well-designed textbooks more effectively (Roth & Anderson, 1988).

### Teaching to enhance motivation

Brophy (1987) has produced a check-list for teachers who are trying to provide adequate motivation through their teaching. He cites three general strategies that teachers should use in all lessons. First, he argues that teachers generally spend too little time at the beginning of a lesson in establishing the value and relevance of what is to be learned. Establishing relevance seems to provide a springboard for maintaining interest thereafter. The next general strategy involves establishing that learning should be an enjoyable experience, rather than a formal requirement of the school system. Finally, tests should be used as ways of checking personal progress rather than demonstrating a rank-order of levels of performance across the class. High performance is, ofcourse, motivating, but the strongly demotivating effects of continued poor performance has been repeatedly noted in the literature. It reminds us that the relationship between motivation and performance acts in both directions, and so one of the best ways of increasing motivation is to find ways of ensuring that students recognize their own progress in their academic achievements.

Brophy (1987) goes on to mention a range of specific strategies which might be introduced into teaching from time to time to add variety and maintain motivation. Many of them stem from the teacher's ability to personalize learning, to make the material more accessible to the student, and more directly related to everyday experience. Establishing relevance also depends on helping the students to establish their own objectives and priorities in relation to the course, and to take an active part in monitoring their own progress and remedying identified weaknesses. The teacher should also try to create suspense or to present paradoxes both of which can stimulate meaningful classroom discussion.

The last two specific strategies itemized by Brophy have been considered important enough by other researchers to give them more centrality in teaching. Brophy suggests that problem-solving should be demonstrated by personal example and that metacognitive awareness should be encouraged. These strategies are central to the attempts to improve study strategies and to encourage self-regulated learning.

### Teaching to encourage self-awareness in learning

One of the traditional ways of coping with the problem of ineffective study strategies was to introduce study skills workshops. A great deal of effort went into devising courses on, for example, speed-reading or "developing your memory". Advocates of these methods often pointed to dramatic improvements, and yet in everyday studying it was more frequently found that the improvements occurred only within the study skills course itself. Transfer to academic subjects was often weak (Selmes, 1987). Indeed some studies have suggested that courses which emphasize the specific skills or individual techniques of studying may encourage a surface strategic approach to learning, which may produce good examination results but will not lead to thorough understanding of the subject being studied (Martin & Ramsden, 1987).

Nisbet and Shucksmith (1986) have pointed out the need to distinguish between skill, strategy and approach in relation to studying. They use the analogy of skill training in soccer to draw attention to the limited utility of skills on their own. To be a skilful soccer player, skills have to be integrated and used appropriately to produce a strategy. They also have to be guided by a game plan which controls the use of strategies which will achieve the goals - literally within the analogy. Similarly, skill in learning depends on an effective integration of specific skills of learning and studying into strategies which take into account the specific purpose in tackling a task set. Guiding the strategies have to be the broader goals which can be seen as the study orientations which have been built up from past experience and which reflect differences in predominant forms of motivation. To be effective, study skills support should involve all three levels, and courses that have done this do seem to be successful (Selmes, 1987; Ramsden & Martin, 1987), at least for students with the necessary motivation (Biggs & Rihn, 1984).

There are two major problems in developing effective interventions in this area. Firstly, the learning skills and strategies, particularly in secondary and tertiary education, are to some extent subject specific. Thus generalized skills will only be useful if they are supported by similar support specific to the subjects or topics being studied. Secondly, the intervention depends on the level of sophistication students have reached. Biggs (1985, 1987) has argued that only the fairly sophisticated learners will be able to benefit from a course which emphasizes metacognitive awareness. Let us take each of these in turn.

Teachers in secondary or tertiary education tend to see their role as presenting students with the content of their discipline. They often find it very difficult to explain learning processes and strategies to their students, and yet this is essential in order to develop metacognitive skills. Corno (1987) has been exploring ways of training teachers to encourage self-regulated learning in their students. This involves teachers in acting out for the class the way they tackle tasks or problems, and promoting discussions among students about why different ways of doing it might be more or less effective. Students are then trained initially to follow procedures in which they are required to ask themselves questions as they tackle each new task. "Am I sure what I have to do?" "What do I know about this topic already?" "How might that knowledge apply to this task?" "How shall I start?" "What should I do next?" "How am I getting on?" "How well have I carried out the task?" "Are there ways in which I could have done it better?" All of these questions have been designed to stimulate an awareness of purpose, strategy and monitoring which form the core of metacognitive awareness. Corno (1987) has at least provisional evidence that students do begin to apply these strategies in other work in the classroom and that academic performance is improved. But these are not the only techniques available; a variety of other strategies have been suggested (Weinstein, Goetz & Alexander, 1988). The remaining problem seems to be that some of this strategy training is not effective for complex academic learning and that, even when it does work, it may not be equally effective with students who lack either prerequisite skills or sufficient motivation. Biggs (1987) argues that such students may have to be taught skills initially in a didactic way, followed by a staged progression introducing first specific strategies and then metacognitive awareness. But that may still not be effective with students who lack motivation. For them it may be necessary to start with counteracting beliefs about their own learning potential or about the external causes of failure.

Van Overwalle and his colleagues (1987) used videotapes of students explaining how they had changed their views about the reasons for their poor academic performance. They were able to show that students who were experiencing low levels of performance were helped by their peers to handle difficulties and to recognize their own responsibility for learning outcomes.

### Contextual influences on learning and school ethos

All of these interventions, however, view the learners themselves as being predominantly responsible for the learning outcomes. The teacher is not given direct responsibility for the learning outcomes. The teacher is not considered directly, except in terms of providing appropriate training courses. Psychologists often seem to pay no more than lip-service to the effects of environment on learning, and yet there is a substantial body of evidence, even whole research traditions, which have demonstrated its effects. In the field of personality, for example, Magnusson (1984) has argued that human behavior can only be understood in terms of the inter-action between the individual and the environment. He has gone on to challenge psychologists to identify and measure influential components of environment to complement the detailed mapping of individual differ-ences which has dominated their research in the past. The recent research on student learning has begun to take up that challenge by describing how various components of the learning environment influence both the approach to learning and the levels of understanding reached by students. Several studies have shown that perceptions of assessment procedures have a profound effect on the type of learning that students carry out, and on the way they spend their time. Thus examinations with a heavy factual bias encourage a surface approach in students, leading to rote learning and limited understanding, while questions requiring explanations and interpretations lead students to interact with their learning material in a deeper way which promotes individual understanding (Thomas, 1986). For example, one psychology student, when asked to explain why he was using what seemed to be a surface approach, explained how he was influ-enced by his perceptions of the requirement to take repeated short-answer tests. He believed that rote learning the "facts" would bring high marks in these tests, whereas he was also clear that a similar strategy would not work with the essay-type examinations at the end of the year where understanding was required (Entwistle & Ramsden, 1983).

Group perceptions of assessment procedures are also influential on study strategies and on time allocation. For example, Gibbs (1983) describes how a psychology department asked for speed-reading courses to overcome a problem they had with first-year students. The students were not doing sufficient background reading. Interviews with the students showed that they believed that the marks they obtained on write-ups of their practical work were crucial in determining their progress into the second year of the course. They had therefore been spending much of their time on writing these reports. In reality, the practical marks had little influence on progress, and changing this perception provided more time for background reading.

Besides the assessment procedure itself, the approach to learning has been found to be affected by the quality of feedback on essays and assignments and by the nature of the handouts and learning materials. Hounsell (1984) investigated the ways in which students wrote essays in two contrasting departments. He found that students were strongly influenced by the comments made by tutors. For example, if tutors emphasize the importance of thinking out ideas and coming to a personal conclusion, then a deep approach will be encouraged, whereas an overemphasis on factual detail creates the opposite effect. Similarly, handouts or learning materials which provide students with "all they have to know", while effective in relation to factual examinations, foster dependency on the lecturer, and again lead to a surface approach (Mahmoud, 1989).

The approach to learning is also affected by students' perceptions of the quality of teaching they are receiving and the freedom they are given in deciding what and how to learn. Students have been asked to describe which aspects of teaching promote a deep approach to learning (Entwistle & Ramsden, 1983). Their answers described what would be generally accepted as the components of a good lecture - pitching the material at the right level, presenting it at an appropriate pace, and providing a clear structure. On top of that, students described the effects of striking explanations and enthusiasm, both of which seemed to create interest and a deep approach almost in spite of the student's initial orientation (Hodgson, 1984). Finally, students mentioned the perceived level of empathy of the teacher as influencing how they learned. What must be strongly emphasized is that the learning environment does not affect students uniformly. Assessment which stresses factual answers pushes most students towards surface approaches, but the strength of that approach is still very much a function of the individual. Also it is not the learning environment in a totally objective sense which influences approaches to learning, but students' perceptions of those environments (Entwistle & Tait, 1990). A telling illustration of this comes from Fransson (1977). He investigated the effects of relevance and of a stressful situation on the approach to reading an article. He showed that it was not the allocation of a student to one or other experimental condition which influenced the approach adopted, but the student's own individual perception of whether the article was relevant or the situation stressful. We shall return to this issue in the next section.

Although the effects of the learning environment were initially demonstrated within higher education, similar effects have since been found at school level. The concepts used to describe student learning have been successfully operationalized through inventories used in secondary schools (Entwistle & Kozeki, 1985) and it has been shown how pupils, like students, see their approaches to learning being influenced both by the style and methods of teaching, by the form of assessment, and by time-pressure (Selmes, 1987). Interesting differences have been found between Britain and Hungary suggesting that formal, fact-orientated examinations at age 16+ in Britain may be pushing pupils into surface approaches, whereas the emphasis on ideas in the Hungarian system may be devaluing the importance of detail and evidence (Entwistle & Kozeki, 1985). More recently, attempts have been made to demonstrate the effects of the overall learning environment in a school on approaches to learning, with promising results (Ramsden, Martin & Bowden, 1989; Entwistle, Kozeki & Tait, 1989). Taking these most recent studies into account, it seems that there are good reasons for believing that the coherent set of concepts emerging from the research on student learning can be adapted for use in studies of secondary education. And although there is less evidence about primary education, what has been done suggests that the concepts can be used fruitfully at that level too (Entwistle, 1987a).

## An integrative model of the teaching-learning process

One of the problems in translating psychological principles about learning into effective action in the schools is that the models used by researchers tend to oversimplify the real-life situation to the point where they cease to represent recognizable reality for the practioners.

The model presented by Walberg within the present volume could be criticized on those grounds. From extensive reviews of prediction studies, he is able to outline an impressively parsimonious list of factors shown to influence educational outcomes. But those factors are presented in isolation, both from each other and from the reality of the social situation within which learning takes place. The resultant implications are then described at a level of abstraction which cannot be readily translated into action at classroom level, and so create a problem in effective communication of the ideas and implementation of any recommendations which emerge.

An alternative approach is to identify factors which not only have ecological validity, but also describe classroom reality in a way that teachers can recognize and at a level of specificity which provides a guide to action. Having identified those factors, as has been done in the preceding sections, it is still necessary to show how those factors may interact. At present it is not possible to map all the complex interactions implied by the research studies, but it is possible to provide a heuristic model to guide the thinking of teachers and researchers in relating interventions in education to their place in the interacting system which is a school or college. Failure to understand the nature of these interactions can be seen as one of the reasons for the all too common experience of interventions which have worked in isolation, and which are supported by an impressive body of theory, being rejected by teachers and administrators.

How, then, can the set of concepts described earlier be put together in ways which will point up directions for future fundamental studies? In an attempt to summarize the effects of individual differences and environmental influences on the outcomes of learning, a heuristic model has been developed (see Figure 1 and Entwistle, 1987b). Earlier, Magnusson (1984) was quoted as asking for a mapping of the factors within the environment which interact with individual characteristics. This model can be seen as an attempt at mapping the learning environment of the school or college by presenting those components of the institutional environment which have been shown to influence, or to interact with, learning characteristics in affecting the outcome of learning. The overall model presents concepts describing student characteristics, teaching characteristics, and departmental or institutional policies and procedures, and directs attention to the influence these are likely to have, in interaction, on learning strategies and processes, and on learning outcomes.

Figure 1. A heuristic model of the teaching learning process in higher education.

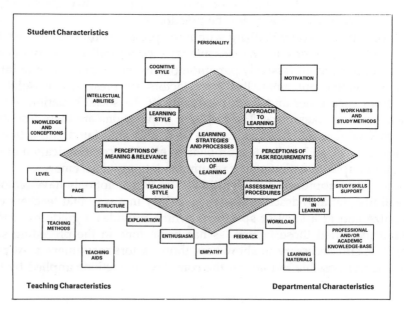

The boxes have been positioned to indicate the relative closeness of relationships. Thus, approach to learning is positioned to indicate its direct functional relationship with learning strategies and processes, and also to show its demonstrated associations with motivation and study methods. "Learning style", used in a more general sense than Pask's, is shown in relation to its component parts, seen as previous knowledge, intellectual abilities, cognitive style and personality. There is a similar attempt in the bottom half of the model to indicate the central position of teaching style and assessment procedures in influencing learning strategies, processes, and outcomes. The meaning of the term "teaching style" has been broadened to include not only preferences for differing methods of teaching and forms of presentation (including teaching aids), but also the components of "good teaching" as perceived by the students. At the moment these components describe only teaching by lecture or teacher talk, but could be extended to cover other forms of classroom teaching and organization.

The positions of the boxes describing teaching have been chosen to indicate probable associations with the student characteristics vertically above them. There are strong logical reasons, and some empirical support, for suggesting that the "level" at which instruction is pitched should be related to a student's previous knowledge and conceptualizations, and similarly that the "pace" of presentation should depend on the student's intellectual abilities. These boxes in the model are intended to emphasize the importance of appropriate matching the content and pacing of courses to the students' existing knowledge and abilities. Continuing round the model, the types of "structure" and "explanation" used can be seen as reflecting the stylistic preferences of the lecturer, which may or may not coincide with those of the students, while "enthusiasm" and "empathy" are seen as reflecting differences in the teacher's personality which again will influence an individual student's perception of the teaching being provided. Again the evidence presented in earlier sections showed how a single mode of presentation would not suit all students. The possibility of developing alternative instructional styles designed to produce a better match between student and instruction is one of the growth points we shall explore in the final section.

It is not possible to establish such a clear patterning in relation to departmental or institutional characteristics, although feedback, workload and freedom in learning, can all be seen as describing aspects of assessment procedures which have been shown to affect students' approaches to learning. The effect of different kinds of study skills support on student learning has already been described in some detail, and taken in conjunction with the research on metacognition and self-regulated learning, provides another important growth point to be taken up later. The position of "learning materials" within the model is less easy to justify from research evidence. Such materials may be more under the control of the teacher and could be placed alongside teaching aids, but its relationship with approach to learning determined its position in the model. The box at the bottom right-hand corner of the model is included as a reminder that the workload and assessment procedures will often reflect established consensus about what is appropriate in that subject area.

A final feature of the model is the positioning of the two "perceptions" boxes. Their position is intended to indicate that the learning environment does not generally influence students in direct or consistent ways. It is an individual student's perception of the situation which has a functional relationship with the student's attitudes and activities, and that perception depends as much on the student's own characteristics as on the more objective features of the environment. Thus, for example, a student who has holistic learning preferences is likely to react favorably to a teacher who has an expansive teaching style which enriches the content with illustrative material and anecdote, while a serialist, in contrast, may consider the same teacher to be a confusing exhibitionist incapable of providing a sufficiently tight and logical analysis.

Much of the research summarized earlier emphasizes the effects of a specific intervention on a defined population of students without specifying the contextual situations. Such interventions, if introduced into the educational system itself, cannot work in the same way. We need to develop a model of the teaching-learning process which allows us to conceptualize interventions in a more holistic way which takes account of several of the most significant contextual variables together. For example, the above model allows us to deduce that there would be no point in introducing even carefully targeted study skills support if the assessment, feedback, and teaching procedures all led students to believe that factual reproduction was the most essential feature of learning. It needs an analysis at the system level within an institution to design procedures which will consistently reinforce and support defined learning objectives. Already there are some examples of this beginning to happen in higher education (Eizenburg, 1988) where a department has defined objectives in terms of learning outcomes, and then looked systematically at teaching content and style, recommended textbooks, handouts, tutorial support, assessment and feedback to ensure that all of these components actively support the desired approaches to learning and studying in the students and so lead to the required learning outcomes. To date, a similar system-level analysis at schoollevel has not been carried out, at least in relation to the set of concepts described in this paper and yet it is clear that students are influenced by aspects of the learning environment beyond those found in the classroom itself. There are also influences which are a product of the institution and come under the heading of "school ethos" or "institutional climate". Recent work on the definition and measurement of school climate, learning environment and school ethos suggests another line for fundamental studies to follow.

## A research agenda for fundamental studies

The starting point of this chapter was an investigation of the effects of teaching on learning, but the research evidence presented has broadened the focus to take in a variety of other factors within the learning environment which also influence learning. The model presented in the previous section can be used as a map not only of those factors, but also of the potential interactions between those factors and specific characteristics of the learner.

These interactions provide some of the most promising growth points for fundamental studies in this area. It is suggested that there might be a series of investigations into some of the more interesting interactions identified in the earlier review sections. The studies suggested have also been chosen to provide a gradual broadening in the definition of the learning environment. The first study focuses narrowly on the interaction between the teacher and the individual learner in the development of understanding. The second looks at ways of developing metacognitive skills and intrinsic motivation in the learner through a program of studies in one or more components of the curriculum, while the final study suggests an examination of the effects of the whole institutional ethos, as perceived by the students, on the quality of learning outcomes. The evidence presented in previous sections has already indicated why the suggested investigations are important and likely to have an influence on both teaching and learning. These three interactions will now be discussed in more detail to indicate the nature of the research questions which might be addressed in fundamental studies.

One of the most basic questions of all relates to the ways in which students develop and demonstrate their understanding of what they have learned. In an earlier section it was suggested that students may not store concepts in the way previously suggested by psychologists. There is accumulating evidence that conceptions are brought into being through attempts to apply knowledge and experience to specific situations, and so they may have no continued existence in cognitive structure. Facts are stored, and so are procedures, but the way these two aspects of knowledge combine to develop abstract understanding is far from clear. And yet the facilitating of understanding is at the heart of educational objectives.

It would be fruitful to use the phenomenographic techniques of research to carry out studies to answer the question "How do students use factual knowledge to develop idiosyncratic forms of representation and personal understanding?" Packs of information could be prepared which students would use to answer general questions designed to test understanding. The stylistic differences in explanation could already be anticipated from Pask's work, but other interesting differences could be investigated, particularly if questions were asked in a way which tested whether a concept was being utilized in different ways in relation to each specific question or situation. This work would be fundamental in the sense of necessarily preceding any investigation of the influence of teaching or assessment procedures on the quality of learning.

This investigation could be extended to the characteristics of teachers which facilitate the development of understanding. Observational studies could be combined with interviews to identify which ways of presenting information encourage the types of reorganizing and restructuring which seem to be essential to the development of understanding. The previous research shows that striking real-world illustrations seem to encourage a deep approach to learning, but the effect of differing learning styles suggests that there would be marked variations in the effectiveness of such explanations. Some students would probably benefit more from carefully structured, logical developments, while for certain individual purposes personal understanding would not be sought and then factual presentation would be preferred. With the advent of the microcomputer it would be possible to store a variety of different forms of explanation, based on the observational studies indicated above, which could be presented in controlled sequence to students whose learning style and preferred approach had previously been identified from inventory responses. In this way fundamental studies could address the question "To what extent does the form of explanation affect the level of understanding of students with contrasting learning styles?"

This question would lead to a fundamental study of the cognitive interaction between teacher and student which could feed into subsequent intervention strategies designed to influence both teachers in the classroom and the design of learning materials - books, classroom materials and computer-based learning programs. The question is posed in a way which reflects a particular view of the teaching-learning process, and one which contrasts markedly with the more behaviorist model presented by Walberg, for example. In his chapter, the quality of instruction is described in terms of "optimal cues", "correctives", and "reinforcement". From a behaviorist perspective, this can be taken to describe good instruction, but it is based on a model of learning which is in sharp contrast to the constructivist perspective adopted here, and would lead to very different implications for teachers.

In looking at the next area, motivation and study methods, the theoretical bases again lead to research questions which are very different to those implied by Walberg's view of learning. Motivation is seen in his chapter as the "willingness to persevere on learning tasks" and that is thought to be enhanced and maintained through the use of rewards, such as tokens. The research reviewed in this chapter suggests that such reinforcement would maintain high levels of extrinsic motivation and so encourage surface approaches to learning. In contrast, intrinsic motivation would be maintained by ensuring that the content had a high level of interest and relevance, and rewards would take the form of enhanced understanding of the world around. The question emerging from the studies on motivation, study skill, and aptitude-treatment research reviewed in earlier sections addresses the enhancement of intrinsic motivation and the development of self-awareness in studying at different ability levels. This question has been framed so as to bring together the evidence on motivation and feelings of self-worth with the work on self-regulated learning and study orientation. The implications for teaching and learning seem to be so convergent that a single research direction can be seen.

This range of studies suggests that there is a way of teaching which would develop what Corno has called "self-regulated learning" and strengthen metacognitive skills in a way which would enhance intrinsic or self-motivation and so support a deep approach to learning. Although the techniques described in the various studies mentioned earlier are rather different, their purpose is very similar - to make the students more aware of the active role they must play in learning, from defining the problem, through reviewing existing knowledge and monitoring progress,to reviewing the quality of the outcome and considering implications for future learning. Couched in abstract terms this may seem idealized, and yet several studies have shown that even ten-year-old pupils are well able to develop this metacognitive awareness which seems to be at the heart of the deep approach to learning. There are, however, caveats in the literature about the extent to which less able, or less motivated, pupils would develop these strategies, and this limitation in generality would have to be investigated.

An interesting question for fundamental studies is thus "To what extent can students of differing ages, levels of motivation, and abilities be taught to use metacognitive strategies, and what effect, if any, does such training have on their performance in schoolwork?" Again there are inventory measures of motivation and approaches to learning available at school level, and the literature indicates techniques which could be integrated to provide a coherent program for teachers to use. Such a program would have to be built up in one or more subject areas, not taught as a separate "add on" unit. It would involve the teacher in discussing with the students how to tackle a series of problems or tasks. The teacher would initially model the strategies used, and then provide a heuristic which would encourage students to develop their own strategies. It would also be necessary to provide opportunities for collaborative learning or discussions designed to draw attention to the strategies and learning processes being used.

To be confident about the effects of these interventions, there would have to be training programs for teachers, as the emphasis on process, rather than content, often proves particularly difficult for teachers to accept and use effectively. It would also be necessary to target the interventions on one or more specific areas of the curriculum and at age levels where substantial interventions would be accepted by the authorities. Again without the interventions becoming an accepted and reasonably substantial part of the curriculum, their effects would be slight and transitory. Finally, ways of assessing the outcomes of learning would have to be developed which emphasized qualitative differences in understanding - as this is the prime target of the intervention. There already exists a variety of such methods of educational measurement, from conventional examinations using open and fairly general questions supported by evaluation, through the SOLO taxonomy (Biggs & Collis, 1982), to techniques which use concept mapping (Novak & Gowin, 1984).

The question posed above may be seen as only partly fundamental. Certainly, the development of metacognitive strategies needs to be understood before interventions are evaluated, but here the idea of such an investigation being carried out within classroom environments may suggest that we are no longer considering a fundamental study. The proposed investigation could, of course, be adapted so as to focus on the use of metacognitive strategies within controlled laboratory conditions, and thus become fully fundamental. It would then, however, lose both ecological validity and practical utility. There seems to be a real danger in drawing the division between fundamental and applied studies too firmly. There can be no absolute divide, and the advantages to be gained by carrying out fundamental studies within the actual classroom context seem to outweigh the need for defining them narrowly. It depends ultimately on the model of educational research that is adopted, and there is by now sufficient doubt about the conventional "scientific" paradigm to tread warily in its application. If we are to use concepts and theories which have demonstrable ecological validity, those concepts and theories need to be developed and tested within the specific context in which we are interested. In some sense at least, if the definition of fundamental studies is kept so narrow that the studies are decontextualized, the opportunities subsequently to devise effective interventions may be jeopardized. Also, if learning outcomes are the result of a complex interaction between learner characteristics and the learning environment, even contextualized examination of one particular component may be invalid, if extrapolated back into the everyday educational context. It is this degree of specificity and complexity that helps to explain the limited success of both psychological and sociological theories in guiding effective instruction.

The final question takes up the thrust of the research which led to the heuristic model, and looks at the influence of learning environment on the quality of learning. The model stresses the importance of considering the effects of the interactions which occur within a whole school or college setting, and in particular indicates how the students' perceptions of the teaching and assessment procedures they experience influence the ways in which they go about studying. The research question which could then be posed might take the form "What influence do institutional ethos and learning environment, as perceived by the students, have on the quality of the learning which takes place within that institution?" The question is phrased in such a way that it could be asked about either a school or a college. There is a great deal of research needing to be done in tertiary education, as well as at school level.

This question can thus be seen to be fundamental in the sense of being general, as well as investigating a fundamental question relating to the way students perceive their learning environments. If such a question is seen to be too general, then it would be possible to identify specific components indicated by the models which have been shown to influence the quality of learning, such as the type of feedback and the form of examination, and then systematically to explore their influence on learning processes and outcomes. The latter approach would be easier to operationalize as the students' perceptions would be less disparate. The broader question seems more interesting and far-reaching in terms of fundamental studies, but it would involve a difficult technical problem in defining and measuring the students' perceptions of institutional ethos. Some preliminary work on this has, however, already been carried out as part of the studies looking at the influences of the learning environment on approaches to learning, both in higher education (as described earlier) and in schools. The learning environment in schools can be measured through self-report inventories drawing on definitions of the learning environment which are either narrowly focused on the teaching and support for learning experienced (Ramsden, Martin & Bowden, 1989) or more broadly based on climate and perceived ethos as well (Entwistle, Kozeki & Tait,

1989). In the latter study it was the heuristic model which suggested the components of the learning environment which should be investigated.

The importance of this line of research would be partly in its own right by providing a better understanding of the interactions between the learner, the teacher, and the learning environment. But it would also be valuable in complementing other studies which investigated learning and instruction either in isolation or within a limited or controlled context. By carrying out analyses at school level it would highlight differences between schools or colleges, as perceived by the students, and might begin to identify which particular features of the institution were related to differences in the way that students within it went about their work. In the British context, the importance of finding out what students think about the institution has been highlighted by the determination of the government to make schools and colleges more accountable to the public for their work. Schools, in particular, will need to be more aware of their local reputation and the systematic exploration of pupils' perceptions would be a useful starting point. In this way what began as a fundamental study might feed into policy issues, but it remains fundamental in the sense that its origins were in the research literature, and the implications of the findings would be wide-ranging.

The stance taken in this attempt to derive directions for fundamental studies has been to argue that those studies should be chosen in ways which are more likely to lead to a successful intervention in the future. A serious problem arises if fundamental studies are chosen from a theoretical perspective which is remote from the everyday context of teaching and learning. There can be no clear idea of whether the interventions such studies might suggest would work equally well in a real-life setting, nor could there be any indication as to whether the interventions would be acceptable to the teaching profession. Such potential barriers to successful implementation need to be considered at an early stage in the planning process, otherwise future support for educational research may be at risk. Increasingly, policy makers are looking for outcomes of research which can be shown to be useful, even if that utility is well into the future.

Fundamental studies are of great importance to the effectiveness of education; they allow advances in research to influence the otherwise rather traditional approaches to teaching and learning which persist within the educational system. But it is important that the relevance of the fundamental studies is carefully evaluated. The design of the studies should be informed by theories which appropriately describe the specific contexts found in education and be directed towards the ultimate purpose of educational research - an improvement in the quality of education.

# References

Ames, R.E. & C. Ames (1984) *Motivation in education.* volume 1. New York: Academic Press.

Ausubel, D.P., J.S. Novak & H. Hanesian (1978) *Educational psychology: a cognitive view.* New York: Holt. Rinehart & Winston.

Bennett, S.N. (1976) Dimensions of study behaviour: another look at a.t.i. *British Journal of Educational Psychology,* Vol. 46, pp. 68-80.

Biggs, J.B. (1985) The role of metalearning in study processes. *British Journal of Educational Psychology,* Vol. 55, pp. 185-212.

Biggs, J.B. & K.F. Collis (1982) *Evaluating the quality of learning: The SOLO taxonomy.* New York: Academic Press.

Biggs, J.B. & B. Rihn (1984) The effects of intervention on deep and surface approaches to learning. In: J.R. Kirby (ed.) *Cognitive strategies and educational performance.* New York: Academic Press.

Bloom, B.S. (1977) *Human characteristics and school learning.* New York: McGraw Hill.

Brophy, J. (1987) Socializing student motivation to learn. In: M.L. Maehr & D.A. Kleiber (eds.) *Advances in motivation and achievement,* volume 5. Greenwich, CT: JAI Press.

Carroll, J.B. (1963) A model of school learning. *Teachers College Record P,* Vol. 64, pp. 723-733.

Cohen, G. (1983) *The psychology of cognition.* London: Academic Press.

Corno, L. (1986) *Self-regulated learning and classroom teaching.* Paper presented at the Annual Meeting of the American Educational Research Association in San Francisco, April.

Covington, M. (1983) Motivated cognitions. In: S.G. Paris, G.M. Olson & H.W. Stevenson (eds.) *Learning and Motivation in the Classroom.* Hillsdale, N.J.: Lawrence Erlbaum.

Cronbach, L.J. (1967) How can instruction be adapted to individual differences? In: R.M. Gagné (ed.) *Learning and individual differences.* Columbus: Charles Merrill.

Driver, R. & G. Erickson (1983) Theories-in-action: some theoretical and empirical issues in the study of students' conceptual networks. *Studies in Science Education,* Vol. 10, pp. 37-60.

Eizenberg, N. (1988) Approaches to learning anatomy: developing a programme for preclinical medical students. In: P. Ramsden (ed.) *Improving learning: New perspectives.* London: Kogan.

Entwistle, N.J. (1981) *Styles of learning and teaching.* London: Wiley.

Entwistle, N.J. & P. Ramsden (1983) *Understanding student learning.* London: Croom Helm.

Entwistle, N.J (1987a) *Understanding classroom learning.* London: Hodder & Stoughton.

Entwistle, N.J. (1987b) A model of the teaching-learningprocess. In: J.T.E. Richardson, M.W. Eysenck & D. Warren Piper (eds.) *Student learning: Research in education and cognitive psychology.* London: S.R.H.E./Open University Press.

Entwistle, N.J. (1988) Motivation and learning strategies.in: R.R. Schmeck (ed.) *Learning Styles and Strategies.* New York: Plenum Press.

Entwistle, N.J. & B. Kozeki (1985) Relationships between schoolmotivation, approaches to studying, and attainment among British and Hungarian adolescents. *British Journal of Educational Psychology*, Vol. 55, pp. 124-37.

Entwistle, N.J., B. Kozeki & H. Tait (1989) Pupils' perceptions of school and teachers. *British Journal of Educational Psychology*, Vol. 59, (in press).

Entwistle, N.J. & K.A. Percy (1974) Critical thinking or conformity? An investigation of the aims and outcomes of higher education. In: C.F. Page & J. Gibson (eds.) *Research into higher education, 1973.* London: Society for Research into Higher Education.

Entwistle, N.J. & H. Tait (1990) Approaches to learning, evaluations of teaching, and perceptions of the learning environment. *Higher Education* (in press).

Entwistle, N.J. & S. Waterston (1988) Approaches to learning and levels of processing in university students. *British Journal of Educational Psychology*, Vol. 58, pp. 258-265.

Eysenck, H.J. & L. Kamin (1981) *The battle for the mind.* London: McMillan.

Fransson, A. (1977) On qualitative differences in learning IV-Effects of motivation and test anxiety on process and outcome. *British Journal of Educational Psychology*, Vol. 47, pp. 244-257.

Gamoran, A. (1987) Organization, instruction, and the effects of ability grouping. *Review of Educational Research*, Vol. 57, pp. 341-345.

Gardner, H. (1984) *Frames of mind.* London: Heinemann.

Gardner, H. (1985) The development and education of intelligences. In: F. Link (ed.) *Essays on the intellect.* Washington, DC: Curriculum Development Associates.

Gibbs, G. (1981) *Teaching students to learn.* Milton Keynes: Open University Press.

Greeno, J.G. (1989) A perspective on thinking. *American Psychologist* (in press).

Gustafsson, J-E. (1987) Individual differences and instruction;micro- and macro-adaptation. In: E. de Corte, H. Lodewijks, R. Parmentier & P. Span (eds.) *Learning and Instruction:European Research in an International Context.* Oxford: Pergamon.

Hiebert, E.H. (1987) The context of instruction and student learning. *Review of Educational Research*, Vol. 57, pp. 337-340.

Hodgson, V. (1984) Learning from lectures. In: F. Marton, D.J. Hounsell & N.J. Entwistle (eds.) *The experience of learning*. Edinburgh: Scottish Academic Press.

Hounsell, D.J. (1984) Learning and essay writing. In: F. Marton, D.J. Hounsell & N.J. Entwistle (eds.) *The experience of learning*. Edinburgh: Scottisch Academic Press.

Jenson, A.R. (1970) Hierarchical theories of mental ability. In: W.B. Dockrell (ed.) *On intelligence*. London: Methuen.

Kozeki, B. (1985) Motives and motivational styles. In: N.J. Entwistle (ed.) *New directions in educational psychology*, volume 1. Lewes: Falmer Press.

Laurillard, D. (1984) Learning from problem-solving. In: F. Marton, D.J. Hounsell & N.J. Entwistle (eds.) *The experience of learning*. Edinburgh: Scottish Academic Press.

Leith, G.O.M. (1974) Individual differences in learning interactions of personality and teaching methods. In:*Personality and Academic Progress*. (No editor named). London: Assoc. of Educational Psychologists.

Magnusson, D. (1984) The situation in an interactional paradigm of personality research. In: V. Sarris & A. Parducci (eds.) *Perspectives in psychological experimentation: Towards the year 2000*. Hillsdale, N.J.: Erlbaum.

Martin, E. & P. Ramsden (1987) Learning skills or skill in learning? In: J.T.E. Richardson, M.W. Eysenck & D. Warren Piper (eds.) *Student learning: Research ineducation and cognitive psychology*. Milton Keynes: Open University Press.

Mahmoud, M. (1989) Contrasting perceptions of an innovation in engineering education. *European Journal of the Psychology of Education*, (in press).

Marton, F. (1988) *Phenomenography and "The art of teaching all things to all men."* Research report. University of Gothenburg: Department of Education.

Marton, F. & R. Saljö (1976) On qualitative differences in learning. II - Outcome and process. *British Journal of Educational Psychology*, Vol. 46, pp. 4-11.

Marton, F. & R. Saljö (1984) Approaches to learning. In: F. Marton, D.J. Hounsell & N.J. Entwistle (eds.) *The experience of learning*. Edinburgh: Scottish Academic Press.

Nisbet, J.D. & J. Shucksmith (1986) *Learning Strategies*. London: Routledge & Kegan Paul.

Novak, J.D. & D.B. Gowin (1984). *Learning how to learn*. Cambridge: University Press.

Pask, G. (1976) Learning styles and strategies. *British Journal of Educational Psychology*, Vol. 46, pp. 4-11.

Pask, G. (1988)  Learning strategies, teaching strategies and conceptual or learning style. In: R.R. Schmeck (ed.) *Learning styles and strategies*. New York: Plenum.

Pfundt, H. & R. Duit (1986)  *Bibliography: Students' alternative frameworks*. Kiel, West Germany: Institut für die Pädagogik der Naturwissenschaften.

Prosser, M. & R. Millar (1989)  The 'how' and 'what' of learning physics. *European Journal of the Psychology of Education*, (in press).

Ramsden, P. (1981)  *A study of the relationship between student learning and its academic context*. Unpublished Ph.D. thesis, University of Lancaster.

Ramsden, P., E. Martin & J. Bowden (1989)  Study approaches and school effectiveness: the influence of school environment on sixth-form pupils' learning processes. *British Journal of Educational Psychology*, Vol. 59, (in press).

Rogers, C.R. (1969)  *Freedom to learn*. Columbus, Ohio: Merrill.

Rollett, B (1987)  Effort avoidance and learning. In: E. de Corte, H. Lodewijks, R. Parmentier & P. Span (eds.) *Learning and instruction: European research in an international context*. Oxford: Pergamon.

Roth, K & C. Anderson (1988)  Promoting conceptual change  learning from science textbooks. In: P. Ramsden (ed.) *Improving learning: New perspectives*. London: Kogan Page.

Schmeck, R.R. (1983)  Learning styles of college students. In: R. Dillon & R.R. Schmeck (eds.) *Individual differences in cognition*. New York: Academic Press.

Selmes, I.P. (1987)  *Improving Study Skills*. London: Hodder & Stoughton.

Slavin, R.E. (1987)  Ability grouping and student achievement in elementary schools: a best-evidence synthesis. *Review of Educational Research*, Vol. 57, pp. 293-336.

Snow, R.E. & D.F. Lohman (1984)  Towards a theory of cognitive aptitude for learning from instruction. *Journal of Educational Psychology*, Vol. 76, pp. 347-376.

Sperry, R. (1983)  *Science and moral priority*. Oxford: Blackwell.

Speth, C. & R. Brown (1988)  Study approaches, study processes and strategies: are three perspectives better than one?*British Journal of Educational Psychology*, Vol. 58, pp. 247-257.

Sternberg, R.J. (1985)  *Beyond IQ: a triarchic theory of human intelligence*. Cambridge: University Press.

Sternberg, R.J. & D.K. Detterman (1986)  *What is intelligence?* Norwood, N.J.: Ablex Publishing Co.

Svensson, L. (1977)  On qualitative differences in learning. III-Study skill and learning. *British Journal of Educational Psychology*, Vol. 47, pp. 233-243.

Svensson, L. (1984) Skill in learning. In: F. Marton, D.J. Hounsell & N.J. Entwistle (eds.) *The experience of learning*. Edinburgh: Scottish Academic Press.

Svensson, L. (1989) The conceptualisation of cases of physical motion. *European Journal of the Psychology of Education*, (in press).

Thomas, P.R. (1986) *The structure and stability of learning approaches*. Unpublished doctoral dissertation, University of Queensland.

Trown, E.A. & G.O.M. Leith (1975) Decision rules for teaching strategies in primary schools: personality-treatment interactions. *British Journal of Educational Psychology*, Vol. 45, pp. 130-140.

Van Overwalle, F., K. Segebarth & M. Goldchstein (1987) *Improving performance of freshmen through attibutional testimonies from fellow students*. Duplicated report, Unit EDUCO, Free University of Brussels.

Watkins, D. (1983) Depth of processing and the quality of learning outcomes. *Instructional Science*, Vol. 12, pp. 49-58.

Weiner, B. (1984) Principles for a theory of student motivation and their application within an attributional framework. In: R.E. Ames & C. Ames (eds.) *Motivation in education*, volume 1. New York: Academic Press.

Weinstein, C., E.T. Goetz & P.A. Alexander (1988) *Learning and study strategies*. New York: Academic Press.

West, L. (1988) Implications of recent research for improving secondary school science learning. In: P. Ramsden (ed.) *Improving learning: New perspectives*. London: Kogan Page.

Westbury, I. (1977) *The curriculum and the frames of the classroom*. Paper presented at the AERA annual meeting.

Witkin, H.A., C.A. More, D.R. Goodenough & P.W. Cox (1977) Field-dependent and field-independent cognitive styles and their educational implications. *Review of Educational Research*, Vol. 47, pp. 1-64.

# The World as an Educational Laboratory

Alan C. Purves
The University at Albany
USA

One kind of educational research that has grown over the years has been that of comparative and international studies. Although historians and anthropologists of education as well as educational planners had been looking at other systems of education for a long time it was not until the 1960s that the idea of comparative studies other than the descriptive came into prominence. One of the major catalysts in that change was the formation of the organization that came to be known as the International Association for the Evaluation of Educational Achievement or IEA. A recent issue of The Comparative Education Review gives something of the history and flavor of the organization (Husén, 1987; Postlethwaite, 1987; Purves, 1987) which I shall summarize briefly. I shall concentrate on the work of IEA in this paper, in part because it represents the sort of research I know best, and in part because I think it is illustrative of the value of comparative educational research as opposed to national or subnational research on the one hand and comparative statistics on the other.

In the late 1950s IEA started as an organization of researchers from around the world who found that they were concerned with a number of issues that could not be studied well within the confines of one school system. The reason for this is that most systems are more or less uniform with respect to such matters as class size, age of school starting, length of the

school year, comprehensive secondary schooling and the like. If one wanted to study the effects of these variables, one needed to design costly and
politically risky experiments. There was however "natural variation" if one
were to go beyond the borders of a single geographic unit. The idea of
comparative empirical studies of achievement and its antecedents and
consequents was thus born.

One of the first problems the group faced was that of creating comparable
measures, tests that could be used across languages and cultures. The initial experiments showed that this task was feasible, so a full-scale study of
mathematics was launched in the early 1960s and was followed by the
"six-subject survey" (reading, literature, science, civic education, and
English and French as foreign languages) in the 1970s. During the course
of the past decade, IEA has conducted a second study in mathematics and
science, a study of written composition, and one of classroom environments. IEA is currently conducting studies of pre-primary education and
computers in education. It is also launching a study of reading literacy, the
first in a series of projected cyclic studies of learning in the basic school
subjects, and is contemplating a study of social values and moral reasoning.

In general IEA's methodology has been one of survey research, with an
emphasis on careful test construction combined with sets of questionnaires
for students, teachers and school heads as well as "national" curriculum
questionnaires and supplementary histories and interviews. Over the
course of its history, IEA has used various approaches to the analysis of
the data and has been among the pioneers of various sorts of causal mod-
elling and analysis. Although the studies are surveys, they are surveys
that take into account and, indeed, are predicated upon the differences
that exist among the schools and systems surveyed. The studies are what
Michael Cole refers to as "comparative" studies, those which take research
out of the laboratory and into the real world, or that see the world as a
"naturally" existing laboratory. The IEA studies enable researchers and
policy-makers to view alternative strategies and structures in education.

In the last decade of this century the sorts of surveys that IEA pioneered
have become commonplace within educational systems as national assess-
ments and various international organizations contemplate the collection
of data on student achievement, particularly in the basic skills, as well as
on other educational indicators. In many cases, they do so with the view of
the world or the nation not as a laboratory but as a competition. Such an
approach appeals to educational policymakers, who are able to tie budgets
to relative success or failure in an educational horserace. They may ask
why it is important to do cross-national comparative research, as an addition to the provision of cross-national indicators for monitoring systems.

I would suggest that there are a number of answers to that question. All of the answers point to the importance of seeing the world as a laboratory containing natural variation. All of the answers would see that the focus of research must be on the educational system as a system involving schools, classes, teachers, students, and communities. Comparatively speaking each of these systems has its unique features; at the same time all have common threads. In particular, all systems must cope with a number of issues, some of which have been raised by prior IEA research, and some have yet to be fully studied. Among the first group of issues I would set the following: exploration of the curriculum and particularly opportunity to learn; exploration of the effects of tracking and streaming; and exploration of the relationship of achievement in a positivist sense to styles and patterns of thinking about the subject. Among the second group I would argue that the following issues could benefit from cross national study: the educational fortunes of ethnic and linguistic minorities; the tracking of efforts to educate the semi-literate underclass; and the changing educational patterns in third world countries. These are all fundamental educational problems which occur in many countries around the world.

## Opportunity to learn

Over the course of their history, the IEA studies have been remarkably consistent in identifying as one of the main variables that lies behind differences between systems of education in student achievement, "opportunity to learn." This phrase has been used to describe the actual class instruction in a subject, which may differ from what is in the official syllabus. Opportunity to learn has been a remarkably good predictor of the relative achievement of large groups, although not as good a predictor of differences between students. As far as I know, it is a feature unique to IEA measures, and one that has been consistently used since the first mathematics study in the early 1960s. The index is based on an indication by the students tested or by their teachers as to whether the material or process or concept measured by a specific item has been presented to the student and how recently it has been presented. The various IEA studies have experimented with different ways of determining OTL. In some cases it has been by a single question; in some by a set of questions that seek to disentangle curricular history; and in some by a series of detailed questions on methods of teaching. There have also been interviews of teachers after the testing as well as interviews and questionnaires given to the students themselves. In two studies the same measures have been given to both student and teacher with a request to estimate the order of importance of various items.

Whatever the method, the result has been to show that at the operational level of schooling there is variation between systems of education as to the opportunity students have had to master a particular concept, learn a particular procedure, or adopt a particular cognitive style, each of which is seen as an important aspect of schooling. The OTL indices have often explained systematic differences in student performance in terms of choice, not chance. If one looks across systems of education, one finds that in mathematics and science, different sub-topics are covered; in reading, literature, and writing different genres and different strategies are stressed; in foreign languages different emphases are placed on the skills of reading, writing, speaking, and listening; in civic education different priorities are set among the various civic and familial values.

Across this variation, the IEA studies have been remarkable in the degree to which they have identified common concepts, common skills, and common values. These might be thought of as the International Basic Skills. The common skills are modified by the tradition and history of a culture and its school system. Even mathematics, seemingly most immune from cultural influence, has been shown in the recently completed IEA study to have cultural overtones that distinguish the learning of algebra in Japan from that in Swaziland or Costa Rica. In reading comprehension, science, and written composition studies, the same picture emerges. Although there may be variation as to the types of texts read or written and the particular linguistic and orthographic systems, such aspects of reading comprehension as analysis and interpretation or of writing as structural coherence and appropriateness of style have universal dimensions. The IEA studies reflect not cultural or educational imperialism but the subtle interplay between national and international definitions of performance in the basic skills.

Opportunity to learn has appeared in a variety of subjects that IEA has studied, and as a phenomenon has had the potential of challenging the idea of growth or development as an explanation of why students within a system do not do well on a particular task. Within a system the argument is often that "they are not ready for it," or are not mature enough to do it. When it is shown that in other systems of education students do perfectly well on the same task, this argument loses its strength. This use of opportunity to learn has not been made fully enough, and the very concept has not been studied as fully as it might. One of the research questions that might arise asks in what other aspects of the curriculum might we see the phenomenon working. It seems that cross-national studies call into question the assumptions about "growth" or "development" that operate within a given culture and show that many of the so-called "universals" of human learning can be reinterpreted as functions of a society's particular curriculum. Such questions need to be sharpened and studied more carefully in future research. They can only be addressed in an international comparative framework.

## The effects of tracking and streaming

The previous IEA studies have shown that students who are in the "lower" or less able tracks or streams of the educational system tend to fall behind. Although this might not seem to be a particularly significant finding, some of the early studies showed that students in non-streamed systems performed better than their counterparts in streamed systems. The reasons for this finding are not clear. They may have something to do with the mix of students and their impact on the teacher, or they may result from the curriculum itself (see Entwistle, this book). More recently, certain analyses of IEA studies have suggested that the curriculum may be the better answer.

In the recent mathematics study and in the Written Composition study, there is evidence in several countries that students in the "lower" tracks are presented with a curriculum that almost guarantees that the students will not achieve at more than a minimal level. These curricula focus on the repetition and drill of very simple material, material that keeps the students attending to the surface features of the subject at the expense of the more important concepts. Students in lower mathematics groups repeat the same sorts of arithmetical exercises and so never really move on to the next unit and to the more salient mathematical concepts. Similarly, students in mother-tongue keep practicing work in writing grammatical and error free-sentences and so never attend to the discourse-level issues of composition.

These findings parallel similar findings in the earlier IEA studies, particularly in reading and literature, where lower track students practiced decoding skills and never got to comprehension and interpretation. In some school systems, these same students were not given materials to read, but films and other mass media and so were denied access to the culture that they were blamed for not having. The analysis of the science data in several systems of education suggests that the same phenomenon occurs in that subject as well; there appear to be major differences in the curriculum depending upon the program in which the students are enrolled.

The question that needs to be examined through the natural laboratory approach is what actual curricular variables operate in those systems that have grouping. Another thrust would be to study those systems in which there is no ability grouping or in which the curricular materials and offerings remain constant across ability groups. What happens when students who are supposedly less able are indeed offered the material that is given to the brighter or more fortunate? There is enough anecdotal evidence across systems of education that the lower group of students can learn if only they are given something of importance to learn. In sampling their school systems, the participating members should seek to identify and single out the schools which appear to be anomalous. Such has been planned as an option in the IEA Reading Literacy Study so that one can single out those schools where students perform higher than would be expected given the social class of the students and the type of school in which they are enrolled. That having been done, the research team can visit those schools and explore in depth the possible explanations of their success.

## Achievement and styles of conceiving the subject

In some of the earlier IEA studies, attention was paid to aspects of achievement besides a cognitive test score. In the first Science Study there was a Test of the Understanding of Science which tapped something of the ways in which the students conceived of the subject science. In the Literature Study there was a response preference measure, which determined the characteristic approach to texts that students had acquired as an aspect of their instruction in literature. In the recent Written Composition Study there was a measure which asked the students to define achievement in writing in their school. There was also an opportunity to examine differences in approach to the composition assignment among students from the various systems to see if there was such a phenomenon as a national style. The Second Mathematics Study was able to determine characteristic modes of conceiving the subject among teachers in the participating systems. The Reading Literacy Study is going to include a measure of reading practices, which can be seen as an index of the uses of reading as learned in the schools and supported by the community.

Different as these studies are, they all suggest that learning in a school subject is not simply the matter of the acquisition of particular skills or pieces of knowledge. Learning a school subject in any system of education bears with it the acquisition of sets of habits and preferences concerning the subject of study. These sets are complex and perhaps culturally determined, but they are more than side-effects of education, they may - in some instances - be the central outcome of learning.

This finding suggests that it is important for researchers to see the extent to which school systems tend to establish communities of learning that are regional, national, or transnational. Is there a common conception of the subject that enables easy communication across regional or national groups or are there some barriers to communication? To what extent do cultural differences occur in the conception of a particular school subject that may enhance or inhibit learning? At a more particular level the issue may be framed as asking whether certain groups of students are limited in their achievement because they have a conception of the subject that is at variance with that which prevails. In composition, for example, certain groups of students appear to see achievement only in terms of handwriting, neatness, and spelling. These are the students who appear to fail to produce meaningful discourse when they write. Is the problem that they do not have a larger view of the subject or is it that the instruction they have undergone fastens on the surface features rather than such aspects of discourse as content structure, or style? It would appear that the problem exists in subjects like mathematics and science as well, where conceptions about the subject field may both be culturally determined and potentially inhibiting of learning for some groups.

Comparative studies at their best seek to uncover the complexity of causes that may underlie the differences in learning of a particular subject by groups around the world. The IEA studies have come to show that learning in any subject is multivalent. Achievement is not a simple matter of a unidimensional score, but it involves the learning of procedures and approaches with respect to the subject. We may say that these and other more detailed studies in particular settings that have followed the comparative approach studies have given empirical proof to the activity theory of Vygotsky and his followers. They have shown that school subjects must be seen as complex activities made up of their constituent acts and operations. Further they are culturally embedded particularly in the procedures and approaches, which constitute an important part of what it means to be a member of the educated group in a society. Across the range of societies in the world these procedures and approaches are not uniform so that the activity of literacy or mathematics, or science, or even education is not monolithic. Educational systems and the subject communities that are contained in them are culturally situated, and a simple test of achievement runs the risk of neglecting the subtle and powerful dimensions of school learning. It is only through the comparative approach in a natural laboratory that these dimensions can be explored and brought to light.

## The educational fortunes of ethnic and linguistic minorities

In most systems of education throughout the world there are ethnic and linguistic minorities. Some of these are indigenous populations as in large nations like the USSR or Indonesia, smaller ones like Finland or Yugoslavia, or new nations that emerged out of artificially carved out colonies such as many of the sub-Saharan African nations. Other minorities are immigrant or "guest" populations as in many of the European nations and others that have taken in large numbers of refugees. Whatever the particular history of these groups, their existence has long constituted an issue and a concern for educational systems. Among the specific concerns are those of the language of instruction, the segregation or integration of these groups in schools or classrooms, the teaching of the "home" culture and its literature and history, and the importance of adult instruction as well as instruction of the children. IEA's Written Composition Study and Reading Literacy Study in particular have extensive background information on the language practices in the students' homes and schools. Such information can clearly be used to compare and contrast systems and to shed light on these concerns.

The approach to these concerns taken by different systems of education has varied; there is even a variety of approaches taken within a system depending on the size and nature of the minority group. To some extent the approaches taken result from political determination, but there are clear educational consequences of these political decisions. In those nations where a large segment of the population only spends a limited number of years in school the political decision to educate the children in two or three languages may result in a populace that is illiterate in several languages. It might prove more effective to concentrate on one language. Comparative research can shed some light on that issue. It may do so by examining systems that have different approaches to the bilingualism or multilingualism issue but that all have a relatively short effective life in school for a large percentage of the population.

Other systems that have immigrant or minority populations can also study the effect of bilingual or monolingual programs and integration and segregation of the language groups by comparative study. These studies can look at performance both in the basic skills of literacy, numeracy, and scientific learning but also at the cultural component of education and the extent to which the ways of thinking of the host culture clash with those of the parent culture of the students. The various systems of education around the globe have clearly distinct practices with respect to these issues. Their effectiveness and their effect clearly warrant study (see Siguan, this volume).

At the same time one must realize that studies of these concerns may elucidate issues and problems that have other than educational ramifications. The treatment of subgroups is often a political question rather than an educational one, and although the research may show the effectiveness of a particular policy or practice, its implementation in another context may prove impossible. Clearly the major political question is the desirability of integration as opposed to segregation. To take the example of the United States and Canada: the former has a long history of assimilation and integration which forms the core of its educational policy; the latter has an equally long history of separate identities and the protection of ethnic and linguistic identities (see Cummins, this volume). Officially the school systems view linguistic and ethnic groups so differently that there is virtually no common ground. This difference does not preclude the importance of cross-national research involving these two systems. It may be that the one policy has a different effect from the other; whether the one system can adopt the other's policy may prove impossible. The usefulness of the research is not to produce an educational solution, but to raise the awareness of the decision-makers to the fact that these are political rather than educational issues.

It is also clear that for other systems of education, the political decision has yet to be made and that research into the effects and consequences of decisions in other systems concerning the education of linguistic and ethnic minorities can help the decision-makers to make more thoughtful decisions and also help to educate the administrators and teachers to implement them successfully. Despite the probability that decisions on this issue are based on a variety of forces, comparative research using the natural laboratory of the world's educational systems can inform those who are in charge of implementing the decisions that have been made at the political level.

### Tracking efforts to educate the semi-literate underclass

In many countries there is emerging a group of people who, while not functionally illiterate, do not succeed in gaining or retaining employment in institutions which require a fair amount of skill (Rosow & Zager,1988). With the proper training, these people can do the work, but too often the schools and the industries fail to provide them with that training and they take lower-level jobs. These are the people who tend to pull down a nation's mean scores on a measure like those produced by IEA. Some of these people choose not to continue school beyond the compulsory level, either because they see no economic advantage to it, or because they have been deemed and doomed as failures by the educational system.

Analysis of the six-subject survey data in New Zealand and the United States (Purves 1978,1980) as well as analysis of the bottom 25% in the more recent mathematics and science studies indicate that the students who are unsuccessful do not necessarily come from the poorest families or the most deprived backgrounds. They are a group that has set relatively low aspirations for itself. The question must be raised as to whether these students as a group have been kept down by "the system," as the tracking issue suggests, or whether they have, in fact, opted out of the conventional set of values. There is an argument by cultural critics that the latter may well be more the case than the former. They refer to this group as being "alliterate," rather than "illiterate," for its members see no advantage to schooling and education in a materialistic culture where these have lost their value. They become the dropouts either in fact or in principle. By law they may stay in school, but they do so as a disaffected subgroup. In many of the Western countries this appears to be the case with an increasingly large population. In some systems of education, there may well be instances where the schools or the employers or some combination of the two is succeeding with this segment of youth. As comparative surveys are conducted in various nations, the national staff should seek to include these exceptional programs in the sampling frame, and perhaps isolate them for analysis to see the extent to which they really are working. Such a proposal means including those programs which often are not included as "schools" in educational systems, because they fall outside the traditional primary or secondary system. Some of these programs are offered by other governmental agencies such as the military, some of them by industry, some by community action groups. Alternative educational programs must be seen as a part of a nation's total educational system and should be included in comparative studies.

## Changing educational patterns in third world nations

A recent meeting of various groups concerned with education in the third world indicated that a number of international institutions, including The World Bank, UNICEF, UNESCO, and UNDP see some alarming shifts in education including a declining status and income for teachers, increasing drop-out rates, and declining performance of various groups, especially women. The concern is great enough for these groups to call for a new thrust in education and particularly the basic skills and a strong effort to reduce what Benjamin Bloom called "The Achievement Gap" between rich and poor countries and between rich and poor within countries.

This new thrust is one that defines the acquisition of basic skills as a human right equal to health and food and shelter. It will seek to impress upon governments and citizens that having the children attend school is not an end but a means; the end is learning. It will seek particularly to focus on the education of those groups which appear to have been denied the right, which is to say women. At the same time such a new policy will force systems of education in the developing nations to make hard choices about where to place their priorities. One of the hardest choices, given a limited economy, is the relative emphasis to be placed on teaching the adult or the child population. Another choice will be on the extent to which education is to be seen as a part of the economy as important as the military or the transportation system.

If education is to be viewed as important in every nation of the world, where should scarce funds be allocated? It is here that international comparative research comes into play. One may say that the resource allocation can be divided along traditional lines: plant and equipment, materials and supplies, and personnel. Each of these is in short supply in many of the developing countries. Some have been ravaged by internal and external strife and have no schools and no way of getting children to school if there were a school. Those that have schools have insufficient desks and chairs or suitable means of keeping the noise of other activities in the community or in the school out of the classroom. Of the second group of resources, many systems of education have not the paper for textbooks, much less consumable paper for teaching writing. Some schools may have one textbook for each one hundred students; and only one chalkboard as well. Libraries are non-existent. Along with other studies, IEA research has shown how important materials are to the learning of students, particularly in reading and writing, but also in science and mathematics. Other research has shown the effect of providing hand-held calculators that teach spelling and words as well as those that have arithmetic functions. In an industrialized nation these are easy to provide. They represent a major item in the budget of a poor nation.

But are buildings, desks, and instructional materials at all useful if there are poorly trained or untrained teachers in the classroom? In many systems of education of the world primary teachers have no training save that provided in the same or another primary school. If they are to teach something of mathematics and science, not to mention reading and writing, they must have knowledge of the subject that they are teaching. This need is most important at the secondary and upper primary level, but it is important at the lower primary level as well. The IEA study of classroom environment has shown this to be the case both in industrialized and in developing nations (Anderson et al.,1989). All of the pedagogical technique in the world cannot make up for ignorance of the subject on the part of the teacher.

Another factor which must be considered in considering the issue of basic education for all is that providing such education may serve to undermine the existing cultures of the society and move the society willy-nilly into a standardizedsociety. In a recent article in The Courier (1988), Frederico Mayor wrote, "...culture should be regarded as a direct source of inspiration for development, and in return, development should assign to culture a central role as a social regulator. This imperative applies not only to developing countries, where economic extraversion and cultural alienation have clearly and sometimes dramatically widened the gap between the creative and productive processes. It is also increasingly vital for industrialized countries, where the headlong race for growth in material wealth is detrimental to the spiritual, ethical and aesthetic aspects of life, and creates much disharmony between man and the natural environment" (Mayor, 1988, p. 5). The thrust of such a statement for educational research and monitoring is that while it may be important to see education internationally as a race that will lead to economic gain, such a single-minded approach may cause great harm. Education leads people away from their past and their family; it is the main cause of alienation as well as the main cause of acculturation. Programs of international cooperative research should take the occasion of the laboratory to look at the costs and benefits of education both in terms of the achievement of students and their attitudes and values. In such a way it may be possible to determine which educational programs serve best to educate people for development without destroying their cultural heritage and cultural pride.

Building buildings, providing materials, training teachers, preserving culture in the face of standardization: all are important to the provision of a basic education for all. Which of these comes first, if not in order of priority in order of emphasis within a budget? Is there any way of helping a nation decide? How can comparative research contribute to these decisions? One way that has demonstrated its usefulness to planners in a variety of educational systems has been monitoring and research using comparable measures of student performance in various school subjects. One can take the concept of the educational laboratory with systems that have natural variation in their allocation of resources and compare outcomes in terms of student learning and retention. One can also use these sorts of data to undertake simulations and on the basis of these inform policy makers of the effects of different allocations of resources.

## Conclusion

The reasons for having international measures of performance that go beyond monitoring to providing a strong research base are several: to estimate student performance according to standards set by an impartial group; to allow for comparisons of similar systems of education particularly with respect to the education of targeted subgroups; to provide comparisons over time using stable measures of both achievement outcomes and the various background variables that might affect those outcomes; and to allow researchers and evaluators to enter into a dialogue with their colleagues around the world.

To an individual system of education, particularly one that has had little experience in doing educational research nationally, the advantages of joining ongoing comparative research projects as opposed to monitoring projects are several:

1 They represent cooperative work in test-construction, created by international teams of experts and based on detailed surveys of the subject domain, so that a participant can learn and share at the same time and not be the recipient of an imperialistic approach to goal-setting and testing;

2 They are designed to be used across cultures and languages both within and between educational systems so that a system can see where it fits in a larger picture and add national options that suit its own circumstances;

3 They provide an international standard of achievement according to which a particular educational system can ascertain the performance of its students, but balanced by detailed student, teacher, and school and system questionnaires to allow for complex analysis and testing of alternative models and for comparative study of the effects of particular approaches to instruction and schooling.

In sum, the approach of cooperative international research studies allows nations and systems of education to join in the comparative education world and to be part of the laboratory for research. It is a laboratory in which the end is the improvement of education and learning for all. It is a laboratory in which each of the systems of education is an equal researcher and in which all are asking questions that can help the others. It is a laboratory which recognizes the similarities and differences among cultures, nations, and their educational systems and seeks to avoid cultural imperialism in educational solutions. It does assume that there is a global definition of learning and schooling, a broad definition with room for variation according to the particular history and aspirations of each participating system of education. This is a view of education and learning that allows for diversity within a larger global unity.

# References

Cole, M. & B. Means (1982) *Comparative studies of how people* think. Cambridge: Harvard University Press.

Husén, T. (1987) Policy impact of IEA research. *Comparative Education Review,* Vol. 31, pp. 29-48.

Mayor, F. (1988) The world decade for cultural development. *The Courier,* November, pp. 4-6.

Postlethwaite, T.N. (1987) Comparative educational achievement research: Can it be improved. *Comparative Education Review,* Vol. 31, pp. 150-158.

Purves, A.C. (1987) The evolution of IEA: A memoir. *Comparative Education Review,* Vol. 31, pp. 10-28.

Rosow, J.M. & R. Zager (1988) *Training; The competitive edge.* San Francisco: Work in America Institute, Jossey-Bass.

# List of Contributors

Prof.dr. Margaret Clifford

University of Iowa, 362 L.C. College of Education, Iowa City, IOWA 52242, USA

Prof.dr. Jim Cummins

Modern Language Center, The Ontario Center for Studies in Education, 252 Bloor Street West, Toronto, Canada M5S IV6

Prof.dr. Noel Entwistle

Department of Education, University of Edinburgh, Buccleuch Place 10, Edinburgh EH8 9JT, Great Britain

Prof.dr. Alan Purves

School of Education, University of Albany, 1400 Washington Ave., Albany, NY 12222, USA

Prof.dr. Miguel Siguan

Institut de Ciències de l'Educacio, Universitat de Barcelona, Plaça de la Universitat, Barcelona-7, Spain

Dr. Paul Vedder

Dutch Institute for Educational Research, Sweelinckplein 14, 2517 GK The Hague, the Netherlands

Prof.dr. Herbert Walberg

College of Education, University of Illinois at Chicago, Box 4348, Chicago, Illinois 60680, USA

Prof.dr. Franz Weinert

Max Planck Institut für Psychologie, Leopoldstrasse 2, D 8000 München, Federal Republic of Germany

Prof.dr. Douglas Windham

School of Education, State University of New York at Albany, 1400 Washington Ave., Albany, NY 12222, USA